ART AND ENGAGEMENT

ARNOLD BERLEANT

Art and Engagement

TEMPLE
UNIVERSITY
PRESS
Philadelphia

Temple University Press, Philadelphia 19122
Copyright © 1991 by Temple University. All rights reserved
Published 1991
Printed in the United States of America

The paper used in this publication meets the minimum
requirements of American National Standard for Information
Sciences—Permanence of Paper for Printed Library Materials,
ANSI Z39.48-1984 ⊗

Library of Congress Cataloging-in-Publication Data

Berleant, Arnold, 1932–
    Art and engagement / Arnold Berleant.
        p.   cm.
    Includes bibliographical references and index.
    ISBN 0-87722-797-7
    1. Aesthetics.   2. Engagement (Philosophy).   I. Title.
BH39.B3945   1991
111'.85—dc20   90-39920
                                              CIP

TO RIVA BERLEANT–SCHILLER

CONTENTS

ILLUSTRATIONS

PREFACE

THIS BOOK WAS BEGUN LONG BEFORE IT WAS CONCEIVED, AND ITS intent and direction may become more apparent if I briefly recount its origins. In an earlier book, *The Aesthetic Field: A Phenomenology of Aesthetic Experience* (1970), I developed a theory of art and the aesthetic that may have seemed somewhat idiosyncratic at the time it appeared. This was a theory intended to account for all the major factors that enter into the experience of art, without prejudging their importance or their divisions, and without taking any one of them as exclusive or even central. So broad a canvas was not fashionable in that heyday of philosophical miniatures. It is not surprising, therefore, that its landscape was visible mostly to people concerned with the creation and performance of the arts, who found that the book depicted clearly and accurately what they had sensed but never articulated.

The central theme of *The Aesthetic Field* is that any attempt to account for art must start from the ways in which art actually works in human experience, in particular with those experiences in which the aesthetic function of art predominates, and therefore with the character of that experience as aesthetic. *Aesthetic* is indeed the broader term, not only because it encompasses natural objects that at times may share with art objects a special place in human perception, but because the term *aesthetic* has its etymological roots in such perception. As "sensation" or "perception by the senses," aesthetics is inescapably bound to the human factor so completely that no consideration of art can proceed in any hope of truth without acknowledging that fact. Aesthetics, then, is doubly inclusive, embracing human perceivers as well as natural objects, and aesthetic experience is the concept best able to accommodate both.

The account offered in *The Aesthetic Field* elaborated that idea around four functions, focusing in turn on the art object, the perceiver, the artist, and the performer. These stand, not as separate elements or constituents that combine with others in aesthetic experience, but as distinguishable dimensions or perspectives of what functions as a homogeneous field of experiential forces.

THE LONG SERIES of essays that followed the publication of that book developed many of its themes, exploring the terrain of aesthetic experience in directions that were guided by the inherently perceptual nature of such experience. This meant that the essays dealt more with empirical questions than with conceptual ones, not so much with general issues in aesthetics as with particular ones about how individual arts like painting, sculpture, and literature, and how specific developments in the contemporary arts, actually work in our perceptual experience. As these studies progressed, certain ideas seemed to emerge out of the very conditions of aesthetic experience as the most effective explanation of that mode of experience.

Central among them was the notion of participatory engagement by the appreciator with the object or circumstance of art. Engagement was not only recognizable as an explicit factor in the work of many innovative artists and schools; it became the principal key in making the various regions of aesthetic experience intelligible. More significant yet was the discovery that aesthetic participation is not an explanatory principle for the contemporary arts alone: it applies to the traditional arts as well, recharging our experience of them. This was troubling at the same time as it was liberating, for the tradition in aesthetic theory since the eighteenth century, when the discipline was identified and defined, is that art consists of objects that possess a distinctive kind of value, aesthetic value. Moreover, to appreciate such objects properly one must adopt an attitude quite opposed to our practical relations with things, which are presumably governed exclusively by considerations of use and consequence. Instead, we were instructed to assume a stance toward art objects that removes all practical interests and allows us to contemplate the work of art for its own sake, with a disengagement that excludes every other consideration.

Now this tradition is not only axiomatic in aesthetic theory; it is bolstered by still more general principles that were preeminent in philosophy long before the Enlightenment and the rise of modern aesthetics. In developing a theory that responds to the unpremeditated experience of art, then, we confront the larger philosophical structure of which the tradition in aesthetics is but one part. We face, in particular, an array of tendentious and obstructive dualisms, especially that of subject and object, which are widely accepted as fundamental truths. Despite Hegel and the succeeding efforts of Bergson, Dewey, and Merleau-Ponty, among others, these dualisms still remain primary philosophical commandments for most philosophers. And they join with other basic convictions, such as the cognitive primacy of science, the universality and exclusivity of truth, the objectivity of knowledge, and the hierarchical order of being, to form the foundation of modern Western intellectual culture.

Aesthetic engagement challenges this entire tradition. It claims continuity rather than separation, contextual relevance rather than objectivity, historical pluralism rather than certainty, ontological parity rather than priority. Unfortunately, however, one book cannot do all things, and while I must set aside a full discussion of many of these larger questions, they shadow the elaboration of aesthetic issues. It is enough here to confront the central tenet of modern aesthetics without having to defy the larger part of modern philosophy. What this book does do is develop the notion of engagement as an explanatory principle in aesthetic theory. And since the arts are always individual and our experiences with them more particular still, my argument does not pursue a primarily dialectical course, even though it rests on a general conceptual structure. Instead I weave a net of instances that I hope grasp the participatory quality of our experiences in the arts and display the capacity of the concept of engagement to liberate and illuminate those experiences.

This book offers, then, not so much an argument from text as an argument from art. It is an argument through which art, both past and present, can acquire new significance and renewed vitality. For the ideas developed here can, I believe, account for whatever has been accomplished by the traditional aesthetics of distance, while accommodating the seemingly disruptive innovations of the past century. Perhaps those for whom this book is intended—scholars, artists, students, all those who consider art and aesthetic experience significant and who think seriously about what that significance is— will find a touch of truth in this attempt to capture and hold that elusive quality.

This preface would not be complete without remarking on the affinity the ideas elaborated in the following pages have with the newly developing perspective of feminist aesthetics. Feminist thought has not evolved far enough yet in aesthetics for its shape to become entirely clear, but I take it as something of a corroboration of the ideas with which I have long been working that their intent and direction find so close a parallel in what is emerging as a fresh alternative to the received tradition.

A final note of clarification is in order. Despite the reference to art in the title, this book moves freely at times between the arts and aesthetic experience in nature, especially when discussing landscape, architecture, and environment. This is not a careless disregard for their differences but a deliberate bridging of what I consider to be another of the misleading divisions that dog aesthetic theory. For the natural world does not stand apart from human presence and action. We are increasingly aware of the inescapable and pervasive effects of human agency, both local and global, on our natural environment. In nature as in arts there is an active transformation of materials in the shaping of experience, and the same conceptual structure of an aesthetics of engagement applies as readily to the one as to the others.

NO AUTHOR WRITES *de novo.* My own intellectual indebtedness is widespread and includes many from whom I have learned by reaction as well as support. In addition, many friends and colleagues have read portions of the manuscript in some of its many metamorphoses and have suggested numerous improvements, and I acknowledge with real gratitude their generous offering of time and effort. They include Rudolf Arnheim, Robert Cantrick, Selma Jeanne Cohen, William Deguire, Sondra Horton Fraleigh, Paul Gray, Morris Grossman, Hilde Hein, Berel Lang, Geoffrey Payzant, Alexander Sesonske, Dabney Townsend, and Gary Washington. The suggestions of the anonymous reviewers for Temple University Press were both important and exceedingly helpful. My collaborative work in environmental aesthetics with Barbara Sandrisser has been richly illuminating. William Pardue has advised me often and well with his open mind and fine editorial eye. But special thanks must be reserved for my wife, Riva Berleant–Schiller. No one could hope for a more exacting editor or a more sympathetic critic. Whatever inadequacies or infelicities still remain I take, of course, upon myself. I am also grateful to the C.W. Post Campus Research Committee for an extended series of grants that provided financial assistance and time for my research, and to the staff of the Witherle Memorial Library in Castine, Maine, for its unfailing helpfulness. Finally, I owe much to Jane Cullen's extraordinary skill and tact, which have blessed the entire editorial process that has led to this book's publication.

ACKNOWLEDGMENTS

PERMISSION IS GRATEFULLY ACKNOWLEDGED FOR THE USE OF THE following materials: Alfred A. Knopf, Inc. for "Six Significant Land-scapes," VI, by Wallace Stevens; New Directions Publishing Co. and David Higham for "A Refusal to Mourn the Death by Fire of a Child in London," by Dylan Thomas; and Grove Press for an excerpt from *Waiting for Godot,* by Samuel Beckett. The following publishers have graciously allowed the use of materials from my previously published work: Cambridge University Press for "Aesthetic Perception and Environmental Design"; University of Cincinnati for "Aesthetic Participation and the Urban Environment"; State University of New York Press for "Toward a Phenomenological Aesthetics of Environment"; Oxford University Press for "The Historicity of Aesthetics"; Kluwer Academic Publishers for "Experience and Theory in Aesthetics" and "The Eighteenth Century Assumptions of Analytic Aesthetics"; The American Society for Aesthetics for "Aesthetics and the Contemporary Arts."

ART AND ENGAGEMENT

Introduction

AESTHETICS IS A STUDY WITH A LONG HISTORY AND A SHORT IDEN-
tity. Like its root discipline philosophy, aesthetics has struggled to
establish both itself and its subject matter, its material and its meth-
odology, its proper problems and its structure, its order of working
and its order of work. Yet aesthetics differs from some other regions
of philosophical inquiry in that neither its origins, its data, nor its
concepts are exclusively philosophical. The very existence of aesthetics as a discipline emerges from the effort to understand the
activities and occasions of the arts and the appreciation of nature.
And the aesthetician can only work by having traveled among their
many regions, sometimes as a sophisticated observer, sometimes as
an anthropologist, sometimes as a scholar, but most of all as a
participant in artistic–aesthetic activities.

Yet aesthetics has not supplied the premises for the world of art,
nor has it received its own from the study of the arts. Nor again can
aesthetics claim independence as a discipline, for many of its leading
ideas have been transplanted from broader philosophical ground.
Moreover, for a variety of reasons the study we call aesthetics is not
exclusively philosophical. Historical, psychological, sociological, and
anthropological modes of inquiry also contribute information on
how art is practiced and experienced, as well as methodologies that

are necessary supplements to the conceptual and dialectical ones of philosophy. More than in most fields of study, we must begin with diversity.

There are, however, certain basic and persistent circumstances that provide us with stable points of orientation. Among these are the occurrence of art in every known culture, a presence that is pervasive and diffuse, and its appearance at every stage of human history, including the most ancient. Indeed, certain of the earliest extant examples, such as the cave paintings at Lascaux, Font de Gaume, and Altamira, and many prehistoric votary figurines, are not "primitive" attempts to be regarded with amused indulgence, but highly sophisticated renderings that reveal a mastery of hand and eye and suggest a lengthy history. Furthermore, an irrepressible impulse impels people toward the aesthetic and the artistic. Sometimes called an aesthetic need, it may appear as small sensory pleasures and attention to perceptual details, which seem inessential and unnecessary to the practical minded, or it may take the form of full devotion to a life in art.

The aesthetic, then, is omnipresent, perhaps even necessary. Not only are these experiences distinctive and valuable; they cannot be excluded from any consideration of human culture. And while we now commonly identify a mode of experience we call aesthetic, we cannot at the same time ignore its ties to the affectional, the religious, the social, the practical, and the technological. The aesthetic dimension penetrates both human history and culture.

Even though the beginnings of both art and culture in general are incompletely known, they certainly were not abrupt. There is no reason to doubt that aesthetic awareness emerged as part of the lengthy process of cultural evolution rather than appearing, like Venus, fully formed at some late stage in human development. But as the arts evolved into historical time and people became more deliberately conscious and curious about them, questions of origins, forms, meanings, and significance were articulated and refined, and various explanations were offered. This is where difficulties arise, not so much with the arts or the experiences related to them as with the accounts that propose to define, explain, and judge the arts.

It is here that this book finds its place. For even if the problems of aesthetics lie more with the explanations than with the experiences of art, the two cannot be separated, since experience and understanding exert a mutual influence. An alternative theory alone

2

Introduction

is not sufficient: in this field no theory can hope to be self-justifying. As an empirically grounded discipline, aesthetics must establish itself on the evidence of artistic activities and aesthetic experience. Yet is not a theory required in order to determine and select the evidence? Facts, aesthetic or otherwise, do not hang about ready to be plucked; they are concretizations in experience that are shaped, recognized, and ordered by the implicit presuppositions in human being and acting and by the demands of particular circumstances. On the other hand, what we select as identifiable and relevant is guided, consciously or not, by the conceptual frame we employ. Are we not trapped in a vicious circle?

This is an intellectual dilemma, however, not a practical one, since in the temporal order of things experience ultimately claims priority. Cognitive activities inevitably occur within the dynamic context of life, and every theory must recognize its origins in these conditions. Yet the fascination with ideas can exercise an attraction that often casts its spell over evidence, especially empirical evidence. Indeed, the history of aesthetics has been written largely apart from the social history of the arts. Aesthetic theory has not only often failed to reflect artistic practice and aesthetic experience; it has presumed at times to decide them. In fact, theories have sometimes attempted to legislate which objects to include and exclude from the domain of art. The persistence of this judicial impulse is more than a sign of intellectual confusion; it also leads to misguided and damaging action. For while societies are correct in recognizing the widespread influence of the arts, they usually fail to grasp their special contribution. Nor do they realize that the richness of art is possible only through creative autonomy.

The theme that guides this study is that the vortex of experiences of art and the aesthetic lies at the center of our thinking about them. These experiences occur in a situation, under circumstances that are concrete and determinative. Furthermore, these conditions have a social cast, regardless of whether art is experienced in solitude or in an institutional setting: As social animals, we carry our sociality with us. Furthermore, the character of such experience does not rest on the separation of an art object from the appreciator and on its isolation in a sacred space. Just as art has ties with other aspects of people's lives, so is it bound to the circumstances within which it works. These continuities are more than mere ties; they are exhibited by an active interplay of the factors involved: perceptual, material, environmental, formative, and performative forces that contribute to a dynamic unity of experience. Most important for us as creators and appreciators of art is the contribution we ourselves make, a contribution that is active and constitutive. That is why I call this an aesthetics of engagement, a participatory aesthetics.

The three parts of this book develop such a view. The first establishes the theoretical and historical background for this position, while the second explains and illuminates the argument through the study of particular arts. The final part inquires into the metaphysical grounding of aesthetics and probes the larger significance of aesthetic experience. The coherence and the continuity of the argument may become clearer by sketching it out in advance, so let me conclude this introduction with a preview.

PART ONE BEGINS by examining the relationship between experience and theory in aesthetics. Approaching this connection historically, the first chapter identifies certain key features of traditional theory: the notion of aesthetic disinterestedness and its correlatives—the isolation of the art object and the object's special status. After looking into the meanings and development of the notion of experience, traditional aesthetics is held up against the experiences and practices of the contemporary arts, where these ideas appear strikingly anachronistic and inappropriate, and where an accurate account of such experience must reflect its participatory quality.

In the second chapter we inquire into the origins of changes in the experience of art resulting from the technological innovations of industrialism and the social and perceptual transformations of the modern world. The significance of these developments for aesthetics lies in the support they give for a unified theory of aesthetics, a view of experience characterized by continuity, perceptual integration, and engagement. These features are expressed in the notion of the aesthetic field, a concept which integrates the four principal aspects of the aesthetic situation—the creative, the objective, the appreciative, and the performative, replacing disinterestedness with engagement and contemplation with participation.

THE SECOND PART of the book develops the ideas of aesthetic participation and engagement in the context of particular arts. As in science no universal claim can be established conclusively by enumerating specific instances, so too in aesthetics. The intent here, however, is not so much to prove aesthetic engagement as to exhibit its value in clarifying and illuminating our understanding and experience of the arts. These chapters therefore examine a number of individual arts, showing how each of them exhibits specific characteristics that are accounted for best by the notion of aesthetic engagement. Each of these arts exemplifies how the aesthetic situation or field leads us to participate in a particular way, one that is appreciative, object-oriented, creative, or performative. Focusing on a single aspect at a time will help us grasp its peculiar power of engagement, realizing all the while that the participatory quality of each aspect is mirrored by all the others. In some arts, moreover, one of these dimensions may become the generative point of the entire field, that feature from which the others are best understood, as performance is for dance and creation for music.

Part Two begins by considering how the landscape painting, as an art object, encourages the viewer's contribution by insisting on the spatial involvement of the perceiver. The engaged perception of space in painting becomes inescapably direct in our actual environment, so we move next to examine how this occurs in architecture and, since buildings are bound to their sites, in environmental design. A study of literary experience follows, examining appreciation through the human factor in the ontology of language, both in its formation and in its artistic and aesthetic uses. Music exemplifies the creative aspect of aesthetic perception, where the composer's activity in generating the musical materials is paralleled by both the performer and the listener. Finally, the embodied action of dance eloquently displays the performative contribution as a process of bodily engagement, not just a psychological attitude, and how somatic participation is essential to the creation and completion of dance. Although each of these arts illustrates a particular dimension of the aesthetic field, we must constantly be aware that the experience of every art is a unified occurrence in which all four facets join without separation.

Because perception is the core of all human experience and understanding, beyond as well as within the arts, it is important to acknowledge both the ontological significance of art and the interconnections that bind art to other areas of philosophy and other regions of experience. Recognizing this, Part Three returns to a more general theoretical mode. Notwithstanding the claim that aesthetic theory must be fashioned in its own terms and rest on the central place of aesthetic experience, such experience is not isolated from the rich complexity of human culture. For art, while self-centered, is not self-contained or self-sufficient. Furthermore, the comprehensiveness of perception in the arts suggests that they may create occasions of such depth, scope, and intensity that they carry their own conviction and generate their own reality.

The final part of the book probes these matters. It reaches toward a view that assigns to art a distinctiveness and a stature equal to other realms of experience and understanding, while recognizing the interrelationships art maintains with these different domains. It also extends the idea of a perceptually grounded ontology that has been implicit throughout the book. This claim is pursued through various arts—literature, painting, and environment, but the most extended discussion is reserved for film. Because cinematic experience involves, explicitly and vividly, the constitutive dimensions of space, time, and movement to generate a reality through total engagement, film is taken as a model of what occurs in all the arts. Along with the other arts, film upholds the ontological legitimacy, indeed, the ontological parity of the aesthetic realm with the human world more generally, and I propose a theory of multiple experiential realities to express this. The final discussion pursues the need and direction of an aesthetics of renewal and considers the implications of taking aesthetics as philosophically foundational, a curious exchange with the usual practice.

THIS BOOK EXHIBITS what might seem to be an odd combination of the most general and the most specific, a juxtaposition of particular studies and comprehensive theory. Yet what better setting than the arts for such a reunion, since the experiences they generate are the occasions of the most unique particularity, at the same time as they resonate in the deepest chambers of human being. Perhaps such experiences show the way to achieving a grand reconciliation of art with the rest of the human realm, where each domain retains its integrity yet none its isolation. This may be more vision than accomplishment, but I hope that both may in some measure be present here.

Aesthetics and experience

PART ONE

CHAPTER ONE

Experience
and
theory
in
aesthetics

FROM THE EARLIEST TIMES ART HAS BEEN INTEGRAL TO HUMAN culture. Both fascinated and perplexed by the arts, people have tried, since the age of classical Greece, to understand how they work and what they mean. Philosophers wondered at first about the nature of art: what it is and how it relates to the cosmos. They puzzled over how art objects are created and they extolled human skills that seem at times godlike in their powers. But perhaps the central question for such philosophers as Plato and Aristotle concerned our involvement with art: the response we have to beautiful things, the moral and salubrious powers of art, and perhaps most of all, the power of art to transform and transcend, leading us into a condition of enhanced perception that may be wondrous, dangerous, and at times overwhelming.

The classical age displayed a richness of discussion that centered on art as an activity: an activity that is at once cosmic, social, and individual; an activity that brings understanding of a sort; an activity that may be salutary and even exalting, as in Aristotle's celebrated discussion of tragedy and its cathartic effects. Since the eighteenth century, however, this has changed. Questions about art have shifted to the idea of experience, paralleling the great change in the focus of philosophy from matters of ontology to those of epistemology. In place of starting from an examination of the nature of the universe and moving to the human position in the order of things, we have come to realize, since Descartes and Kant, that all inquiry has its inception in a human locus. Now, at the end of the twentieth century, we have finally recognized that the human factor in every kind of awareness and knowledge is structurally unavoidable. Art has become both a symptom of this change and a standard for grasping it.

The scope of our claims has narrowed, then, and while the human place has become less cosmic, it is more pervasive and personal. Whatever the world be, we can only encounter it and know it as humans. Thus we may be less likely to ask what makes something art than to consider how our experience of art is to be explained, and even when we pose the former question, we answer it in terms of the latter. Theories of beauty have given way to doctrines of emotion, meaning, communication, with even symbol being taken as the embodiment of feeling. And questions that purport to be about art objects, like the search for aesthetic qualities, turn out to be attempts to locate experiential properties of these objects, since properties such as "delicate," "graceful," "elegant," "lovely," and "beautiful" require aesthetic sensitivity to be perceived.[1]

Writings on aesthetics and the arts have proliferated since the Enlightenment, a tribute to the ceaseless activity of artists, the broadening of their public, and the ever strong influence of art and the uses to which that influence has been put. One can identify in this literature a continuing body of doctrine that derives from formulations shaped during the eighteenth century, when modern aesthetics first emerged. This was a time of broad intellectual change that affected the arts as much as anything. Early in that century, the various arts, some of which until then had been bound with the mathematical and other sciences, with other quondam liberal arts, and with crafts, coalesced into a generally accepted set of fine arts in which they were compared with one another and organized by the same principles.[2] And in the writings of many of the same men who were codifying the body of fine arts, a coherent set of beliefs about art emerged which, by the latter part of the eighteenth century, had achieved the status of a separate discipline called "aesthetics." This was a seminal period that redirected the course of the philosophy of art and established the field as we know it today.[3]

Adapted and transmuted in the subsequent two centuries, this theory of the fine arts has rarely been challenged. The pattern of thought that developed at this time has become integral to discussions about art, hardening into a set of axioms that have since acquired the stature of unquestioned and inviolable dogmas. Three, in particular, are pertinent here: that art consists primarily of objects, that these objects possess a special status, and that they must be regarded in a unique way. A brief look at some of the writing of this period will illustrate these characteristic themes.

The work of the British theorists of the eighteenth century deals not so much with characterizations of art in general as with the types and locations of beauty and the manner in which it is apprehended. That beauty is a characteristic of objects, to which the mind supplies meaning and order, was beyond dispute. The task lay in identifying such beauty, in determining in which objects beauty occurs and what traits of imagination are needed to respond to it pleasurably. As Shaftesbury wrote of the painter in 1711, "His piece, if it be beautiful, and carries truth, must be a whole, by itself, complete, independent, and withal as great and comprehensive as he can make it." Art, then, is concerned with beauty, and beauty is associated with an object.

Related to this idea is the requirement that the art object be demarcated from its surroundings and set off as an independent and integral work, instead of being diffused across "the walls, the ceilings, the staircases, the cupolas, and other remarkable places either of churches or palaces," as Shaftesbury put it. "We may give to any particular work the name Tablature when the work is in reality 'a single piece, comprehended in one view, and formed according to one single intelligence, meaning, or design; which constitutes a real whole, by a mutual and necessary relation of its parts, the same as of the members in a natural body'."[4]

Hutcheson and Reid developed this characterization further. Hutcheson sought to inquire into the quality in objects that excites our ideas of beauty and harmony, which he discovered in pleasing formal relations, especially as they are found in what he called the compound ratio between uniformity and variety.[5] And Reid, toward the end of the eighteenth century, tried to determine what is common to all objects in which beauty can be found, a condition he located "in the moral and intellectual perfections of mind, and in its active powers."[6]

Now such beauty, these men held, is not to be found in the

material from which art is fashioned but appears only when that material acquires something that beautifies it. Art is what beautifies matter, and since there is no principle of beauty in the physical object, that principle of meaning, regulation, and order must be supplied by the mind. Moreover, a particular sort of attention is necessary to apprehend such beauty, one which considers the object for its own sake without regard to further purposes.

Here arose the famous notion of 'disinterestedness': an attitude denoting the perception of an object for its own sake without regard to further purposes, especially practical ones, and requiring the separation of the object from its surroundings in order that it may be contemplated freely and with no distracting considerations. Disinterestedness began to emerge as the mark of a new and distinctive mode of experience called 'aesthetic,' a kind of awareness distinct from more commonly recognized alternative modes, such as instrumental, cognitive, moral, and religious experience.

It was in the work of Kant, however, that the concept of aesthetic disinterestedness became fixed and assumed a distinct and integral place in aesthetic theory, just as aesthetics itself was integrated in his philosophy into a comprehensive system. While Kant remained true to the classical view of art as an activity of making, he described beautiful art as a product that pleases us solely in the act of judging it, not by pure sensation or by its conformity to a concept such as that of having a purpose.[7] For Kant distinguished aesthetic perception by its separation from interests that have a practical concern or end; it is distinct from the apprehension of objects in ordinary experience. Taste, he held then, is the faculty of judging or representing an object by a satisfaction or dissatisfaction that is entirely disinterested, and it is the object of such satisfaction that is called 'beautiful.'

So it came about that the experience of art took on central importance and that this experience was attainable through the use of the special attitude of disinterestedness.[8] By separating the experience of beauty from sensory pleasure or ordinary emotions, Kant effectively removed it from a locus in human affairs and attenuated its grounding in somatic activity to the point of dematerialization. And by making taste disinterested, he provided the theoretical impetus for isolating art from commerce with the world of human activity and setting it in its own region beyond the command of practical

affairs. Art, however, retains some resemblance to the realm of practice, Kant admitted, through the judgment of taste, which exhibits
"purposiveness without purpose."[9]

From this formative period in the history of modern aesthetics
there emerged an identification of the art object as separate and
distinct from what surrounds it and isolated from the rest of life. As
Münsterberg put it much later, "To isolate the object for the mind,
means to make it beautiful, for it fills the mind without an idea of
anything else: . . . this complete repose, where the objective impression becomes for us an ultimate end in itself, is the only possible
content of the true experience of beauty."[10] Such an object requires a
special attitude for its proper appreciation, a disinterested attitude by
which the object is regarded in the light of its own intrinsic qualities
with no concern for ulterior purposes. This is a tenet echoed regularly through the halls of academe by such phrases as Bullough's
well-known notion of *psychical distance* and Ortega y Gasset's less
gracious *dehumanization.*[11] Stolnitz summed up two centuries of
discussion when he defined the aesthetic attitude as "disinterested
and sympathetic attention to and contemplation of any object of
awareness whatever, for its own sake alone."[12]

Although formulated in the eighteenth century, the doctrine of
disinterested contemplation has its roots in the distant past. Aristotle's contemplative model of cognitive experience still rules the
realm of aesthetics, and many share with Aquinas the conviction that
we grasp the beauty in art with the same intuitive directness and
certainty as the axioms and proofs of logic: "Clarity is for beauty
what evidence is for truth."[13] The art object thus stands whole and
pure, and we must contemplate it with the attitude appropriate to an
observer. One can read the history of the philosophy of art as a
reflection of the powerful impact of this contemplative ideal, which
has continued to the present day in attempts to identify art with
language, symbol, and symbol systems.[14]

One might read this list of aesthetic axioms as a mere reiteration
of obvious truths and wonder at the value of documenting a tradition
so well established as to seem unquestionable and irrefutable. We
shall pursue these axioms more directly later. But if they presume to
describe the *experience* of beauty, and if experience is to provide the
basis for aesthetic understanding, we might expect the first order of
business to be a clear, unassumptive query about the characteristics

of such experience. For experience is the central term in aesthetics, and all that we can say about art and the aesthetic is in some way an elaboration of this notion. In attempting to describe experience, however, it is essential to escape the prevalent tendency to regard it as a purely subjective event, a tendency that emerges in phenomenology as strongly as in traditional empiricism. Let us start by attempting to disentangle the concept of experience from the hereditary characteristics it has acquired during the past two centuries.

To the Western philosophical mind the term *experience* connotes sense experience, and the appeal to sensation as the source of knowledge, or *empiricism*, as this is known, suggests in turn the major tradition in British philosophy. What we have inherited from that tradition (it too, like aesthetics, a product of the seventeenth and eighteenth centuries), is a view of experience as the composite product of separate, discrete sensations. Whether these unitary perceptions are called "ideas that we receive from sensation" (Locke), "ideas actually imprinted on the senses" (Berkeley), "impressions" (Hume), calculable units of pleasure or pain (Bentham) or, as with more recent writers, sense data or other immediately given percepts, what is alleged is that these units are what we experience directly and immediately.[15] Furthermore, we derive all knowledge from these elements by combining and ordering them into the more complex structures of our cognitive world. Now such units of perception are sensory ones, and it is from this trait that experience is said to have a subjective ground, for is not sensation something that can be traced to the mind? Is it not a personal, inner awareness, an effect caused by impinging forces from the world outside?

If, however, we apply to the question of experience the same Occamist rigor that the empiricist tradition urges us to direct toward logical and metaphysical claims, it is clear that such an account of experience is neither descriptive nor simple. Like traditional aesthetics, it prejudges our experience by imposing on it a division between person and world. Yet this dualistic tradition of separating consciousness from an external world, so deeply ingrained in modern thought, cannot be assumed as given. For it presumes a structure in experience that, for all its initial plausibility, rests on a particular historical and cultural tradition not shared in other times and places.

Yet this pattern of separation continues to prevail in the way the arts are explained and treated. In the effort to keep them distinct from other activities and objects in human culture, our aesthetic encounters are usually channeled along a carefully paved course through official cultural institutions—galleries, museums, concert halls, theaters. Such confinement not only often restricts the force of the arts; it conspires to erect obstructions that inhibit our openness to artistic modes that do not conform to those requirements. Moreover, it forces traditional aesthetic theory that has been modeled on its constraints to scurry after in a vain attempt to keep up with the irrepressible inventiveness of artists. By attempting to decree the acceptable modes of artistic action and appreciative response, traditional aesthetics ends by legislating itself into irrelevance.

Our Western involvement with science and technology, where the atomistic pattern of experience seems so effective, may in fact have provided us with a misleading paradigm. For the experience of the arts exhibits a unity, and holistic experience occurs here in ways which are sometimes subtle as well as obvious and compelling. The contemporary arts, in particular, frequently insist on experiences of engagement by provoking us into movement or action or by forcing us to adjust our vision and imagination. One can attain such experiential unity, moreover, with the traditional arts as well as with the recent ones.

A clear alternative to the dualistic claims of the empiricist tradition lies, then, in the claim for a continuity of experience, joining perceiver with the world in complex patterns of reciprocity. The universal scope of this view has been emerging slowly during the past century, ranging across the social sciences, the physical sciences, and philosophy. But it is in art that the continuity of experience is exemplified most strikingly. Elaborated in aesthetic theory, experiential continuity in the arts can serve as a model for other areas of inquiry.

The rise of the idea of experiential continuity as an alternative to this tradition of separation in modern philosophy has been gradual and groping. We are still impeded by a dualistic conceptual structure and its corollary, the reduction of experience to a subjective response. Perhaps we can avoid the pervasive dualism of the modern period and begin to grasp the meaning for aesthetics of the continuity of experience by identifying some of the significant stages in its emergence. For art is one of the regions of culture in which this continuity is a significant, perhaps a necessary explanatory concept. Moreover, by discerning the stages by which experiential continuity has emerged here, through intuition and empathy to involvement and engagement, we may begin to see a significance that goes beyond the aesthetic realm.

When Henri Bergson writes of the difference between relative and absolute knowing, he is identifying an alternative between the dualistic relation with a separate object and the unitary condition of direct apprehension. The first, he claims, offers knowledge that is external; the second, knowledge that lies within. But Bergson's reference to knowledge is unlike our common, more literal use of that term. For him knowledge is a condition of awareness, a grasping of something, not a proposition or a statement of fact. Even so, Bergson's fascination with the different ways of knowing an object is nonetheless still an intellectual preoccupation. Despite his agreement with common sense that reality is independent of the mind, his account of knowing offers an answer to the question of how we can gain an awareness of something by placing it within a cognitive frame, and his concern is with the mental act of knowing an object by a kind of "intellectual sympathy," as he calls it.[16]

There is more to the experience of art, however, than mental involvement, and others have pursued ways in which the whole person, not just mind, intellect, or consciousness is engaged. One thinks of the notion of *Einfühlung*, which Theodor Lipps developed about the same time that Bergson was writing. For Lipps, *Einfühlung*, or empathy, begins not with a separate object with which we then have aesthetic enjoyment and not with such pleasure taken in an object, but with both the object and the pleasure drawn together in a single act. "Empathy is the fact that the antithesis between myself and the object disappears, or rather does not yet exist." This is more than a psychic unity, for even though Lipps retains the notion of contemplation in his account, empathy is a concept that incorporates movement or activity. This activity is bound up with the observed object, both by being derived from it and by being inseparable from it. When empathy with a physical movement takes place, there is a consciousness that is wholly identical with the movement. "In a word, I am now with my feeling of activity entirely and wholly in the moving figure. Even spatially, if we can speak of the spatial extent of the ego, I am in its place."[17] There is an identity here, yet there is no passive identity or purely visual assimilation, nor does it involve a private sensation or pleasure in an object. It is rather the activity of feeling oneself into the aesthetic object, an activity that engages not just our attention but also kinesthetic sensations, such as the muscle tensions that are so insistent a part of dance appreciation.

Dewey exhibits a still more explicit recognition of total organic involvement in art. The biological, evolutionary model underlies his account of experience and, when he turns to art, he employs the same factors. Whether one's interests be scientific or aesthetic, "the ultimate matter of both emphases in experience is . . . the constant rhythm that marks the interaction of the live creature with his surroundings." The function of art is consciously to restore "the union of sense, need, impulse and action characteristic of the live creature." Such an occurrence is integrated and consummated in what Dewey calls "*an* experience," the distinguishing mark of the aesthetic.[18]

Aesthetic involvement is carried further yet in Maurice Merleau-Ponty's discussion of perception as a synthesis that finds unity and wholeness in our sensory grasp of objects. Such a synthesis involves the "body as the field of perception and action" and yet goes beyond what is directly perceived to a whole, a totality that is ultimately the world itself. In his description of seeing, Merleau-Ponty carries this idea of physical engagement to art, particularly painting. "Since things and my body are made of the same stuff, vision must somehow take place in them; their manifest visibility must be repeated in the body by a secret visibility."[19]

More recently Mikel Dufrenne has continued to extend this theme of perceptual unity. In aesthetic experience the spectator assists in revealing the aesthetic object, an object that is both a thing and its meaning and that exists through the perceiver and not independently. Yet it is only in perception that the being of the aesthetic object is realized. Not constituted by consciousness, it nonetheless exists only for a consciousness able to recognize it. Like Merleau-Ponty, Dufrenne argues that this produces a relation of subject and object in which each exists only by means of the other, a kind of reconciliation of the two. There is no opposed physical object here whose presence is externally related to the appreciator. One must enter into the work in an intimate fashion, active not as a pure spectator but as an involved viewer.[20]

These characterizations of aesthetic experience vary in the degree of engagement they recognize between perceiver and object.

They may even admit, as Dufrenne does, of a paradox between the appreciator's absorption in the object and the distance imposed by its independent identity.[21] Whatever their differences, they reflect a development that extends aesthetic experience well beyond a state of mind that is separate and distinct from the aesthetic object, beyond a psychological attitude or an act of consciousness. They join in stressing involvement, ranging from multi-sensory synaesthesia to somatic action and continuity with the object.

The notion of unitary perception in aesthetic experience has thus gradually taken form as an alternative to the theory of disinterestedness. Yet the efforts to shape this notion remain bound to the very theory they intend to challenge. Its development has followed an uneven course, often hampered by vestiges of an incompatible past difficult to recognize and set aside. Even though the proposals we have just reviewed reject key elements of traditional aesthetics, they often retain other features of that theory—its psychologism, its concentration on the spectator, its essential passivity, its acceptance of the autonomy of the art object. Yet perceptual unity is an essentially different idea, inconsistent with the tradition of disinterested contemplation. The maturation of this idea, moreover, complements a parallel development in the arts of the last hundred years: their assimilation of perceiver and object in appreciative experience.

Now the purpose of aesthetics is to clarify and explain our experiences with the arts, and all theoretical assertions must stand ultimately on their ability to do this. While art of the past might appear to corroborate the customary explanations of traditional aesthetics, this is only because their appreciation has been impeded and distorted by doctrines that misrepresent aesthetic activity.[22] But when we consider the history of the arts from the perspective of the present, the inadequacy of the traditional doctrines is striking. The arts of this century demand a transformation of theory.

These arts pose an intimidating challenge to traditional theory. For our initial fascination with the contemporary arts often turns into bafflement when we attempt to understand and explain the disconcerting array of materials and perceptual activities with which they confront us. Traditional aesthetics is uncomfortable with sharply new materials, such as plastics, electronic sounds, and found words and objects. It has difficulty accounting for artistic developments such as process art, where the product is secondary to the activity of producing it, and in explaining artistic activities that have purely ephemeral objects or no identifiable objects at all. Nor can traditional theory easily absorb the deliberate elimination of the customary devices of order from various arts. Even the distinctions among the arts have broken down, and we are often unable to decide where a new development belongs: whether, for example, environments are sculpture or architecture; assemblages are paintings or sculptures; Happenings are theater, painting (as an outgrowth of action painting), or an entirely new art form synthesizing elements of theater, sculpture, dance, painting, and music; and where, if anywhere, performance art can be placed. In fact, multi-media developments like performance art seem deliberately to rebuff the usual classifications of both artists and their art, as music, dance, theatrical spectacle, film, and poetry merge with the creative artist, performer, and audience into an inseparable flow. And among the conventional arts, too, basic distinctions no longer hold. We find it difficult to draw a clear line between design, decoration, illustration, and fine art, between musical sound and noise, and between architecture and environmental sculpture.

Thus the evolution of the arts in the twentieth century has often been described as experimental, controversial, even chaotic. This is hardly the first time in history that artistic innovations have evoked confusion and dismay. Still, in our own period there is a greater variety of diverse, independent, even conflicting movements and strands of development than in any previous age. Some commentators have extolled the new for its differences and its freshness; others have condemned it for its iconoclasm, its sensationalism, or its opportunism. But the artistic impulse toward fresh perceptions persists and, with the passage of time, history has accommodated itself to innovation and change by enlarging its embrace, as the "wild beasts" of the present become the masters of the recent past.

Yet the contemporary arts exhibit more than an expansion of styles, materials, and techniques, for technical innovations do not stand alone. They influence more than the forms of the arts: They affect the manner in which we engage with and appreciate art. And it is here in our relation to the arts that the most profound transformations have occurred, for artists have altered our very ability to identify what art is and our capacities for experiencing it. These are the changes that carry the most significance for aesthetics. By modifying what we accept as art and by reordering the conditions and character of our experience of it, these developments have at the same time undermined the customary beliefs through which people have appreciated, understood, and esteemed art. In the face of all this it is presumptuous for the theory of the arts to decree what qualifies as art and aesthetic. The converse is more appropriate: Aesthetic theory must examine artistic practice carefully and consider how best to respond to this alteration and enlargement of the traditional station and experience of the arts.

It is precisely in accounting for many of these new developments that the traditional axioms of aesthetics have shown themselves increasingly inadequate. During the early years of this century, art movements arose that contradicted one or another of the received principles. By mid-century, however, the arts had developed to the point where these principles were no longer simply inadequate but had become utterly irrelevant in general. Let me illustrate their unsuitability by holding up each of the three eighteenth-century principles that we identified earlier against developments in the recent history of the arts. Many of these have become movements that have by now assumed "official" status and have been absorbed into the mainline history of the arts, where their very presence in that history denies those received principles.[23] While we shall consider these axioms separately here, many artistic developments refute them all. For, indeed, these are not independent principles at all but interdependent supports of a single obsolete philosophical structure.

The assumption that art consists primarily of objects has been challenged and undermined in both obvious and subtle ways. With increasing frequency during the past century, the art object has become less important in the aesthetic situation and at times has vanished altogether. In the visual arts this change appears clearly in the sequence of movements that began in the late nineteenth century and has continued to the present: impressionism, cubism, futurism, dadaism, expressionism, abstract expressionism, optical art, conceptual art, Happenings, and performance art. It was an evolution that started with the dissolution of the representational object within the traditional painting, shifted to the perceptual experience of the painting, and concluded with the disappearance of the painting itself. Braque's bold assertion was a symptom of this change: "I do not paint objects," he stated, "I paint the relations between objects." And

Matisse made a similar claim, saying that he paints not objects but the differences between them. Let us look at this sequence of stages more closely.

Impressionist painting began the process. It dissolved the substantiality of things into atmospheric appearances, from the pointillism of Seurat, whose dabs of brilliant, pure color needed to be mixed by the eye to form a semblance of the coherence and solidity of things in sunlight, to Monet's multiple versions of haystacks, the cathedral at Rouen, lines of poplars, the Seine, and other landscapes under the momentary conditions of the passing sun, suggesting a painterly exemplification of Berkeley's dictum of the century before, "To be is to be perceived."

Yet the dissolution of the pictorial object, separate and independent, only began with the Impressionists. The apparent solidity and permanence of objects do not just dissolve under the fleeting changes of light and atmosphere. These ephemeral objects also inhabit the transitory domain of duration, and painters rendered the very temporality of the perceptual process in various ways. Analytical cubism flattened out the thickness of things by delivering a multiplicity of perspectives simultaneously on the same picture plane, while the futurism of Boccioni, Balla, and Severini portrayed the world by fragmenting objects into the dynamic patterns of motion. In a similar fashion Duchamp's descending nudes unfolded into nothing more than their movement, so that the painterly object was no longer a coherent whole ignoring temporal change but an abstract construct conceptually conjoined from its passing presence.

The perceptual process took a psychological turn in the work of the Expressionists, whose subjects were transfigured by their emotive significance as the painter's heart beat through his hand. In surrealism the painter's oneiric world dominated the visual one, and painting relied more on a metaphorical than a literal image. René Magritte clearly illustrates the key role of imaginative consciousness. A master of the realistic image, he nonetheless did not develop his art out of his ability to render what is directly seen. The effectiveness of Magritte's sensibility lies rather in exciting an awareness of what is not seen at all but is contributed instead by the viewer. Birds in a cage, Magritte once remarked, are a known and expected combination. We can get a more interesting image if we put a fish or a shoe in a cage. "But though these images are strange, they are unhappily accidental, arbitrary. It is possible to obtain a new image which will stand up to examination through having something final, something right about it: it is the image showing an egg in the cage."[24] What Magritte observes reflects the truth of any effective metaphor, where the revealing juxtaposition is its most general condition.

In the third quarter of the twentieth century these developments expanded into the many modes of non-objective painting and sculpture. Trends such as abstract expressionism, optical art, and color field painting require active involvement in the visual perception of ambiguities in linear configurations, and of patterns, textures, and color relationships in order for the work to function at all. Moreover, appreciative engagement is not confined to the visual arts. In speaking of modernist fiction, for example, Annie Dillard observes that the art object's "doing, however internal, requires a perceiver to complete its value." Similar instances can easily be drawn from the other major arts.[25]

Now these disappearances of the object occur within the enduring boundaries of larger things, and it may be argued that even though objects may vanish within a painting, the picture as an art object remains. Many instances appear, however, in which that very object begins to disintegrate. In the installation piece *Les fausses confidences* (The False Confidences) (1983), Giulio Paolini has placed a number of merely primed canvases in a low arrangement, while a slide image is projected above them, exemplifying the liberation of the image from the art object.[26] There are other works in which the entire object recedes into insignificance, becoming merely the occasion for exciting a condition of awareness. Dada illustrates this in those instances where the art object is trivial or obscure, leading appreciation to rest on the meanings associated with it rather than on the object itself. Dada is more than a parody of the sanctimonious attitude toward art that its name signifies: It is a revitalization of aesthetic experience by transferring attention from the exhausted art object into the realm of meaning.[27]

Consider Marcel Duchamp's *The Bride Stripped Bare by Her Bachelors*, the *Large Glass* (1915–1923). Offering "a mechanistic and cynical interpretation of the phenomenon of love," this sculpture of oil, lead wire, foil, dust, and varnish on two large glass panes superimposed to form a vertical panel offers its strongest impression iconographically rather than visually. Only when explicated as the ideally projected working of two love machines, utilizing a hermetic iconography that draws from Duchamp's earlier works, does its message of sexual futility emerge.[28] Yet visual perplexity is not the only condition in which meaning supersedes the object. Duchamp's *Etant Donnée* (The Door of the Given: 1. The Waterfall 2. The Illuminating Gas) (1946–1966) is his counterpart to the transparency of the *Large Glass*.[29] This sculpture takes an obvious subject matter—it is a realistic diorama of a meadow with a nude lying suggestively supine in the foreground—but makes it accessible only when the viewer looks through a pair of tiny peepholes situated in a dark corner. Thus the position of the spectator turns him or her unavoidably into a voyeur and adds the peculiar significance of experiencing *that* meaning to the perceptual consciousness of the object.

The dadaist transformation of the art object into its meaning is extended to its fullest degree in conceptual art. Here meaning so dominates aesthetic consciousness that the object often devolves into trivial gestures, as in Sol Lewitt's *Six Thousand Two Hundred and Fifty-Five Lines* (1970), a surface covered with thirty-three rows of short, parallel vertical lines drawn freehand, or in Vito Acconci's *Step Piece*, a record of a daily sequence of steppings onto and down from a stool at a steady rate of speed, performed as a daily series for a month.[30] In fact, the object may disappear altogether, as in Richard Fleishner's conceptual sculpture, *Sited Works,* in which photographs of striking natural and human-made shapes were placed at various sites at which the viewer was asked to reconstruct their presence imaginatively. Happenings were another recent phase in the dissolution of the independent object. This development was somewhat akin to theater, except that there was often no audience but only participants who pursued in a largely improvisatory fashion the directions contained in a scenario.[31] Currently, performance art continues in a similar direction, providing an occasion for display and participation in which the object is replaced by activity. Protesting against the commercialization and exploitation of the art object, the work of performance artists is deliberately ephemeral. Moreover, it characteristically overrides the conventional boundaries between the traditional arts by employing mixed-media performances, so that even if there were an object, it could not be identified. The various forms of process art, like action painting, earth art, conceptual art, and performance art de-emphasize the final product and stress the activity of making and grasping art. Just as Newton proved in 1666 that color was not a property of matter but rather of light as it interacts with objects, artists in this century seem to be showing us that art is not a property of objects but emerges from the perception by human beings in interaction with objects or events.

Theater provides many clear illustrations of the rejection of the second axiom of traditional aesthetics, the principle that accords a special status to art objects. Some artists in this century have been intrigued by the ordinariness of things, by those very features that make them undistinguished, and where significance lies not in what is presented but in what rises up, as it were, between the cracks. The tragic hero becomes a nondescript, unsuccessful salesman; the dramatic situation is discerned in the transcript of a trial; the poetry of language is sacrificed to the dull mundanities of common speech. *Waiting for Godot* is probably the best-known example of this dethroning of the object, where there are passages in which eloquence of word and gesture, so closely associated with the traditional theater, is notably absent. Action, furthermore, is virtually nonexistent, and the force of the situation emerges from the intimations that rise out of the seemingly pointless reiteration of banalities and, perhaps even more, from the silences that interrupt them.

ESTRAGON:	Ah! (Pause) You're sure it was here?
VLADIMIR:	What?
EST:	That we were to wait.
VLAD:	He said by the tree. (*They look at the tree.*) Do you see any others?
EST:	What is it?
VLAD:	I don't know. A willow.
EST:	Where are the leaves?
VLAD:	It must be dead.
EST:	No more weeping.
VLAD:	Or perhaps it's not the season.
EST:	Looks to me more like a bush.
VLAD:	A shrub.
EST:	A bush.[32]

Similar instances in theater where art emerges from the depiction of the ordinary include such well-known plays as Beckett's *Krapp's Last Tape* and *Happy Days,* and Albee's *The Zoo Story, The American Dream,* and *The Sandbox.* Ionesco's *The Bald Soprano* is composed entirely of inane phrases taken from an English grammar book.

Dada again seems deliberately to deny any special status to art objects. Duchamp's readymades are often cited and frequently ridiculed, yet their artistic significance is nevertheless widely acknowledged. Much of the eloquence of the readymades lies precisely in their ordinary and undistinguished appearance and in the playfulness with which they twit serious aesthetic expectations. Bicycle wheels and urinals parody our search for significant form and our perception of aesthetic qualities. As for uniqueness, a readymade is by definition a standardized object, and placing it on a pedestal merely thrusts its ordinariness upon the viewer.

There are yet more recent instances of art that denies the claim to distinguished stature. One can recognize such art in the assemblage, which may use prosaic, everyday objects in sculptures and on the surface of paintings; in *musique concrète,* which utilizes often chance arrangements of the sounds that constitute the aural ambience of our industrial culture or constructs musical works by manipulating spoken texts electronically; in pop art, which presents the unadorned forms, surfaces, and images that pervade popular culture; in found poetry, fashioned from chance arrangements of words obtained from mundane sources; and in *objets trouvés,* sculpture made out of the detritus of industrial society. Moreover, older and recent technologies alike have generated lithographs, woodcuts, photographs, movies, books, and music recordings for which there is no original but only copies, thus dispensing with the hallowed traditional traits of uniqueness and rarity.

Most interesting of all, however, is the ingenuity with which many artists have contradicted the precept that art objects must be regarded with a special attitude. The experience of art is indeed distinctive, and the doctrine of disinterestedness attempted to promote this by putting a frame of sorts around art, thereby isolating it from the rest of human objects and activities and placing it in a special realm free from practical demands. This frame is primarily a psychological one, a shift in attitude that leads the appreciator to attend to the qualities of the art object without concern for the usual meanings and uses it may have in ordinary experience. Much of the recent history of the arts, however, reads as an intentional denial of disinterestedness, for artists have shaped works in every medium in which the active participation of the appreciator in completing the artistic process is essential to the aesthetic effect. This is not just a matter of bringing attention and interest to the situation but of making a perceptual, sometimes even a physical contribution to the work.

Disinterestedness no longer identifies what is distinctive in the aesthetic situation. With increasing insistence over the past century, artists have been moving toward producing work that denies the isolation of art from the active involvements of daily life. Joining with ancient traditions in the practice and use of the arts, they have seized on the *connections* art has to human activities, instead of stressing its differences and discontinuities. For one need not dissociate oneself from practice and use in order to take something on its own terms, as disinterestedness would have us do. Aesthetic experience thus becomes rather an emphasis on intrinsic qualities and lived experience than a shift in attitude.

This emphasis on qualities and experience is not confined to special, narrow conditions but can be extended everywhere. Moreover, perception now stands in the forefront of active experience instead of merely providing cues for action and meaning, as it does in other situations. Most important, artists have been forcing us to realize that entering the world of art requires the active engagement of the total person and not just a subjective cast of mind. Such engagement emphasizes connections and continuities, and it leads ultimately to the aestheticization of the human world. Art thus remains distinctive without being separate. Just as the doctrine of disinterestedness is the central principle of eighteenth-century aesthetics, subsuming under it the belief that art refers to objects that possess a special and distinctive status, so the idea of aesthetic engagement has become the keystone of the new artistic sensibility.

Appreciative engagement occurs in different ways, depending on the period, style, and artistic modality. In the modern period artists have made this involvement explicit, and many forms of participation may require a variety of overt actions. The most obvious instances are those in which the appreciator must perform some particular act in order for the art work to function completely. The patterns and colors of Yaacov Agam's corrugated paintings change as the viewer walks by, and the paintings are entirely different when seen from the right or the left, the transformation itself becoming part of the experience of the work. Appreciating certain sculptures requires walking into or through them, climbing upon them, or repositioning their parts. One is expected to clamber up or sit on Mark di Suvero's ride 'em pieces, such as *Homage to Brancusi,* a wooden desk chair set on a steel rod, and *Atman,* which incorporates a swinging platform (*see illustration*), while his arrangements of balanced steel beams must be pushed into motion. Again, there are wall sculptures of polished metal that need the reflected image of their viewer to be complete. Wall pieces, paintings, and sculptures are common that respond to environmental stimuli, emitting sounds, echoes, or light at the approach of the appreciator.

While these are innovative uses of overt participation, visual art that uses more traditional forms and technologies may work in similar ways by requiring an active perceiver. Calder's stabiles can be contemplated from a distance, to be sure, but they often can (and should) be walked through as well as around, so that their spaces, planes, mass, and curves can be perceived in continual rearrangement in relation to the body, just as happens with his mobiles. In the one case the wind is the activator; in the other, the viewer. Indeed, the three-dimensionality of most object sculpture requires a circumambulating perceiver to activate its potentialities of shifting surfaces, planes, and interrelations of volumes. Barbara Hepworth makes this explicit when she confesses, "I love working on a large scale so that the whole body of the spectator becomes involved." While painting does not usually take the form of shaped, three-dimensional canvases, the same participatory involvement is necessary. Jasper John's paintings of superimposed numbers are more than a writhing mixture of shapes and colors; they intrigue one into deciphering the forms of the figures, just as cubism requires the viewer to reassemble the multiple planes into a perceptual consciousness of three-dimensional objects. Indeed, such active discernment is a demand of all painting, from recent color field and minimalist art to traditional landscape and portrait painting, where the distance and direction of the viewer, as well as an activating eye, set the forces of the painting in motion. Music, commonly considered an art of receptive enjoyment, has developed modes in which the audience must complete the work by singing or by making percussive sounds. Even in its more conventional forms, music demands an active contribution by which the listener joins in the sequence of sounds shaped by the composer with an active awareness that regenerates the original order of experience.

Innovations in theater have also appeared that disrupt dramatically the conventional protection of distance. Theater-in-the-round, now commonplace, breaks down the conventional separation between audience and performers by dispensing with the proscenium arch and having the audience surround the stage. This usually requires the actors to enter and exit through the audience, a practice that has also been adopted in more traditional theater. Major reforms that recast the conventions of theatrical production are most prominent, however, in the modern movement that began with Artaud and moved through Brecht, Joseph Chaikin's Open Theater, Julian Beck and Judith Malina's Living Theater, and Peter Brook's *Marat/ Sade*, to Jerzy Grotowski's ritualistic theater and, later, his paratheatrics, which abolished any distinction between the actor and the spectator. This development in modern theater might be taken as exemplifying Stanislavsky's comment that you don't *lose* yourself in a role, which would be mystical; you *find* yourself in a role.

A striking instance of theatrical participation was the Open Theater's production of *The Serpent: A Ceremony*. After a compelling pantomime in which Eve finally succumbs to the temptation of the apple, the stage was suddenly filled with an orgy of apples and actors all rolling about, the members of the entire company presenting apples to each other. Then the apples and the actors spilled off the stage, and the players moved among the audience, offering the same treacherous temptation to the bewildered onlookers. The playwright, Jean-Claude van Itallie, expressed this changed theatrical mode well: "The playwright's work is not so much to 'write a play' as to 'construct a ceremony,' " in which the actors 'are in some sense priests or celebrants, and the audience is drawn to participate with the actors in a kind of eucharist."[33]

There are, however, still more subtle modes of participation that take us far beyond the psychological form of appreciative enjoyment found by assuming an attitude of psychical distance. Detective novels that must be read and solved at a computer are only a more explicit use of the reader participation that all novels require. The modernist novel, for example, along with some notable precursors, makes the reader a collaborator in the fictional process. One is no longer entertained by a narrative whose clear line carries an orderly sequence of continuous events. In place of a plot developed in a more or less direct manner, situations, events, and perceptions are described, which the reader is compelled to fit together in order for the novel to become coherent.

Joseph Conrad's *Chance* (1913) may be taken as a precursor of the modernist novel in this respect. It is a tale whose reader must arrange the constant shifts of scene and time in order to fit the narrated events into their chronological sequence. The present-tense account with which the novel begins slips into the background until the very end, while the narrator, Marlow, supplies chapters from the strange history of Flora de Barral. Some of the occurrences are related as Marlow observed them, others as they were told to him by different people who entered Flora's life at critical points, and all are skillfully drawn together with a surprising conclusion in the fictional present. Conrad's technique of fragmentation itself exemplifies the quality of chance that is the motif of the story. Moreover, it also forces the reader to collaborate more directly in the evocation of character and situation than would a simple narrative.

The classic modern case of novelistic fractionalizing is undoubtedly *Ulysses*, in which nearly eight hundred pages of florid detail depict characters, dialogue, situations and, more than anything, the ruminations of its actors. Yet such colorful abundance may obscure the fact that Joyce's expansive novel pursues a regular temporal narrative, encompassing but a single day in the life of Leopold Bloom, a day rich in the company of Dublin's distinctive types and local culture. The reader must contribute to the work's coherence by discerning the order hidden amid the thick flow of events and thoughts.

Recent literature profusely illustrates this same fictional collaboration. One thinks of the *nouveau roman*, fiction that is highly descriptive of things and events but always through "the eye which sees them, the thought which re-examines them, the passion which distorts them." In fact, as Alain Robbe-Grillet put it, "the objects in our novels never have a presence outside human perception, real or imaginary; they are objects comparable to those in our daily lives, as they occupy our minds at every moment."[34] His novel, *The Voyeur*, is exemplary. With dispassionate precision Robbe-Grillet describes the return of a watch salesman to the island on which he had been born long before and where he has gone for a day of business. Through tireless detail, the author enumerates in a mundane, disconnected, and repetitious sequence Mathias's arrival, his colorless attempts at salesmanship, his dull conversations and trivial thoughts. It is a confusion of memories and actual events, which only ends with his departure. Joining with Mathias's consciousness, one begins but gradually to realize that, amid this welter of perceptions and reflections, he is likely responsible for the one notable event that occurred in the entire course of the novel, the death of a young girl, who was apparently raped and murdered. The indefiniteness of consciousness remains to the end.[35]

There is, then, a rich strand among the novels of this century in which the regular recounting of occurrences found in traditional narrative has little interest for the writer. Instead of reality we are given "hallucinations provoked by reality," as Gide once described his own work. The lines between what happens and what is imagined are indiscernible, and we are placed in the state of the characters, a "plane of delirium," in Céline's apt phrase, in which emotions and not objects are captured. Céline's work itself offers the reader no objective narration, no difference between the things and events that take place and the full scope of the jostling emotions they evoke.[36] One is cast into the tawdry, seething undersurface of Parisian life, petty and mean but absorbing in its details and characters. No dispassionate gaze is possible, no curious but white-gloved gentility; one can touch that world only by entering it.

Other cases of demanding fictional participation are easy to find. There is Nabokov's *Pale Fire,* a novel that flickers simultaneously among the incidents in an epic poem, in the life of its poet, and in that of the poem's commentator, which are all evoked in the exegesis of the poem. In Lawrence Durrell's *Alexandria Quartet,* each of the four novels purveys its own distinct perspective on the same events as they have been fashioned through the eye and mind of a different participant. For the work to attain its complete effect, the reader must join together and encompass, if not reconcile, the accounts. The parts of Durrell's *Avignon Quintet,* a more recent "quincunx" of five novels, as he calls it, are interconnected in still more complex involutions. Such novelistic fragmentation is hardly new. It gives a discursive charm, for example, to Laurence Sterne's *Tristram Shandy* and Tobias Smollett's *The Expedition of Humphrey Clinker,* both from the eighteenth century. But in the modern novel such techniques have become a recurrent theme.[37]

Still other arts share a particular need for participation to attain appreciative fulfillment. There is film, which captures the consciousness of the viewer and joins it with the moving eye of the camera in a living sequence of events. There are architecture and urban design which, contrary to our usual expectations, do not offer contemplative objects but require human activity to complete them, perceptually as well as functionally. Dance carries irresistible somatic appeal, as the viewer's empathetic attention accompanies the dancer and may even break out involuntarily into overt movement.

Such experiences in the arts as these did not appear spontaneously. Like all cultural phenomena, they are part of an evolutionary process that still continues. We shall grasp these developments better if we consider the origins of such changes in our experience and the social and perceptual transformations that characterize them. These developments, moreover, possess theoretical importance, for they suggest the recasting of aesthetics into a unified theory that reflects the continuity, perceptual integration, and engagement of our new encounters with the arts. Let us see how these have come about.

CHAPTER TWO

The unity of aesthetic experience

THE ARTISTIC TRANSFORMATIONS THAT CONTRADICT THE INHER-
ited aesthetic of the eighteenth century are no anomaly in the history
of the arts. They must not be dismissed as deviant, an unhappy
though temporary digression from the true and proper course of
things. They move, in fact, close to the far older tradition of artistic
integration that is still a vital part of non-industrial cultures. Yet the
philosophical landscape that has dominated both understanding and
appreciation for some two centuries has shaped an aesthetics of
separation, isolation, contemplation, and distance. So powerful has
this doctrine been that criticism, explanation, and response have all
been directed and determined by its principles. And so thoroughly
have these principles infiltrated our thinking that no doubt remains
and no alternatives seem conceivable.

Yet both theory and appreciation must rest on what happens in
art, and the artistic developments of the past century are part of a
transformation in perception and understanding that compels us
toward a different aesthetic. We have seen how these shifts in art
objects and artistic practices require a new mode of response, an
appreciative attention that may extend to the point of active participation. This takes many forms, as many forms as there are arts
and art objects. Some modes of participation are direct and overt,

others are more subtle. Yet all carry us far beyond the psychological model of contemplative enjoyment that is found in the conventional attitude and toward a unity of experience. If there is one distinctive trait of art, traditional as well as contemporary, it is its ever-insistent demand for appreciative engagement. Disinterested contemplation has become an academic anachronism.

Why has so bold a change occurred in the experience of art? Are these developments the result of the ongoing evolution of the arts? Are there special and distinctive conditions in the modern world that have impelled the arts in new directions and intensified that process? It may be that both are the case. To help meet these questions, let us consider more closely some of the forces that have contributed to the shift of recent art away from the more conventional patterns and forms of objects and appreciation.

Of the many sources of such change, two hold special interest. One is the succession of technological innovations that industrialism introduced; the second, the social and perceptual transformations of the modern world. New materials, objects, and techniques that arise out of the technology of industrial production have entered into the art world and profoundly influenced both the vocabulary and the practice of artists. At the same time, fundamental social changes in the modern world have reshaped our perceptual activities in the arts into new and different forms. These developments help account for the appearance of nontraditional materials and techniques in the arts, and they may explain the encouragement of experiences in art that previously had little place or recognition.

Art is one of the powerful elements in human culture, and its evolution has significance not only for its own future but for understanding the larger society as well. Furthermore, the arts are both a symptom and a sign of cultural change, and at no time has this been more evident than today. For the arts, both popular and high, pervade modern societies in unprecedented variety and scope. Moreover, the attention they receive is more focused and the range of their public and their effects probably greater than at any time since the classical age. Yet the influences are reciprocal, because social and technological developments have themselves deeply affected the practice and experience of the arts.

It would be strange to expect that the arts could stand unaffected by the industrial transformation of modern society. What is surprising is how long traditional ways of making and enjoying art have been able to persist unaltered. But now that such changes are upon us, we find it as difficult to explain them in traditional terms as to account for the power of a nuclear generator by the principle of the lever. Industrial technology has transfigured the art object, just as it has transformed other objects of human making and, more subtly and profoundly still, our relationships with them. Yet in what ways?

Features that are typical of art objects of the past are not difficult to single out. They arose in large measure from the fact that these articles were produced by skilled craftsmen using relatively simple hand tools.[1] These objects combined intricate workmanship and unique design with high cost resulting from the large amount of labor required to produce them and their consequent rarity. Because of their manner of production, traditional art objects possessed signs of human workmanship and fallibility, often displaying considerable irregularity and providing maximum opportunity for unstudied, intuitive decisions in the process of fashioning them. And since this art performed a variety of functions, such as contributing to religious worship or recording people and events, artists were forced to accept severe limitations on their choice of subject matter, on their ability to abstract, and on the sorts of audience responses they could evoke.

At the same time the fine arts possessed a celebratory character, for they were associated with ritual and various forms of social privilege. This encouraged the development of a sharp distinction between people's practical activities, which demanded an unqualified commitment to utility, and the artistic activities of aesthetic enjoyment, which were cut off from practical affairs and regarded for their own intrinsic worth. Along with such regard went a sharply defined difference between the objects of beauty and those of utility. Art objects were treated with special care. They were treasured, honored for their age and for the status they conferred on their patron or owner, and safeguarded as possessing inherent and permanent value. Moreover, these traits were not only descriptive features of past art; they carried a powerful normative connotation as well. It was just such features that art was expected to possess.

Industrial technology changed all this. It generated an entire set of new features in the things that surround us, and these traits have been reflected in the contemporary arts. In place of unique objects possessing an intricate structure, produced by hand in small numbers and at great cost, we now have uniform articles manufactured in enormous quantities, having simplicity of design and economy of price. The irregularity and fallibility of traditional art objects and the intuitive manner by which they were formerly fashioned have given way to a flawless precision governed by careful calculation. And instead of objects treasured for their age and permanence, we value the polished newness of things that are expendable in the light of changes and improvements.

As happened with the traits of art produced by traditional means, these new features have also come to assume the character of aesthetic standards and have given birth to new materials, objects, and techniques of artistic production. The emancipation of the arts from subservience to historical accuracy and devotional purposes has encouraged their propensity to abstraction. At the same time, their integration into the traffic of daily life has replaced the isolated object of art with one absorbed through its function into the course of ordinary human activity. Artists now make free use of materials from the new technology, such as plastics, acrylics, machine parts, electronic sounds, Styrofoam, and foam rubber. They utilize everyday articles, such as newspapers, kitchen utensils, and theater marquees, and ordinary situations, such as factory work and assembly lines. They employ impermanent materials in the form of tree leaves, paper, light, balloons, and such elements of mass culture produced by this new technology as comic strips and street noises. Visual artists are drilling, welding, dripping, and splashing. Composers are electronically manipulating recorded sounds and synthesizing new ones. And artists in many media are composing, designing, writing, and drawing by computer. Behind the use of the materials, objects, and techniques of an industrial culture lies the inspiration of the science and technology that produced it.

This is hardly a recent tendency, for we sometimes overlook how responsive many of the arts have long been to the material transformation of the modern world. We forget how, a century ago, Seurat, Signac, and Cross developed pointillism as a method of producing paintings that drew upon the mechanical techniques of modern technology, the analytic method of scientific inquiry, and the principles of optics. We fail to recall how Zola regarded the novel as the model of a scientific experiment and transformed the novelist into an observer and an experimentalist, and how at the same time the naturalistic novel responded to the ideas of evolutionary biology and revealed the conditions of an emerging industrial society.

Science and technology have continued to exercise a profound influence on theories of artistic production and on their results. In their paintings Léger and the other cubists moved from the geometry of the machine to the geometrization of nature, while Gropius and the Bauhaus discovered in the machine the modern medium and principles of design. More recently, painters have applied scientific concepts and terminology to their work, such as the optical artists associated with the *Nouvelle Tendance,* who create uniform patterns of many small geometric units, which they call *periodic structures,* and speak of elements of their works as *information* and of their compositional arrangement as *programming.* Composers, too, have responded in similar ways when they term the musical score *time–space* and use graphs, statistical charts, symbolic codings, and laws and formulas from mathematics and the physical sciences. Technological tools like the computer and the music synthesizer are now commonplace, and recording on magnetic tape has both assisted performers and replaced them.

Recording techniques have themselves transformed the musical object through the variety of ways in which it can be manipulated, such as by the balance of microphones, echo chambers, multi-track recordings, and the splicing and editing of tapes. It can even be said that recording has turned music into a group product, the result of a collaboration between the composer, the performer, and the sound engineer. Some commentators have even claimed that recording has made the live concert an anachronism.[2] Recording has so changed the requirements of performance that recorded music has become a different art from live music. Tempos, for example, are regularly taken faster to help eliminate dead spots. In a live performance one can observe the player preparing during a pause for what will follow, while the recording replaces this visual spectacle by pushing ahead to the next notes. Moreover, the technical excellence of recorded performances usually results from a collage spliced together out of many takes. The music no longer lives and grows as a freshly re-creative act; it is constructed instead like a machine product.

Mechanical precision and standardization have also assumed other forms, as when minimal, optical, and certain pop artists use repeated patterns and mathematical exactness of line and arrangement. Even when objects of contemporary art appear to deny these features, as sometimes occurred with Happenings, in pop art, and now in performance art, these art forms are still most understandable as commentaries on and reactions to the technological transformations of industrialism and the mass commercial culture that has accompanied it, rather than as spontaneous developments.[3] The Industrial Revolution has finally reached the arts.

While it is true that the mechanization of the arts may seem at times to diminish the personal creative element, this is not a sign of the intrinsic failure of technology. It rather suggests new forms and directions to a creative imagination. Electronic technology, for instance, has led to new types of musical composition, since synthesizers can produce and combine sounds in ways that musical instruments could never do directly. And there are parallels here with other contemporary arts. Traditional techniques of sculpture reflect a craft technology in which the individual sculptor designs and executes his own marble from the crude unshaped block of stone. As bronze became a desirable material, the sculptor began to produce wax or clay models from which molds were made and bronze cast by artisans. The point has now been reached at which sculptors not only have others make castings from their models but also have them make sheet-metal sculptures from small paper cutouts, as Picasso did, and build large constructions from designs and sketches, as was David Smith's practice. Some artists now utilize the new and discarded prefabricated products of an industrial technology, at times simply selecting and mounting the pieces, as in the work of the dadaists, constructivists, and junk sculptors.

Yet probably the most striking and suggestive parallel is in the transformation of the dramatic arts by the advent of photography and the motion picture camera. While traditional theater has continued to function, though perhaps more weakly, with less influence, and to smaller audiences, a new technology has produced a new art in which the actual movement and discourse of people is replaced by the presence of images fixed on a celluloid strip and shown in rapid succession so as to create the illusion of movement. A mechanical process has displaced the old rapport between actors and audience, but a new and powerful experience has been created in which the film audience is able to dispense with the conventional and sometimes stiff illusions so necessary to the appreciation of traditional theater. Instead, through superb mechanical contrivance the audience loses touch with itself and enters a new world.

This transformation of the materials and objects of art through the pervasive influence of industrial technology has been paralleled by new perceptual activities resulting from fundamental social changes. Aristocratic art has had to react to increasing democratization. No longer is art fit only for kings: It must satisfy the new masses, the financial demands of the star system, and the pressure through unionization of performing artists for a solid and steady income. Arts management has shifted from the impresario to the corporation. Demographic isolation has given way to enormous concentrations of population, joined further by the media into national and international audiences. Local and regional cultures have become obscured by mass industrial culture and its transnational magnifications of the production, distribution, and consumption of art.

The relationship between these social changes and artistic practices and perception is still obscure, but their effects are undeniable and profound. As they have combined with industrial technology, social changes have generated new modes of making and perceiving art. One such development is vastly greater inclusiveness, both in the type and range of perceptual qualities and in the objects admitted to aesthetic perception. We are asked to perceive the interaction of color areas arranged in stripes or panels and to discriminate among the subtle gradations of value in monochromatic canvases. Electronic instruments have greatly expanded the frequency range, timbre, and rhythmic intricacy of the sounds we encounter. We are blinded by lights, startled by mirrors, inflamed by an uninhibited vocabulary of dance gestures, transported in fascinated absorption by film. We walk through sculptures, readjust our sense of spatial order in environments and in daring architectural structures, sit alongside the performers in a theatrical event. We are made to view the sacrilegious, the obscene, the mundane, the commercial; to hear the sound of traffic or of dripping water; to vibrate bodily from the impact of intense volume of sound or cringe before the physical force of high frequencies.

Not only have the contemporary arts vastly extended the range of the traditional aesthetic senses and objects, they have also drawn on sensory capacities never before allowed or at least recognized.

Certainly the appeal to our tactile and kinesthetic sensibilities represents a major shift in expanding the limits of aesthetic perception beyond the traditional aesthetic senses of sight and hearing. Along with the enlargement of our sensory responsiveness has come the breakdown of aesthetic prohibitions, and none is more significant than that against the sensual.[4] It is easier to be a visual spiritualist than a tactile one and with the inclusion of the contact senses, the overtly erotic has been admitted and intensified in dance, sculpture, film, and the novel. As sexuality has become more commonplace in the arts, artists continue to press the boundaries of art beyond the current taboos against sexual deviance, the violently grotesque, excreta, and death.

This enlargement of aesthetic sensibility has produced at least two major shifts in the perceptual experience of the contemporary arts. We have already explored one of these in some detail, the ways in which appreciative distance has been bridged and appreciation changed from contemplative enjoyment into active participation. For aesthetic engagement has joined together the object and the appreciator, the artist and the art object, the creator and the perceiver, and all of these under the active influence of performance. It is interesting to consider how the arts have deliberately overridden the perceptual separation among the main factors in aesthetic experience. The art object has succeeded in imposing itself inescapably on the appreciator when the listener can no longer remain contemplatively removed in the face of amplified music of deafening volume, when sound environments envelop performers and audience together, spotlights flash blindingly on the spectator, actors and dancers enter through the audience and at times from among the audience, environments are constructed into which one must enter or through which one must pass, sculptures and assemblages are fashioned whose mirror surfaces incorporate the viewer into the work both as image and as participant through the very act of perceiving them, optical art twists the eyes in painfully futile attempts at conformity, plotless films demand that the viewer give dramatic shape to the passage of time—the list could be continued indefinitely.[5] In similar ways the creative artist and the object are integrated, as in action painting and performance art; the creator and the perceiver have joined together, as in some forms of modern, ethnic, and improvisatory dance and in audience participation theater; and the performer has been assimilated with all the others, as in Happenings, performance art, and computerized novels. Through patterns of continuity and reciprocity, all the elements of the aesthetic situation have combined to form a unity of experience.

Yet another shift in perceptual experience consists in the deliberate integration of features from ordinary life into art. The relationship between life and art has always powered the novel and has been a tenet of the avant-garde since early in this century, but in many of the contemporary arts it has become a main theme.[6] One of the most striking ways in which art is made to reflect these features is through the use of chance elements. Aleatoric music, action painting, literary works that require the reader to choose from among alternative endings, all incorporate the fortuitousness of ordinary experience in an artistic format. Art and life have also been integrated by artists' use of the materials of everyday life, such as prosaic events, commonplace objects, and ordinary speech. There is the music of John Cage, which incorporates every kind of noise in its sonic material. Cage, who observed that "one could view everyday life itself as theater," himself became an influence on the development of Happenings.

While a passing artistic phase, Happenings both exemplified the new perceptual aesthetic and influenced the movements that followed. The Happening not only synthesized all the elements of the aesthetic field into a single creative activity but deliberately drew its themes and materials from the ongoing course of ordinary life and from industrial objects and activities. The audience became a part of the work as the spectators were drawn into the action and forced to respond to a new environment, to a strange adventure, to a parody of customary things and events. The Happening may have reached its fullest extension with Regis Debray, who regarded a revolution as a coordinated series of guerrilla Happenings. Some of his admirers, in fact, took part in Happenings as training for future happenings when they would use guns and grenades. Here Wilde's dictum about life imitating art finds its ultimate exemplification.

The *objets trouvés* used in collages and sculptures intentionally draw in associations from prosaic sources of the most unlikely sorts, leading to parody, satire, or the direct criticism of social beliefs and practices, as well as to an enhanced awareness of one's daily environment. Contemporary dance choreographers often develop their art out of ordinary activities and commonplace gestures, as in Merce

Cunningham's "How to Pass, Kick, Fall, and Run" which, incidentally, uses Cage's music, or in Twyla Tharp's "Push Comes to Shove." This interplay with the conditions of daily experience has long been part of film, and nowhere with such intensity as in much contemporary cinema, with its attention to the visual details of ordinary things and places. In portraying real surfaces with free movement in time and space, the film approaches the directness and randomness of life. The television documentary and drama exploit the capacity of this medium to lead the viewer into intimate contact with particular people and human situations. The images used in pop art and video art, too, derive their force from their association with the objects and events of ordinary life. Robert Rauschenberg, for example, denies any division between "Sacred Art" and "Profane Life," and insists on working "in the gap between the two." Indeed, as he once remarked, "There is no reason not to consider the world one gigantic painting."[7]

Theater has joined the other arts here. Everything is a fitting subject, and in the most candid, graphic terms, from liberalism and race relations to homosexuality, deformity, martial problems, and the sex act. The distancing logic of a plot has receded and in its place appear the ordinary details of life that we never trouble to notice, such as the series of movements by which a man sits in a chair or a woman handles a cup or moves her lips, actions of whose significance Harold Pinter is a master. Dramatic shape is replaced by the mystery of the mundane, and instead of resting on a structure that the playwright has provided, we must move on the crest of our own attention.[8] Feminist poets, black poets, and beat poets are united in their intolerance for poetry that is removed from the hard pressures of daily life and respond with highly rhetorical works.

Nowhere is it more apparent how art has become integrated with the lived environment than in the two arts that, perhaps more than any others, embody the artistic vitality of the present: architecture and film. Auguste Renoir had once commented that "painting, like carpentry or iron work, is a craft and as such, subject to the same rules." And artists have always known that the arts embody a technology that involves, with etymological literalness, a joining or a fitting together. But it is in modern architecture and the film, offspring of our industrial technology, that this integration has asserted itself most strikingly. Both architecture and film embody an aesthetics of function, the one as an explicit concourse for human activity, the other as an absorbing creation and commentary on it. The steel and glass skyscraper, for example, is a mechanical building, a "machine pure and simple," as Frank Lloyd Wright called it, and it has a reflexive force as both the embodiment of industrial activity and a monument to industrial power. Gropius compared the low-ceilinged, air-conditioned cells of the modern skyscraper with the low-ceilinged, humid cells that form the underpinning of the Gothic cathedral. As the latter reminded us of our humble position before God, so the former reminds us of our humble condition before the dollar. While history and fantasy have returned with postmodern architecture, the functional aspect has not disappeared but only receded behind the surface, where it has always been present. And film, perhaps the most extraordinary artistic flowering of our technological age, functions as an eloquent depiction, commentary, and influence on human customs and modern culture.

By stressing their continuity with the technological aspect of artistic production and the functional aspect of social uses of the arts, the contemporary arts have again reaffirmed their affiliation with the basic activities of human life. In a multitude of ways, the aristocratic diffidence of the traditional arts has given way to democratic acceptance and involvement. Whatever the order of influence, life and art have become inseparable.

This lengthy catalog is being continually supplemented by what has become a major motif of the arts of this century—the deliberate dethroning of art and its reintegration into the course of normal human activity. This gives the contemporary arts both a humanistic and diabolical aspect. The childlike, the primitive, the fantastic and dreamlike, the utterly simple have appeared in painting, sculpture, and film accompanied by their obverse: the offensive, the grotesque, the brutal, the scatological, the perverted. Gone is the ideal of beauty and in its place appear the mundane and subterranean. Music, dance, and the plastic arts have joined the other arts in a kind of theater of life in which we are told nothing and presented everything.

Industrial technology, then, has radically altered the methods and objects of the arts, while social and perceptual changes in the modern world have overridden the conventional separation among the component factors in aesthetic experience. These changes have encouraged the return of the high arts from an exalted but isolated position in the domain of social life to the more integrated yet central position that has been their usual place in the rich tapestry of every other civilization. While still different factors have undoubtedly been at work in shaping the human world and the art of our time, the techniques of industrialism and the inescapable changes in human life and experience they have caused are certainly among the most powerful and pervasive forces affecting the art of our day.

What is the significance for aesthetic theory of the developments that have transformed the arts? Can we not regard the innovations we have just reviewed as mere exceptions, perhaps even aberrations in the history of the arts? Might they not be but a facile appeal to self-indulgent and childish interests or a surrender to the inconstant tastes of a sensation-seeking public, cynically exploited by artists and entrepreneurs?[9] And how are we to regard the set of axioms that has dominated our thinking about art for the past two centuries, the legacy of aesthetics' origin as a discipline? Will an aesthetics of engagement abandon all that has special significance in the arts in a futile quest for acceptance and inclusiveness?

Whatever course we follow, these changes in artistic and aesthetic practice cannot be left floating freely above the theory of the arts. Nor can we legislate away innovation by appealing to traditional concepts and principles or modifying them by *ad hoc* explanations that leave their basic structure intact. These changes are not peripheral, mere aberrations in the conservative course of high art. Rather they carry art's leading impulse forward and extend its force and scope. At the same time, by setting ourselves to account for these developments in the arts, we are not making a prior commitment to their value. Great achievements in the arts appear in the same modes as lesser ones, and aesthetics should explain rather than judge. More important than greatness for us here are the forms and processes the arts have taken. For judging the new and different by the standards of the old and customary will easily establish their failure. Such "proof," however, follows from tendentious criteria and the question-begging inherent in any procedure that determines its conclusion in advance. It would be far more useful to judge value at the conclusion of an inquiry rather than at its beginning. In art we are too ready with value judgments before we have discovered the peculiar bent of a work and learned how to engage with it. Value is the result of the outcome of that process, of how effectively an object functions in the aesthetic situation. Deciding on value in advance preempts the possibilities of experiencing the new and unexpected and limits our ability to grasp them.

Yet an aesthetic that accommodates the fundamental changes that have been taking place in the arts is not compelled to repudiate the art of the past. A new theoretical context may, in fact, revitalize the traditional arts by making them more accessible to a modern sensibility. As art is not eternal, neither are the modes of perception and consciousness with which we experience them. That is why the interpretive richness in good art leads us beyond the qualities inherent in the object alone and makes that art relevant to new conditions. Art can thus outlive the theories by which it has been explained and gain in force through a more inclusive aesthetic. An aesthetic theory that can join the contemporary with the traditional arts will help us re-establish contact with our artistic traditions so they are not so much the repository of obsolescent curiosities and sanctified monuments as living forces in a present enlarged by historical resonance.

There is an alternative to the Enlightenment's aesthetics of distance and disinterestedness, which is a history more than a tradition in Western culture. Although its origins are most ancient and its sources deep, the idea of human immanence in the world has long flowed as an undercurrent. It appears in animism, the belief that spirit inhabits all things, both living and inanimate, human and nonhuman. It lies at the heart of Dionysian ecstasy, which the contemplative tradition from classical times on has always viewed with suspicion and hostility. It is found in mysticism, that inexpressible merging of person and place, of human and universe. It can be discerned in the cohesiveness of ritual that binds together a social group through the sacred objects and acts of ceremony. It appears in the shared social activities of the marketplace, the sports arena, the parade, the circus. It lies at the heart of acts of friendship and love. Engagement is the signal feature of the world of action, of social exchange, of personal and emotional encounters, of play, of cultural movements like romanticism and, as is our claim here, of the direct and powerful experiences that enclose us in situations involving art, nature, or the human world in intimate and compelling ways.[10]

In spite of the complexity of our present encounters with the arts, a theoretical order emerges from this empirical ground. Arranging itself around the idea of engagement, it unfolds into an account that by its breadth, inclusiveness, and fluidity is able to respond to the richness of objects and experiences in the modern arts as well as the traditional ones. While the model of separation and distance may serve useful purposes in analysis, scholarship, and criticism, that standard misleads our experience of art by placing it under external constraints. Contemplative theories impede the full force of art and misdirect our understanding of how art and the aesthetic actually function. A theory of engagement, in contrast, responds directly to the activities of art as they occur most distinctively and forcefully.

Appreciation does not emanate from a mental beacon trained on an object of art. Rather, an essential reciprocity binds object and appreciator as they act on and respond to each other through an indivisible interplay of forces. Appreciative perception is not merely a psychological act or even an exclusively personal one. It rests on a mutual engagement of person and object that is both active and receptive on every side. A comprehensive theory must incorporate the reciprocity that animates the aesthetic encounter, for intimate bonds join the perception of an object and the object of perception into an indissoluble unity of experience.

The history of the arts offers vivid examples that bear out the demands art makes in appreciation. Renaissance Madonnas, from whose dais open steps unfold, invite the viewer to approach. The west portal of the cathedral at Chartres extends outward and its flanking jamb statues shepherd one inside. The tradition of seventeenth-, eighteenth-, and nineteenth-century landscape painting in western Europe, as we shall see in the next chapter, shapes the scene so as to lead the viewer into its space. Indeed, the entire arts of dance, music, and architecture require an essential contribution from the person appreciating them.

This participatory impulse, unofficially present in the arts of the past, has been grasped as a basic force by artists in this century. The impact of dadaism, surrealism, and pop art does not reside in the object or the image but in their interplay with the meanings and associations the viewer is obliged to contribute. This locus of appreciation extends further in conceptual art, where the object recedes into insignificance or disappears altogether. We have spoken of paintings and sculptures that require the active intervention of the appreciator, theater that merges actors with audience, novels that require the collaboration of the reader for their coherence and completion, music that absorbs the listener into the sound experience—and the documentation is constantly growing.[11] Perceptual engagement has become a major feature of the contemporary arts.

Aesthetic engagement, then, joins perceiver and object into a perceptual unity. It establishes a coherence that displays at least three related characteristics: continuity, perceptual integration, and participation. Continuity contributes to this unity by the inseparability (although not the indistinguishability) of the factors and forces that join to give an identity to aesthetic experience. Perceptual integration occurs in synaesthesia, the experiential fusion of the senses, as they join in a resonance of meaning and significance. And the appreciator participates in the aesthetic process by activating the unity of the factors that compose it. How do these modes of engagement work?

The notion of continuity reflects the understanding that art is not separate from other human pursuits but is assimilated into the full scope of individual and cultural experience without sacrificing its identity as a mode of experience. Art objects share a common origin in human activity and in productive technology with other objects that do not ordinarily work in an aesthetic context. In addition, social, historical, and cultural factors influence the kind of work artists do and the uses that are made of their art. Aesthetic perception is bound up with the range of meanings, associations, memories, and imagination that permeate all perception, while aesthetic experience is part of the entire spectrum of human experience. There is mutuality here, too, for our dwelling in the aesthetic situation affects the broader social and personal uses of art, and these uses, in turn, influence the character of appreciation.

A profound sense of continuity appears in the rediscovery by artists of the power of art in preliterate cultures to work in ritualistic ways that bind people to earth and cosmos. Some contemporary sculptors and environmental artists emulate the kinds of patterns in which prehistoric cultures shaped mounds of earth and arranged stones that seem to embody a cosmic significance. The influence of such ancient art both exemplifies and symbolizes these artists' recognition of the social significance and function of art.[12] Continuity is found, too, in a renewed interest in murals and in the aesthetic resonance of sites and artifacts that goes far beyond the geometry of land surveys and the preservation of antiquities. The music of India, Bali, and other non-Western cultures exercises a deep influence on many present-day composers, as that art continues to flower from its ancient roots in ways that far exceed the regular and bounded parameters of most Western music of the past three centuries. Continuity recognizes, then, that art and its experience are not sequestered but enter into the rich activity of ongoing human culture more easily than we may have realized. Once we acknowledge this, we can begin to understand how art both affects and responds to those forces that make human culture so fascinating and unpredictable. All this affirms the intimate relation between art and life.

What is generically distinctive here is not the objects of art but the situation we call aesthetic. Yet there is continuity here, too, for aesthetic experience has connections with other modes of experience—practical, social, or religious—although its qualitative features combine in a distinctive and identifiable fashion.[13]

Perceptual integration, the second trait of aesthetic engagement, is the means by which we grasp the continuities in aesthetic experience, the ways in which all the elements in the aesthetic situation join in the procession of a unified experience. Not only have the conventional distinctions become obscured between the creator of art, the aesthetic perceiver, the art object, and the performer; their functions have tended to overlap and merge as well, and they are experienced as continuous. In art, as in modern society, traditional roles have blurred.[14]

Moreover, the aesthetic field exhibits not only an integration of the different factors in this kind of experience but a fusion of the various sensory modalities as well, a phenomenon known as synaesthesia. The psychology of perception has joined phenomenological philosophy in undermining the common division of sense experience into separate channels of sensation, each governed by its dominant sense. Still, a backward tendency in aesthetics and criticism continues to subsist on this repudiated convention, dividing the arts and aligning them with the sense or senses that appear to dominate each. So we have the visual arts, the musical or sonic arts, the spectator arts of theater and dance, and the lower, practical tactile arts or crafts. An irresistible impulse of artistic innovation in this century has been to deliberately break art away from these sensory channels, and this tendency has accelerated. Early efforts, such as Scriabin's combining of perfume and color with music and Rimbaud's discovery of the colors of the vowels, have multiplied in many directions into talking sculpture, sounding wall panels, theatricalized musical performances, and performance art that synthesizes a wide range of artistic materials and sensory qualities to become a contemporary cliche in multi-media events. Most important, though, is the fact that these are not so much combinations of familiar elements as new syntheses, unities of experience that make free use of the actual integration of the various sense receptors in the act of perception.

Yet what adds to the marvelous complexity of perceptual experience is that it is more than sensory in its qualitative content. As human beings we are cultural creatures, unable to sense without the presence of associations and meanings. The very process of sensory development is, in fact, a process of acculturation through which ideas and beliefs become embodied in our direct experience. These meanings and attitudes are not merely intellectual constructs or internal accompaniments of sensation but are subtly infused into our sensory experience. Through trained awareness the viewer can activate the perceptual qualities of color, line, sound, and spatial relationships. By reconstructing the images that poetic discourse evokes, the reader can re-embody the poet's sentiment. By contributing the meanings and associations that surround dada and pop art, the beholder can reconstitute the aura of consciousness that lies at their center. And by recognizing the ingenious variety of self-reflexiveness that has become frequent in the arts of our day, several levels of awareness can work simultaneously in intriguing interplay.

To understand the continuity and integration of experience is to be conscious of these factors as a presence in our actual sensory engagement in the world. New ideas mean new perceptions, and the exclusivity of the intellectual and sensory realms recedes into the history of obsolete ideas, along with other dualistic mythologies of objectivity. The integration of experience has become a hallmark of the arts and a challenge to aesthetics.

Engagement, finally, the central feature of the new aesthetic, stresses the active nature of aesthetic experience and its essential participatory quality. This involvement occurs in many different orders of activity—sensory, conscious, physical, and social—but it is most pronounced in aesthetic experience. The way the arts actually function, in the past as well as the present, reflects such involvement. For aesthetic engagement is grounded on a tradition far older and stronger than any to which the theory of aesthetic disinterestedness can appeal. Indeed, the principle of engagement reflects most of the history of the arts as they have functioned in diverse societies. Aspects of that tradition are found in Western cultural history in the original Greek notion of *mimēsis* and in Aristotle's theory of catharsis, and it is reflected in writers as different as Schiller and Nietzsche, and more recently in Dewey, Merleau-Ponty, and Derrida.

All this suggests the importance of a participatory model that recognizes the aesthetic reciprocity of both perceiver and object in the aesthetic situation. The notion of experiential unity is central here, for art does not consist of objects but of situations in which experiences occur. A unified field of interacting forces involves perceivers, objects or events, creative initiative, and some kind of performance or activation. Its principal factors—appreciative, material, creative, and performative—delineate the various dimensions of an integrated and unified experience.

The concept that best expresses the integral yet complex experience we call aesthetic is the *aesthetic field*. Here the four factors represented by the object, the perceiver, the creator, and the performer are the central forces at work, affected by social institutions, historical traditions, cultural forms and practices, technological developments in materials and techniques, and other such contextual conditions. To single out any one of them as the locus of art is to misrepresent the whole of the aesthetic field by a part. All are essential to a descriptive rendering of aesthetic experience because they have a constitutive effect on such experience. Art objects are not inherently different from other objects, but they possess features that make them effective in the aesthetic situation in which they become art. A field theory of aesthetics is thus very different from the tradition of eighteenth-century thought. Art is not in the object alone. As Wallace Stevens observed, "One is not duchess/A hundred yards from a carriage."[15]

However, an aesthetics of engagement cannot be established by historical analysis or abstract argument alone, nor can it hold for the arts by virtue of its internal coherence or inherent reasonableness. An empirical theory requires an empirical argument, and this must be built on individual cases. The best support for this alternative aesthetics comes from a close scrutiny of how the four dimensions of aesthetic experience join together in active engagement in the particular arts. Let us turn at this point, then, to the arts themselves.

Each of the chapters in Part Two will illustrate the engaging power of one or more of these dimensions—appreciative, creative, material, and performative—through the examination of a specific art. However, all four are simultaneously present, and any art could exemplify the other dimensions of what is a single experiential process. These chapters will help reveal the richness of the notion of engagement. Most important of all, they testify to its value in a reconstruction of aesthetics that can restore to the experience of art its transformative power.

Engagement in
the arts

PART TWO

CHAPTER THREE

The viewer in the landscape

PAINTING IS THE ART OF OBJECTS *PAR EXCELLENCE.* PAINTINGS ARE things, stretched canvases covered with colored oil, paper saturated with tinted water, firm surfaces coated with pigments that have been mixed with a vehicle so they can be spread, blended, and fixed in place. Paintings are typically hung on walls or placed on racks. They are produced individually by artist craftpersons, valued for their uniqueness, judged by their intrinsic properties, appraised for their ability to command a price on the auctioneer's block, considered by the astute a sound investment of stable value, collected to join other treasured things. So much is painting thought of as an object that paintings are the typical referent of the term *art* and the painter is taken as the prototypical artist. The precious products of an untidy process, paintings receive the benefits of our object-centered society. They have become cherished acquisitions, badges of affluence and culture.

As an object of making, judging, and valuing, so too is painting the exemplary object of aesthetic appreciation. Stationary, silent, circumscribed by its frame, the painting stands ready for our gaze at a respectful and proper distance. Within the art of painting, certain genres in particular lend themselves to being thought of as appreciative objects: landscapes that frame the view of a prospect seen from a distance; portraits that render the appearance of persons distinguished by nobility, wealth, achievement, or self-esteem; still lifes that group common articles in appealing arrangements of shapes, volumes, colors, and textures. We typically stand before these works in respectful silence, regarding their subjects with curiosity, delight, and perhaps understanding. Painting seems to accord completely with the tradition of aesthetic theory for which disinterested contemplation is the appropriate mode of appreciation. How can this "single piece, comprehended in one view, and formed according to one single intelligence, meaning, or design; which constitutes a real whole," as Shaftesbury put it, how can this object be taken as a partner in the process of aesthetic engagement?[1]

We have seen how the doctrine of the disinterestedness of aesthetic perception has stood as a dogma of Western philosophy for well over two hundred years. Certainly no art seems to exemplify the appropriateness of disinterestedness more than painting. Whatever difficulties this doctrine may have when applied to the modern arts, representational painting would seem to be its exemplar. Yet the preceding chapters have shown that the doctrine of disinterestedness and its correlative ideas derive less from a close examination of the occasions on which we engage with objects of art in characteristically aesthetic ways than from an intellectual tradition in Western culture that imposes on the aesthetic its preconceptions about the various domains of experience. These ideas determine the approach we take to art and shape the kind of experience we have. Nowhere is this more the case than in painting, the art that seems to fit the classical account so perfectly, and perhaps in no genre is it displayed more clearly than in landscape painting. Indeed, Friedländer has claimed that in landscape painting, along with the still life, "the desired autonomy of art is most readily secured."[2] For both our customary ideas about art and our experience of it, landscape painting stands as a model case.

Yet despite the strength of conventional experience and doctrine, this prototypical art of contemplative distance exemplifies the concept of *engagement*, and it does so in ways that are as effective as they are surprising. In landscape painting, a traditional genre in an art of great traditions, aesthetic participation leads us to reshape our understanding of how paintings can function in appreciative experience. Participation transforms what may appear as a distant and gentle pastoral into an active scene which requires the involvemen of the viewer to render it complete. Through the positive engagement of an appreciating perceiver, this supposedly preeminent art of objects accomplishes its most effective work.

As in most painting, the landscape uses the same array of painterly techniques and qualities that have received so much critical discussion. Color, line, texture, mass, light, composition, brushwork all contribute to a pictorial effect that the discerning eye can follow. A full description of participatory appreciation would pursue each of these, showing how the viewer engages in a collaborative process with its perceptual capacities and forces.[3] Yet none of these features is more basic than that of space, in painting generally but particularly in the landscape. Moreover, not only does every painting possess spatial properties in some fashion; space also appears in one form or other in every art. In addition, space is often used to exemplify the traditional attitude of pictorial appreciation for, as we saw earlier, disinterestedness is commonly expressed by the spatial metaphor of distance. Yet there have been major changes in both our scientific and philosophical understanding of space, and these changes hold implications for aesthetic perception. So, too, does a reexamination of the pictorial experience of space from the standpoint of descriptive phenomenology. Taken together, these offer powerful evidence for replacing the concept of disinterestedness with a quite different one. This discussion will pursue both influences.

The usual treatment of space in painting assumes the classical model of Newtonian physics. It is a conception that Newton developed by extending the system of Cartesian coordinates into a universal order, where it became an all-embracing system of uniformly moving spatial coordinates connected with uniform temporal continua. Within the inertial frames of reference, particles that are not affected by external forces move at a constant speed and in an unvarying direction. In this system both space and time are objective and absolute. Space is a medium that is abstract, universal, and impersonal, a medium in which discrete objects are placed and in which they can be located clearly and irrefragably.

Despite the radically different orientation of modern relativity physics, common sense continues to struggle along under the Newtonian conception. We still tend to see ourselves as inhabitants of a Euclidean universe, preserving the fictions of simultaneity and the absoluteness of space and time. More important here, we persist in the Cartesian illusion that we can stand apart from things, regard them from some remove, and remain unimplicated in their processes. Not yet having accommodated ourselves perceptually to the vastly altered world of Einsteinian physics and quantum mechanics, we continue unwittingly to apply this repudiated spatial orientation to pictorial, as well as to ordinary, experience.

The spatial mode of classical physics takes on certain characteristic forms when applied to aesthetic perception. Space, as an abstract, universal, and impersonal medium in which discrete objects are placed, assumes here the pattern of distance, embodied both in the attitude of a perceiver and in the domain of the art object, itself. This distance develops not only as a space that separates perceiver and object but as a division between them, as well. It may be expressed by describing the space in which the perceiver is located as real space while that of the object is illusory, or by using a notion such as Bullough's psychical distance to represent a psychological separation between viewer and object.[4] The perceiver becomes primarily a visual awareness that adopts a contemplative attitude toward an isolated object. From the physical arrangements for aesthetic appreciation provided by museums, theaters, and concert halls, and the arrangement of space within a painting conceived as a self-contained entity, to the disinterested attitude the perceiver is expected to adopt, this has been the dominant and all-embracing model. And its application to pictorial space in the form of linear perspective is both subtle and instructive.

The evolution of pictorial space is a rich subject to which art historians have given considerable attention. We learn that pictorial space was absent in the visual art of Egypt, Crete, and India; that it was limited and idealized in Greek and Roman art; and that it began to emerge as an important component in the West during the Middle Ages.[5] Space first appeared in paintings in the form of imaginative landscapes constructed as settings for mythological or religious figures and events, both landscapes and personages usually being depicted as flattened planes rather than as solid objects. Distance was neglected, the size of figures rather than their spatial distribution designating their importance. With the Renaissance, figures took on solidity, although the space of the landscape remained typically a theatrical backdrop for more significant subject matter. Although the idealized and imaginary background landscape persisted into the fifteenth-century *Book of Hours* and in the paintings of Leonardo, it was replaced by a more realistic spatial setting in Dürer and the Breughels. From the early fifteenth century on, Flemish, Dutch, and Italian painters moved landscape forward in the painting to become its subject, encompassing human figures and activities and often overwhelming them.[6]

Joined to the interest in physical space and the emergence of the landscape was the development of pictorial techniques for rendering depth accurately. Early in the fifteenth century Brunelleschi worked out the principles of linear perspective and Alberti codified them soon afterward.[7] Linear perspective is a carefully studied technique that rests on the visual perception of distance.[8] Starting from the eye of the viewer, a triangle is constructed along imaginary lines that recede in space to converge at infinitely distant vanishing points. The artist thus projects objects in pictorial space based on the height of the observer's eye and its distance from the painting. And while the perceiver is a necessary factor in the perspectival array, it is to function only as a distant observer.

The theory of linear perspective was developed with such mastery that it has continued to the present time as the model for the realistic apportionment of pictorial space. Other techniques like aerial perspective do little to alter the cast of the spectator as an observer from afar from whose vantage point objects assume their appropriate positions. Linear perspective thus signified a visual approach to space. It solidified in graphic form the primacy of vision as the preeminent sensory modality, a status that reflected its history of superiority and the long-standing metaphorical identification of sight with the cognitive process. That process, too, has traditionally been a distant, contemplative act, and the objectivity of the observer of landscape coalesces with the impartiality of the knower of nature.

Our usual understanding of space continues to reflect the same scientific and artistic traditions and to share similar premises. We still understand and account for spatial perception in common experience largely in Euclidean terms, taking space as independent of the perceiver, with fixed and unchanging orthogonal coordinates, and within which distinct and separate objects are located. The Renaissance model of linear perspective, moreover, continues to underlie the psychology of perception. Our perception of depth and of the distance of objects is still explained primarily in visual terms by binocular disparity, that is, the difference between the retinal images of both eyes, and by visual movement parallax, or the juxtaposition of images seen from different positions.

The changes that modern relativity physics has made in the conception of space, however, are well known. Matter and space are "fused into one single dynamical reality," which takes the form of a dynamization of space. Space is incorporated into "a type of becoming which, together with its dynamical temporal unfolding, still possesses a certain . . . *transversal* extent or *width*."9 Space and time are now understood as a continuum that is curved in the presence of a gravitational field and in which the time and position of events can be fixed only relative to the location of the observer. Thus the perceiver's placement is critical. One's location not only makes a difference in the knowledge of events; it makes a contribution to *what* they are. Thus we can no longer speak of things as if they occurred independently in absolute spatial and temporal frames. Any specification of occurrences depends on the presence and position of a perceiver.10

There is a suggestive convergence in the findings of relativity physics with current psychology of perception. Both take the perceiver as the central reference by which space is determined. While the visual model of perception continues to predominate in psychological theory, other somatic contributors to spatial perception are slowly being recognized. We are coming to understand how vestibular stimuli, which affect the sense of balance, along with auditory, tactile, olfactory, gustatory, and especially kinesthetic sensations of movement and muscle tension, have a profound effect on depth perception. Indeed, the psychology of perception is accepting increasingly the idea that one's body, not just one's vision, acts as the reference from which the distances of objects are judged. Recent approaches to the psychology of perception, such as those of the Gestalt and transactional schools, provide additional reasons for recognizing the human contribution to the world we perceive. This work has demonstrated the essential role of the act of visual perception in determining shapes and patterns. Such cases as discerning closure in a figure, determining the position of the cube in a Necker diagram, and judging the dimensions of the Ames room are not merely perceptual curiosities; they exhibit how our visual acts help determine the kind of object that is actually present to us.11

The appearance of things in hyperbolic non-Euclidean visual space provides an alternative account for what Arnheim has called the *Newtonian oasis*, the proximal zone of perception in which objects possess their familiar physical shapes.[12] Hyperbolic visual space does not "correct" actual spatial perception by this Newtonian standard. It recognizes that the many qualitative differences in the way phenomena appear depend on their distance and relation to the viewer. Unlike nearby objects, distant ones tend to become compressed, so that they seem flat and with their surface planes turned toward the viewer, much as when they are viewed through a telescopic lens. Distant objects appear closer together; their size is difficult to estimate, and the viewer must depend on local cues. The more distant depths are, the more shallow they appear to be. Moreover, horizontal planes do not appear flat. When the plane is below eye level, it assumes the concavity of an enormous bowl; when it is above the viewer, it appears like a shallow arched vault. The space of appearance is far different from the space of Euclidean geometry.[13]

But perception is not entirely a sensory phenomenon. The recent current of interest in hermeneutics has made us realize more clearly than before how meaning never stands alone and how the knower contributes through the interpretive process to the very nature of what is known. Interpretation is ubiquitous, and it is becoming evident, moreover, that this is as true of the physical, spatial world as it is of the social and cultural one, of facts and of perception as it is of texts. The hermeneutical character of cultural knowledge is now well established, yet a dependence on interpretive consciousness is not true of historical and social beliefs alone. Facts are themselves hermeneutical; like all forms of meaning they are human constructions. Thus the impartial, objective knowledge we have been accustomed to ascribe to the results of scientific inquiry appears to be going the way of the absoluteness and objectivity of space and time. Scientific knowledge is itself the product of a hermeneutical process and therefore is constituted in part by the human knower.[14]

There are many strands, then, that converge on the recognition of the perceiver as a contributing factor in the determination of space–time and distance. The individual is no longer a spectator, distantly removed from objects and events and viewing them with uninvolved objectivity. The spectator has been transformed into an actor, wholly implicated in the same continuum in which everyone else is involved. We have now come to recognize our contribution to the world we inhabit through action, perception, and consciousness, whether involving scholarly research, scientific inquiry and knowledge or, as in the case here, aesthetic experience. Thus the coalescence in modern physics and related disciplines of matter, space, and time and their continuity with the perceiver produce a realm that harmonizes the dimensions of the human world into a single, total domain. Another expression of the same idea is to speak of the human world as an inclusive perceptual field in which perceiver and object are conjoined in a dynamic spatiotemporal continuum.

It might seem that so altered a conception of the world nonetheless leaves its appearance untouched and merely accounts for it differently, much as happened when the general theory of relativity supplanted Newtonian physics. But that is only apparently so. We do not have just an expanded, more inclusive view. There is a radical difference from that earlier shift, for now the contribution of the perceiver as an integral part of the constitutive process changes the very nature of things. How the world is known makes a difference in what is actually there as well as in how it is perceived. This has forced us both to revise our understanding of the nature of the world and to recognize our transformed perception of that world. Indeed, what is most startling is to discover that these verge toward becoming the same thing.

We stand at this point at the intersection of epistemology and metaphysics, where far more difficult questions are raised than can be dealt with here. Indeed, a large share of the history of philosophy since Kant bears on such issues as these, and they are central to much philosophical investigation today. The implication of the knower in what is known is a major claim in this century, supported scientifically by relativity theory, quantum mechanics, and the psychology of perception, and interpretively by phenomenology, pragmatism, deconstruction, hermeneutics, and feminism, among current intellectual movements. Yet our concern here lies mainly with perception rather than with knowledge and, more particularly, with the perception of space in landscape painting. Moreover, in the phenomenological investigation of spatial experience we find a descriptive account that is consistent with this changed picture of the human world. It is an account that bears directly on our experience of landscape painting and transforms that experience into something quite unlike what we have been led to expect and therefore to see.

The phenomenological approach to the perception of space develops the same continuity of perceiver and object as relativity physics, but it does this from a philosophical examination of primary experience. Descriptive phenomenology takes its cue from the observation that objects are not independent of the perceiver but rather, as Edmund Husserl put it, "each conscious process *means something or other* and bears in itself its particular *cogitatum.*" To be conscious, then, is to be conscious *of* something. This is what is meant by the intentionality of consciousness. Rather than this being a strange and unaccustomed condition, the presence of the object in consciousness is held to emerge from an unassumptive examination of how consciousness actually operates. Such perception is, in fact, original and primary. "The being of the pure ego and his *cogitationes* . . . is antecedent to the natural being of the world."[15] Applying this strategy to the perception of space leads us to regard space not as neutral and objective, but rather as continuous with the act of perception. Space becomes both shaped by and inseparable from the perceiver, a conception strikingly similar to the space of modern relativity physics.

There is, then, the classical account of visual space—space as it is known "objectively" in reflection, and there is "the vision that really takes place."[16] Maurice Merleau-Ponty expressed the phenomenological awareness of space effectively when he analyzed depth as more than "the link between the subject and space. . . . The vertical and the horizontal, the near and the far are abstract designations for one single form of *being in a situation,* and they presuppose the same setting face to face of subject and world." The perception of distance "can be understood only as a *being in the distance* which links up with being where it appears." Perceiving distance, then, presents no problem, for distance is "immediately visible provided that we can find the living present in which it is constituted." Thus "it is reflection which objectifies points of view or perspectives, whereas when I perceive, I belong, through my point of view, to the world as a whole, nor am I even aware of the limits of my visual field."[17]

In "Eye and Mind," Merleau-Ponty directs these ideas to the perceptual experience of painting. Things are an elongation of the body, "they are encrusted into its flesh." Thus a blending takes place between the seeing and the seen. I do not look at a painting as I look at a thing; "I do not fix it in its place. . . . It is more accurate to say that I see according to it, or with it, than that I see *it.*" Similarly, the space in which I live is not the "network of relations among objects" nessed by an outside observer or formulated by a geometer. "It is, ther, a space reckoned starting from me as the zero point or degree ero of spatiality. I do not see it according to its exterior envelope; I live in it from the inside; I am immersed in it." Depth is no longer a third dimension but "the experience of the reversibility of dimensions, of a global 'locality'—everything in the same place at the same time, a locality from which height, width, and depth are abstracted, of a voluminosity we express in a word when we say that a thing is *there*."[18]

Both our understanding and our perception of space, then, have changed and become fused. From being thought of as an absolute and independent medium known in itself alone, space has been transformed into a condition that includes the perceiver as a constituent. This works to reshape not just physical space and our awareness of it, but all spatial perception, transforming our encounter with pictorial space as well. What was a spatial experience that artists and writers occasionally intuited has now gained theoretical support from both science and philosophy to become what many consider the most accurate view of our world. Euclidean–Newtonian space and Einsteinian–phenomenological space lead, then, to vastly dissimilar ways of ordering the world and thus of experiencing it. Their influence on the arts can be traced in many directions, since space is an important aesthetic dimension in every art. But perhaps in none is it more apparent than in pictorial and environmental perception, where space is a central factor.

When these different modes of apprehending space are applied to landscape painting, two alternative schemata of representation and perception begin to emerge. One is a predominately visual idea of landscape, which I shall call the panoramic landscape; the other, a more intimate, participatory landscape. The panoramic landscape had its origins at the beginnings of the pictorial landscape when, in the fifteenth century, renderings of the natural and the human scene began to appear in the backgrounds of devotional paintings. Before the techniques of linear perspective had been refined, painters like van Eyck represented extension in space by depicting their landscape backgrounds as if they were seen from above. This vantage point also had the convenience of raising the horizon far up the painting, thus incorporating still more space into the scene, at the same time as it conformed to the way of seeing of the time.[19] As the knowledge of linear perspective began to develop two centuries before Newton, the means became available to represent space with greater verisimilitude. Indeed, painting, and especially landscape painting, would seem to be the perfect exemplification of the grasp of space that Newton codified and universalized in his *Principia* of 1687. And in its use of linear perspective, representational painting appears to embody directly the philosophical views that were developed in the century following Newton as the theory of aesthetic disinterestedness. So much is this the case that disinterestedness might be regarded as the philosophical equivalent of linear perspective. Thus traditional experience, traditional theory, and traditional practice combined to produce a pictorial object designed for contemplative appreciation.

The panoramic landscape vividly expresses Newtonian space. It emphasizes physical distance and breadth of scope, offering a primarily visual experience that both rests on a sense of separation between viewer and landscape and conveys that separation in pictorial form. There are two different spatial modalities involved here, that of the viewer and that of the landscape, and these are kept distinct, incommensurable, and separate. By dividing these spaces sharply, the panoramic landscape encourages little visual continuity; instead, an abrupt break occurs between the spatial location of the viewer and the space of the scene being contemplated. Nothing leads the eye smoothly either into the picture space or into the actual space of the landscape. The viewer is a remote observer from whose eye distance is measured and perspective begins. Such a viewer is totally disengaged, gazing contemplatively upon a landscape from which he or she is utterly removed. Moreover, the experience here is entirely visual: the landscape is something to be seen, and its appeal lies typically in its great vistas and awesome distances. We are presented with a grand spatial array into which the beholder is not tempted to set foot but can only gaze at from a respectful distance.

Visual renderings of space commonly reflect this sense of things, and the conventions of linear perspective remain their basic technique. Drawings, for example, continue to rely on perspective, even when they use isometric techniques to offer three faces of objects in an attempt to convey their solidity. Architectural elevations, in fact, relinquish any effort to convey the spatiality of buildings and deliberately reduce the three-dimensional space to two by depicting but a single surface of a structure. While these techniques have their specific, limited purposes, they nonetheless reflect a visual, insubstantial sense of space through the abstraction of surfaces, the physical isolation of objects in a Newtonian world, and the dispassionate and distant ordering of linear perspective.

Paintings reflect this doctrine of separation and distance when they depict scenes as if they were being observed from some vantage point, often an elevated one, a location unconnected with the landscape under view. The space of the painting is separated sharply from the space that lies before and around it, as if carefully observing Alberti's fifteenth-century advice to see the frame of the picture as a window casement through which to look out to the world beyond. Alberti, himself, moreover, instructed the painter to regard the window plane as the place at which an infinite number of straight lines of sight converge from the scene beyond, thus transferring the three-dimensional scene onto a two-dimensional plane.[20] It is easy to see how paintings that follow this prescription conform to the usual definition of a landscape as "a picture representing a section of natural, inland scenery . . . seen by the eye in one view."[21]

Such paintings exhibit pictorial features that present an objectified space and encourage a disinterested attitude. The landscape space begins abruptly at some point in the foreground of the painting, originating at the picture plane and unconnected with the viewer. While the foreground area may lead into the body of the painting, that greater space is often divided into separate, uncommunicating areas, the objective and divisible space of classical physics. The desideratum seems to be to regard the landscape as a totality, visually objective and complete. Division, distance, separation, and isolation are equally the order of the art and the order of the experience, for the features of the painting shape the character of our perception.[22]

These pictorial conventions of landscape are familiar enough, although once the landscape was established as a genre, instances of the panoramic landscape became relatively infrequent, especially among landscape painters of the first rank. Albert Bierstadt's *Scene in the Tyrol* is a typical example of the panoramic landscape (*see illustration*).[23] The edge of a hilltop meadow with grazing cattle bounded by a ruin occupies the right foreground. Beyond and below in the middle distance lie, in succession, a wooded area, a plain, a lake and, in the far distance, snow-capped mountains. There is little continuity between the meadow and the remainder of the painting, which looks like a painted backdrop for the set of an early film. What is most pertinent here is that the scene in the foreground is quite removed from the viewer of the painting, both in the direction of one's gaze and in the plane of the ground. The painting offers a sentimental scene completely discontinuous with the observer, providing us with an object eminently suitable for contemplation.

In the United States, the depiction of such romantic, sometimes grandiose landscapes typifies the work of the Hudson River school and the followers of the French Barbizon school, including painters such as Cole, Church, Kensett, Bierstadt, Durand, Blakelock, and Inness. *Kindred Spirits*, Asher B. Durand's tribute to his mentor, Thomas Cole, is a self-reflexive comment on contemplative disinterestedness (*see illustration*).[24] A striking emulation of Cole's earlier *Mountain Scenery*,[25] it adds to Cole's composition the figures of Cole and the poet William Cullen Bryant on the left side of the painting. These figures are standing on the ledge of a cliff that juts out from a wooded height. Under his arm the painter carries an easel, whose frame points toward the mountains beyond. He is turned slightly toward Bryant, who gazes thoughtfully across the chasm at their feet to the high cliff just beyond. The distant mountains in the center of the painting are carried into the foreground by means of a cascading brook unnoticed by these spectators, which flows from the mountains' inner reaches to the bottom edge of the painting. It is a wildly beautiful scene, yet one from which the observers in the painting are safely apart and the observers *of* the painting even more safely removed. Nothing carries the painting beyond its frame. For all the uncultivated nature within, the scene is pruned neatly within its borders. There is no effort to extend the landscape beyond the painting to the space of the observer. It is enclosed in its own special space by a kind of topiary aesthetic.

In the previous century, the same one that saw disinterestedness established as an aesthetic principle, two painters appeared, one of whom depicted the panoramic landscape to perfection, while the other broke through its fatal flaw to enable us to enter the very scenes he painted.

When we view Canaletto's paintings of Venice, the resemblance is perfect. His "View of the *Salute*," which embodies both perfect perspective and topographic exactitude, cannot be misinterpreted. That is why the painting has no meaning. No more meaning than an identification card. When Guardi shows scattered rubbish and bricks bathed in shimmering light, the alleys and canals that he has selected are insignificant. He shows us a commonplace wharf as a studied decomposition of light. Canaletto puts his brush in the service of his native town; Guardi is concerned only with plastic problems, with light and substance, with colors and light, with unity amid diversity through rigorous imprecision. Result: Venice is present in each canvas [of Guardi]—as it was for him, as it is for us, *as it has been experienced by everyone and seen by no one.*

Sartre's characterization depicts the difference perfectly.[26]

Nowhere is the contrast between the panoramic and the participatory landscapes expressed more eloquently than between these two contemporaries. Canaletto's renderings are documentations, accurate and self-contained. Purposefully painted from a few feet above eye level, they remove the viewer from the scene and offer brilliant objects that provide a vivid portrait of what Venice once looked like. We may inadvertently approach Guardi in the same way, but then we miss his extraordinary effect. The *Piazza San Marco* (*see illustration*) seems to depict an ordinary afternoon in that famous square.[27] No noble, tragic, or dramatic scene, this, and worth little comment. Yet as one gradually approaches the painting, the orthogonals become less pronounced and the space, instead of dissolving or flattening out, as happens with Canaletto, opens up to embrace the viewer. One is a mere spectator no longer; we step into the square and join its activities. We approach a yellow-coated courtier, we notice a pair of gentlemen engaged in conversation on our left, we observe a street urchin receiving alms from a man on our right. This is no documentary held before us; it is the real space of eighteenth-century Venetian life into which we have entered and can move.

For an aesthetics grounded on visual distance, such a unity of perceiver and landscape must seem to be an idiosyncratic aberration or a private delusion. Yet it is possible to set aside Newtonian objectivity and turn to the capacities most landscapes have for perceptual engagement. When we allow ourselves to participate with the landscape, the accounts of painters and writers who have grasped such experience no longer appear quaintly unscientific. One of the most extraordinary descriptions in literature of the continuity of pictorial

and environmental experience was written by a novelist not pron
fantasy or surrealism but whose subtle discriminations of perce
tion and consciousness are unsurpassed. In *The Ambassadors*, Henry
James gives this account of Strether's day of solitary escape from Paris
to the French countryside.

> He had taken the train . . . *to* a station . . . to give the whole [day] . . . to
> that French ruralism, with its cool special green, into which he had
> hitherto looked only through the little oblong window of the picture-
> frame. . . . He could thrill a little at the chance of seeing something
> somewhere that would remind him of a certain small Lambinet that
> had charmed him, long years before, at a Boston dealer's [on Tremont
> Street]. . . . The train pulled up just at the right spot. . . . The oblong gilt
> frame disposed its enclosing lines; the poplars and willows, the reeds
> and river . . . fell into a composition, full of felicity, within them; the
> sky was silver and turquoise and varnish; the village on the left was
> white and the church on the right was grey; it was all there, in short—
> it was what he wanted: it was Tremont Street, it was France, it was
> Lambinet. Moreover he was freely walking about in it. He did this last,
> for an hour, to his heart's content, making for the shady woody
> horizon and boring so deep into his impression and his idleness that
> he might fairly have got through them again and reached the maroon-
> coloured wall [of the dealer].
>
> He really continued in the picture—that being for himself his situa-
> tion—all the rest of this rambling day; so that the charm was still, was
> indeed more than ever upon him when, towards six o'clock, he found
> himself amicably engaged with a stout white-capped deep-voiced
> woman at the door of the *auberge* of the biggest village, a village that
> affected him as a thing of whiteness, blueness and crookedness, set in
> coppery green, and that had the river flowing behind or before it . . . at
> the bottom . . . of the inn-garden. He had had other adventures before
> this . . . and had meanwhile not once overstepped the oblong gilt
> frame.[28]

Instead of dismissing this account as an indulgence in fictional
hyperbole, we might consider it an inverse description of pictorial
experience, more an involvement in landscape as painting than in
painting as landscape. In fact, James's description presents these as
but alternative directions to the same destination and, once this is
recognized, the difference between them dissolves. What we have is
a symmetry of experience between painting and landscape. We enter

the landscape to find ourselves in a painting in quite the same way as we discover the landscape in a painting. Experientially, these are identical.

The difference between fiction and actuality disappears, too, when we read Kandinsky's recollection of his visit to the district of Vologda. This painter's motive is to create precisely the same experience through paint that James created through words.

> In these wonderful houses I experienced something that has never repeated itself since. They taught me to move in the *picture,* to live in the picture. I still remember how I entered the room for the first time and stopped short on the threshold before the unexpected vision. . . . When I finally entered the room, I felt myself surrounded on all sides by painting into which I had thus penetrated. Probably not otherwise than through these impressions did my further desires take shape within me, the aims of my own art. I have for many years searched for the possibility of letting the viewer "stroll" in the picture, forcing him to forget himself and dissolve into the picture.[29]

What we have here is not so much an act of imagination as of perception. A serpentine road or river does more than organize the landscape and provide visual interest and variety. It does even more than serve to draw the eye into the painting. As a path it becomes the occasion for the perceptual movement of the living body into the landscape. The road beckons to the viewer in the same way that a spoken word commands our attention and a question compels an answer. Artistic license was not the justification for Cézanne's claim that a picture contains within itself even the smell of the landscape; it was his conviction that through the effective use of pictorial qualities a painting creates the total sensory field of experience. Moreover, even the use of perspective in visual art is an implicit recognition of the position and hence the participation of the observer. Perspective does not require a precise and immobile spectator but is remarkably able to accommodate a wide range of viewing positions. De Vries's classic diagram assumes that visual projection originates at the eye of the beholder, who stands at some distance from the drawing, and that the lines of projection diverge to encompass the full picture plane. His drawing depicts the perspectival lines converging from that plane toward a distant point (*see illustration*).[30] Yet if the spectator moves toward the figure in the foreground, the viewer no longer stands at the terminus of the lines but can, in effect, enter and move about in the space they enclose. Perspective is able in this way to accommodate a participant observer. The psychologist James J. Gibson has noted that "the visual field expands as you move toward something and contracts as you move away from it."[31] By entering the space projected outward toward the observer, perspective opens up the pictorial space and includes us in it, in reverse analogy to the way molded figures emerge from the flat canvas when we step back from its immediate surface.[32] Our movement, then, activates the life of the painting: "In order to perceive things we need to live them."[33]

An observational attitude toward the panoramic landscape mistakenly leads us into thinking that as viewers we must encompass an entire painting in our visual field. Many landscape paintings actually require an intimate distance quite different from what most viewers are accustomed to adopting, a position too close to permit a view of the object as a whole. To stand back at some remove from the painting is to become a spectator, not a participant, since this intervening space effectively dislocates the perceiver and prevents engagement. At close range, however, the landscape surrounds us, occupying the periphery of vision as it would if one were standing in that actual space. Indeed, artists have often painted the outer areas of their landscapes with the indefiniteness of peripheral vision—the fuzziness of the clouds in a van Ruisdael, the blurred edges in a Guardi. Even with the landscapes of Cézanne and Monet, which require the viewer to stand at an even greater distance from the paintings than most galleries provide, participatory perception requires that we look not at the painting as an integral object but *into* the painting, into its space. Then foveal and peripheral vision reappear as we join our perceptual field with the pictorial space.

Whatever the physical distance between the viewer and the canvas, the participatory landscape requires that we look into the space, that we enter it, so to speak, and become a part of it. In the forest interior of Jacob van Ruisdael's *A Forest Marsh*, for example, the trees that fill the canvas become a presence that is felt, rather than being merely visual objects. We must look in front of and past them, while their tops appear overhead at the edge of the visual field. In the Guardi *Landscape* (1775–85), to take another case, we can move into the shadow of the central group of twisted trunks which, from a distance, appear to dominate the painting.[34] Seeing them from such close range, however, we find ourselves looking at the human activities before and beyond the trees and not at the trees themselves. What seemed at first to be a dramatic natural landscape becomes a human landscape alive with action.

For landscapes seen in this way, a remarkable inversion of importance takes place. The apparently salient features may move out of focus as the rest of the landscape becomes central in our vision. Paintings with exceptionally large canvases force this involvement upon us. In Monet's *Nymphéas*, the presence of a figure within the painting "would define the scale of the picture from the *inside* in terms of the proportions of the human body," while as it is, without any figure, "the picture's scale depends on its relation to the human body of the spectator *outside*."[35] Moreover, by moving some distance away from the painting, the pictorial configurations cohere into water, lily pads, and blooms, and the proportions of the scene form a balance in scale with the body. Constable's *The White Horse* is too huge a canvas for us to encompass in a single visual field, even if we stand at the opposite wall of the gallery.[36] Moving closer, it is the painting itself that encloses the viewer, as we walk along the riverbank in the foreground and become a part of the rustic activity before us.

The participatory perception of landscape painting requires, then, a shift away from the conventional attitude associated with the contemplative model. We must begin by regarding the space of the painting as homogeneous with that of the viewer, adopting a stance that places us on the same horizontal plane as the foreground of the landscape and at a distance, angle of direction, and eye level that permit the perceptual space of the viewer and of the painting to become continuous. In Salomon van Ruysdael's *Country Road* (*see illustration*), what is an unremarkable rural scene when regarded from a distance opens up to accept the viewer as one moves close to the painting.[37] As if traveling along the road depicted, we notice the small herd of cows in the foreground moving toward us, the horsemen farther on moving down the road in the opposite direction, and the hay wagon still farther off, outlined against the sky on the crest of a rise in the road. We have become another figure in that pastoral place and time.

Having no access to the landscape, the lover of forest and stream, the friend of mist and haze, enjoys them only in his dreams. How delightful then to have a landscape painted by a skilled hand! Without leaving the room, at once he finds himself among the streams and ravines; the cries of the birds and monkeys are faintly audible to his senses; light on the hills and reflection on the water, glittering, dazzle his eyes.[38]

So wrote Kuo Hsi in the fifth century of an experience impossible for Western eyes governed by the aesthetic of distance and contemplation. In art of the Far East the Western convention of contemplative distance is not found. In its place are various techniques for encouraging participation. Like Roman landscapes, some Chinese landscapes bring the viewer into the picture by extending the foreground so that it comes up to one's very feet.[39] Chinese scroll paintings, moreover, are impossible to be seen by the eye in one view. They must be unrolled or walked along, as we join the painter in a procession through the hills and across the water, enjoying the various but restricted views and noticing the different activities taking place about us. The Japanese use of axonometric drawing incorporates multiple points of view into the same painting. It is a technique that encourages immersion, since there is no favored position from which we can survey the entire scene. We must stand as if within it and turn our heads in different directions to take in what is around us, just as we would do were we in that very place. The Japanese mastery of the axonometric technique makes possible an experience inaccessible by linear perspective. The capacity of the oriental landscape to engage us is illustrated with whimsical eloquence in the old tale of an ancient Chinese painting master. When it was time for him to die, the master gathered his disciples around him, spread a large sheet of rice paper on the ground, took his brush, and in a few strokes created an entire mountainous landscape with a path. Then the master arose, bade farewell to his followers, and walked off into his own landscape where, after a backward glance, he finally disappeared around a bend in the path.

Western art has long been directed by visual theories that discourage such experience, although ironically, as we have seen, artists themselves have proceeded quite independently of such ideas. There have been occasions, however, when notions about the nature of painting arose that overcame the estrangement of the beholder from the scene that person is regarding. One instance occurs in the writings of Diderot and his contemporaries in France, in which two seemingly paradoxical conceptions of the art of painting appear. The first is a dramatic conception that negates the presence of the beholder before the painting by representing figures entirely absorbed in whatever they are doing or feeling. The second, however, is a pastoral conception that urges a heightened quality of "absorption, sympathy and self-transcendence," and uses quite explicitly the fiction of the beholder's physically entering paintings of landscapes.[40]

One can see for oneself the same action on the viewer in genres other than the landscape. In a portrait the type and direction of the subject's gaze tend to elicit an appropriate response in the eyes of the beholder. A direct look may be disconcerting or confrontational, as those who first saw Manet's *Déjeuner sur l'herbe* discovered. An averted gaze makes one look tentatively at the person so as not to be too forward or bold, while a downcast gaze evokes from us a look of superior strength.[41] Paintings of the Madonna and Child in late Gothic and early Renaissance art make a different sort of gesture to us. Beginning with Cimabue and Giotto, these figures typically sit on an elevated throne approached by several steps. While these personages are flanked by angels or other figures, the steps are usually empty: They face the viewer as an invitation to mount them and approach the holy pair.[42] This is a pictorial use of a common architectural practice. Michelangelo's *Campidoglio,* for example, spreads a staircase out to welcome one into a stately enclosed square. Caravaggio's paintings often seek to engage the spectator directly in the action. The youths in some of his early works "do not merely address themselves to the spectator—they solicit him." In both *The Lute Player* and *The Musician,* for example, he places a violin and a bow in the foreground of the picture with the neck of the violin extended outward, an invitation to the spectator to join the musicians.[43] Rubens's landscape of his villa draws the viewer into the space as an invitation to visit, while Braque spoke of "inverting the pyramid of vision" in his *Houses at l'Estaque,* where cube-like blocks of houses move outward toward the viewer. The spectator of Vermeer's *The Artist in His Studio* must peer over the artist's shoulder to view his work in progress. Cartier-Bresson emulated this last device for participation in his photographs of people in the act of viewing something, making us join the crowd in the photograph as we gaze at it.[44]

When we come to theory from painting rather than to painting from theory, we can see with a clearer eye how our understanding has long been directed by our conceptions and not our perceptions. With the relativity and indeterminacy of space as a dominant intellectual force of our age, we can begin to correct that imbalance, for space is a principal dimension of all perception. Including the viewer as a necessary and formative constituent in a space has consequences not just for painting of the landscape but for all painting and, indeed, for all art. We now understand space differently and this change enables us to experience it more freely and more personally. Our perception of landscape has been transformed, both within painting and without.

It is true enough that viewers may adopt different modes of perception toward the same landscape. Although painterly technique can encourage a panoramic or participatory experience, the painting alone is not enough. Paintings require a beholder, and the mode of the viewer's bodily perception, multi-sensory and kinesthetic, is the pivotal factor in the experience of engagement. Panoramic and participatory landscapes do not determine their alternative spatial modalities only through the choice of subject matter or the use of particular devices or techniques. What makes them truly distinct lies in how they require and evoke different modes of perception. We regard the panoramic landscape with the contemplative stance of disinterested awareness, where measure, control, and distinct boundaries are enhanced by the objectivity of distance, both physical and psychical. Nevertheless, an aesthetic has begun to emerge that defines the perceptual mode appropriate to the participatory landscape, although its characteristic experience has been recognized in the West since classical times. Such a landscape requires an aesthetic of engagement in which the experience of the body as it moves in space and time creates a functional order of perception that fuses participant and environment. Yet this touch of the Dionysian has been suspect in the Apollonian tradition that has dominated Western thought, and the history of aesthetics has labored long under a rationalistic burden.

Is, then, the perception of the pictorial landscape the contemplative view of an independent and objective world that the panoramic landscape portrays? Is it the complement to this, a highly subjective experience in which we use the scene to evoke moods and fill it with our memories, as Friedländer would have us do?[45] Or is the landscape a realm in which we travel through our active perceptual interplay with the pictorial features of the painting? To claim the last of these is not to appeal to customary experience; it is to call for the enlargement of experience, something the arts have constantly pressed on us. Art does not legislate experience, it invites it. And the choice of the mode of experience, like Mill's recognition of its quality, can only be made by the person who has encountered the alternatives. To be engaged with the landscape is to participate in its space, a space not external to an observer or opposed but reaching out to encompass the viewer as a participant. One does not contemplate such a landscape, one enters it. "Landscape is invisible," Erwin Straus has written, "because the more we absorb it, the more we lose ourselves in it. To be fully in the landscape we must sacrifice, as far as possible, all temporal, spatial, and objective precision."[46]

Braque once commented about Cézanne that "you have only to compare his landscapes with Corot's, for instance, to see that he had done away with distance and that after him infinity no longer exists." This is the studied consequence of Cézanne's own deliberate identification with the landscape: "The landscape thinks in me," he once admitted, "and I am its consciousness." The participatory landscape requires a new way of seeing, a new way of perceiving pictorial space as continuous with the viewer instead of opposed. This is a mode of perception that traditional as well as contemporary art offers us, if we are but prepared to attempt it. Theory can serve here as a guide, freeing us from a confining model of aesthetic perception and preparing us at the same time for an expansion of experience that enlarges both art and awareness. It is undoubtedly true, as Goethe remarked, that "people see what they know." The task, then, is to enlarge our knowledge so as to expand our vision. The implications here are universal for, "Does not 'the eye altering alter all'?"[47]

This study of landscape painting provides a model for exploring other related artistic modes. For example, the same perceptual dynamic holds for the cognate art of landscape photography, although its generally smaller scale requires an intimacy less common in painting. Photomurals, however, can expand scale to life-size proportions and may give greater insistence to the forces that encourage participation. Landscape photography joins painting in achieving what art in general may do—reveal aspects and dimensions of human experience with a clarity and force that are absent under ordinary circumstances.

When paintings, moreover, are regarded as experientially active, they come to exemplify the workings of features that also occur outside painting in the larger world in which we live. What is true of our engaged perception of painting and photography holds true for our perception of the physical environment, since the same features can act in all these situations in similar ways. When we deal with the aesthetic perception of the physical environment, the involvement of the human organism in the spatial perception of landscape painting takes forms that are not so much different as more overtly active. Here architecture and environment become the embodiment of the pictorial landscape. And while the synaesthetic, active character of aesthetic experience is true of all the arts, this is nowhere more literally the case than in environmental perception, where space, a perceptual presence in every art, as in all experience, becomes the actual medium within which we act. This is the realm we shall explore in the next chapter.

CHAPTER FOUR

Architecture
as
environmental
design

HOWEVER MUCH THE OTHER SENSES JOIN IN THE PERCEPTUAL EX-
perience of landscape painting, vision predominates. Because it is
necessary for pictorial perception, the visual is the leading sensory
strand, for without sight the kinesthetic, haptic, and other modalities
of sensory awareness cannot join in. Even so, when we view a pictorial landscape as a participant, the senses combine synaesthetically,
and the painting changes from a contemplative object into a world
that we enter and in which we engage. Strether's experience of the
French countryside becomes our own.

The perception of the physical environment resembles the experience of landscape painting, although differences appear in its
sensory modalities, in the force and directness of what is present to
us, in the overtness and movement of engagement. The objects of the
ordinary world often impose themselves forcibly on our thoughts
and actions, and our involvement with them is likely to be active as
well as reciprocal. Environmental perception, moreover, holds implications for action that bridge the traditional gulf between aesthetic
pleasure and practical action. As the painting is transformed from
an object into a region of active experience, our perception of environment turns us from imaginative participants into real agents
whose salient sensory modality is kinesthetic. We become actors in

the theater of landscape, to use a metaphor popular in the sixteenth and seventeenth centuries.[1] *We* are the performers in the art of environment.

As soon as we step from the painting into the world instead of from the world into the painting, we meet conditions more insistent and unavoidable than those of pictorial art. Moreover, environmental experiences are not only sensory: in the human transformations of the natural landscape lies a history of cultural activity far more pervasive than we usually realize. These alterations of the landscape assume patterns that have been guided by habit and local tradition as well as by broader social and technological trends, for the cultural landscape began to replace the natural one with the emergence of human society. This human landscape of culture and history is embodied not only in the forms of buildings and roadways but in the bucolic countryside as well; not just in cultivated fields but in places remote and wild; not in the physical configuration of our surroundings alone but in the haptic layer of sounds, smells, and substances that fill our ears and lungs and are absorbed deep into our bodies.

When we come to consider architecture more specifically, we gradually realize that it cannot be considered merely as the art in building but that architecture must be construed inclusively as the creation of the built environment. And because no aspect of the human habitat is unaffected by our presence, there is no exaggeration in saying that architecture and the human environment are, in the final analysis, synonymous and coextensive. A cultural aesthetic is at work here on a collective art. Furthermore, as the painting as object has dissolved into a world of perceptual experience, the environment can no longer be regarded as an external location but as a physico-historical medium of engagement, a dynamic field of forces continuous with human life.

These broad ideas need to be detailed, so let us pursue a path across this still obscure terrain to explore the aesthetics of the human environment. We shall center first on architecture and on various ways in which a building can relate to its site, ways that suggest different models of environmental experience. Examining how these models are expressed in the design of the human habitat will lead to a metamorphosis of the architectural structure into an environment of engagement.

Buildings are human constructions. They use materials and

techniques; they take form and develop relationships among themselves and with their sites in ways that can reveal the ingenuity of imagination as well as an adaptation to the exigencies and opportunities of time and place. Vernacular architecture reflects the temper of a people and the quality of their lived world in ways that also appear in the companion folk arts of music, dance, epic, costume, and in the crafts. That is why architecture has central importance for both anthropology and philosophy: It is rooted in the ground of human activities and the requirements for survival, and it both defines and embodies how "man dwells on this earth."[2]

Yet we live in a self-conscious age in which traditional building has become anachronistic and the local artisan builder has been replaced either by the engineer or by the architect schooled in techniques and styles that have lost their bond with history and region. When architecture has not embodied bureaucratic anonymity in dully conventional boxes or imitated the classical orders in an effort to acquire at least the appearance of probity, it has become internationalized. Movements in our century like the Bauhaus and the International Style have left their origins behind to appear often as ungracious and derivative forms in the most unlikely places. Even postmodernism, that recent phase of architectural fashion, becomes in its less imaginative and playful appearances a mere commonplace book of unhinged design features, floating free of their original meanings, functions, and settings.

Architecture consists most fundamentally in reshaping the earth's surface. The physical presence and social use of architectural forms and structures belie many of the traditional distinctions and diremptions of aesthetic theory, such as those between form and matter, beauty and function, work and appreciation, even between art and morality. The rootedness of a building in the ground and its social function are its basic and determining conditions. Let us begin with the first of these.

A built structure may be related to its site in different ways not always the result of a conscious design decision. Sometimes the placement of a building is the consequence of zoning regulations or physical constraints imposed by the size and shape of its lot or the conventions of its neighbors. Yet in these cases as much as in those in which the site of a building is chosen by the architect with deliberation and care, placement displays a particular kind of vision, the perception of things in certain ways and not in others. The siting of a building, as much as its architectural design, is a physical statement of personal and cultural beliefs about the human place in the world. Buildings stand, indeed, as the embodiment of such beliefs. They depict the human abode in a variety of contrasting ways: aloof, dominating, separate, hostile, self-enclosed, in equilibrium, continuous, integrated.

A building that stands alone is an isolated object. It may aspire to lofty monumentality, as with a skyscraper or cathedral, which by an upward thrust looks to the space above it, whether from motives of spirituality or economy. The space surrounding singular structures is the result of incidental circumstances. It may be made abstract or spiritualized, transfigured into colored light admitted through stained glass in the forms of religious personages or parables. Or the ambient space may be attenuated into distant regions, where from an observation platform one gains panoramic views but cannot see the building's immediate setting or its site. Similarly, when a dwelling or small building stands in bare isolation on its plot, the surrounding space frequently does not exist for perception. This may occur either because the structure is blind to its site—left unornamented and barren, enclosed by grass, pavement, a parking area, or roadways—or because the building is contiguous with other unrelated structures. Such a conception of architecture may be described as *monolithic*.

Connecting a building with its immediate surroundings softens the abrupt boundaries of its walls and boldly expands its limits. This may result merely from the gesture of placing the skyscraper or cathedral on a plaza. Often the setting is not so grand, as when a house rests gently on its plot amid foundation plantings. A wall, a fence, or a road typically provides a clear edge to the site and defines the limits of the surrounding space. In the most memorable cases, a setting may be elaborated deliberately and with sensitivity, suitable to the scale and significance of the structure. The formal pool of the Taj Mahal and the gardens of Versailles are among the most eloquent developments of the conjunction of building with site. We may think of this as a *cellular* conception of architecture, in which the building is the nucleus of its site and both, together, form an integral unit. As a cliché of suburban housing developments, clusters of these cells may spread over vast areas without ever attaining greater form or acquiring the identity of place, remaining, as in the Los Angeles basin, loosely connected pieces of domestic protoplasm of a still inchoate creature.

The need for greater harmony in the built environment appears in the complex organization of structures that creates its own total and self-contained environment. This *organic* conception of architecture takes many guises, from the building–plaza complex that may include an arcaded entrance, planters, outdoor seating areas, sculpture, and perhaps a fountain, to the shopping center and the industrial park; from the medieval walled city, architecturally and socially self-enclosed, to the new town, in many ways its modern counterpart. The college campus can be a particularly felicitous instance of the organic model when it is conceived and built as a total environment, as in the case of Jefferson's University of Virginia; Ramee's Union College in Schenectady, New York; Thom's Trent University in Peterborough, Ontario; and Stone's State University of New York at Albany. The organic conception may even take a visionary form, as in Schulze-Fielitz's Space City or Soleri's arcologies, where the construction of a total urban environment is upward, housing all city functions in a multi-tiered, largely self-contained structure.[3]

A still different model of architecture is one that elaborates a structure sensitive to the distinctive physical features of its location, incorporating them into the design and reaching toward a unity of building and site. Here the building complements its site, carrying out its suggestions, incorporating its features, assuming a place through adaptation rather than imposition. This *ecological* conception integrates structure and site by blending the building into the physical and qualitative features of the natural landscape to achieve proportion and harmony.[4] From Mediterranean villages that have accreted to their sites over long centuries, fusing to rocky mountainsides, embracing protected harbors, or nuzzling among hills, to the New England farmstead that seems to have grown out of the contours of the land, vernacular architecture and its derivations typically express this respect for the landscape, adapting and adjusting over time to the economy of conditions and need. Contemporary architects have sometimes consciously followed this model, as in Frank Lloyd Wright's classic Fallingwater, which incorporates into its design the overhanging rocky strata of its brook site, John Andrew's design for Scarborough College, which wraps around a steep hillside, and Paolo Soleri's Arcosanti, where a pueblo-like cliff dwelling of concrete structures harmonizes with the sun, stone, and the Native American historical presence in the American Southwest.

These four relations of building to site—monolithic, cellular, organic, and ecological—are familiar, and while they may be combined at times, they exemplify different sensibilities to environment. Yet these types do not just represent ways of seeing, ways of sensing space and mass and of apprehending the qualitative characteristics of the building site. And these physical and perceptual relations embody more, too, than ways of building. They provide ways of being, for each of the different architectural patterns originates in a distinct conception of the human environment. Each provides an embodiment of that conception and, most important of all, each shapes and directs the experiential world of its inhabitants. Architectural structures, then, do not stand alone but must be related to environmental experience. What is such experience? What is environment?

We can look in vain for an explicit definition of environment in the writings of cultural geographers and cultural ecologists, where we would most expect to find one. The usual practice is to adapt our common sense understanding to the purpose, taking environment to mean the physical surroundings. Philosophers tend to be more explicit, yet those few who face the demands of definition tend to retain the same division between people and their surroundings. All such proposals suggest the definition of environment sanctified in the *Oxford English Dictionary* as "the object or the region surrounding anything." Cartesian dualism remains alive and well.[5]

Yet the actual patterns in which the human world takes shape display forms of grasping environment that are far more varied than those that conventional usage has made orthodox. In constructing their habitats, people have created different kinds of environmental order that reflect the contrast in attitude and experience between disinterested contemplation and aesthetic engagement. There is a scope here that resembles the range of relationships of building to site from isolation and division through degrees to continuity and integration. At least three patterns of environmental experience can be identified in discussion and practice: contemplative, active, and participatory.[6]

Like the panoramic landscape described in the preceding chapter, the *contemplative* paradigm has become the standard for environmental experience. This attitude toward art, originating in classical philosophy and assimilated into the structure of modern aesthetics, lies at the heart of the notion of environment as surroundings, importing a visual model to explain our apprehension of space. The ideas of the art object's separation from what surrounds it and the special attitude of disinterested contemplation that is required for regarding the object's intrinsic qualities have become silent partners in most discussions of architecture and environmental design.

Adopting a contemplative attitude, environmental experience takes the form of the gaze of a spectator removed, even distant from the world being observed. Attention is directed to how objects are placed in spatial emptiness and especially to how they will be seen in relation to each other.[7] This attitude appears in the monolithic and cellular conceptions of building, where a structure is isolated either alone or on its site: a house on its grassy lot with hardly a shrub to soften its stark geometrical contours, a skyscraper in austere solitude on its plaza. Contemplation produces a spectator attitude toward architecture, in which the appearance of a building seen from a distance is the standard by which it is known and judged, and it is expressed in architectural models and perspective drawings. Visual buildings may be facades primarily, in which the third dimension is a practical necessity, incidental to their beauty, and the exterior is distinct from the interior, or they may dissolve into pure surface, as in the curtain-wall skyscraper.[8] Such buildings, moreover, often confront us with continuous planes of monotonous regularity, in which the only imperfection is an insignificant opening for access. The same visual influence takes a contrary form in the monumental public building of classical design whose entrance is its most prominent feature, yet whose site on an escarpment, emulating the Parthenon, places it in lofty dominance atop a pedestal and makes access difficult. Such structures usually stand in isolation, often opposing the viewer with grandiose symmetry. On a more modest scale appears that monument to petit bourgeois aspiration, the development house: its brick facade limited to the front, which is visible from the street, separated from its neighbors by a fence or hedge, and gazing outward through a picture window that mirrors its visual isolation.

Certain traditions in garden design display the same contemplative structuring of experience. The appeal of French gardens lies in the formal designs of manicured flower beds and geometrical pools, where carefully articulated patterns of color and shape are confined within sharply defined borders. These are gardens best seen from a distance, where the eye can identify the forms and encompass the full array. Renaissance Italian gardens share a similar formal attraction. Their artful blend of architecture and planting, with clipped hedges paralleling stone balustrades, formal pools, statuary, fountains, descending terraces, and lines of poplars conveys a controlled humanistic balance of the natural and the man-made. Objectivity and harmony of place pervade the scene.

The contemplative environment is spread before us, too, from the scenic outlooks constructed as amenities for the modern automobile traveler. Usually bounded by a barrier wall, these are places designed for one to pause on a journey to enjoy the view of a distant landscape. Like the urban panorama viewed from the isolated vantage of an observation platform, these outlooks, at their best, offer an impressive picture of the surroundings from a commanding height. Yet the landscape they present is inaccessible, open to the eye alone, having no continuity with the viewer nor allowing any direct access.[9]

Urban design is replete with examples of the contemplative, visual approach to space. It appears when the cellular conception of building is extended by combining the structure on its immediate site with other similar ones in the grid pattern of city streets. The urban vista also expresses a visual design experience, where a broad, unbroken view can impress an image on our consciousness so vividly that it becomes one of the most powerful identifications we can have with particular cities. Prospects of Park Avenue in New York and the Champs Élysées in Paris are striking cases of visually compelling urban space. Ceremonial malls and plazas frequently appeal to the sense of sight. The reflecting pool and the mall from the Lincoln Memorial to the Washington Monument offer a great expanse that the eye can cross but not the foot; the Place de la Concorde is imposing to see but unapproachable, having become a great traffic circle. The contemplative visual model can even subsume an entire city, as in Baron Hausmann's redesign of central Paris into avenues radiating outward from the Place de la Concorde and in L'Enfant's similar plan for Washington, while Brasília is almost totally a visual city. Cities are filled with a multitude of visual designs. Because visual perception is rectilinear, these grand avenues, boulevards, and malls are straight lines. We do not see in curves or around corners, hence the drama of sight requires ruler-edge rigidity. The eye becomes the effective organ of space, as since the seventeenth century it has been the metaphorical organ of thought.

Custom and frequency give great weight to this classical view, even though it is but one way of experiencing environment and embodies no necessary or irrevocable truth about the world. Still, the contemplative approach is established so securely that it has conquered the very concept of environment. The objectification of environment, however, is the product of an intellectualist tradition that grasps the world by knowing it and that controls the world by subduing it to the order of thought. Such a strategy may have secured the assent of philosophers and scientists but it has not won over the ranks of artists. Wallace Stevens's response, appropriately offered in his "Six Significant Landscapes," is as eloquent as it is explicit:

> Rationalists wearing square hats
> Think, in square rooms,
> Looking at the floor,
> Looking at the ceiling.
> They confine themselves
> To right angled triangles.
> If they tried rhomboids,
> Cones, waving lines, ellipses—
> As, for example, the ellipse of the half moon—
> Rationalists would wear sombreros.[10]

It might seem difficult to think of any alternative for urban aesthetics to the static, axially oriented visual space of Renaissance and Beaux Arts planning. This is a problem, however, only if we accept the spectator model of experience. Urban vistas are not spaces of the body, they are spaces for the eye, spaces to be seen but not inhabited. *"Pelouse Interdite,"* read the signs in French gardens. Experience, however, does not always cooperate with the classical view of separation, and even the French on rare occasions set aside grassy areas for people to lie on. In recent years, moreover, a changing sense of environment suggests the need for a theoretical shift toward overcoming the passivity and separation of the standard theory. It is becoming increasingly clear that environment, far from being a contemplative object, collaborates in human perception and action. This enlarged understanding carries aesthetic as well as practical implications.

"Vision is born from what is happening in the body," Dufrenne once remarked.[11] The eye is but one factor in our perception of space, an awareness that we grasp through multiple sensory channels. If environment is more than a visual object but is apprehended synesthetically and somatically, what has it become, and where can we locate it? Now that we can no longer regard environment from without, what happens when we enter the landscape, not through the magical beam of the eye but through the overt movement of the body in actual space? Can we even *enter* a landscape? Is it a discrete space, a space with boundaries we can cross? And if we move, do we move within borders or does our motile position become the center from which environment assumes its forms, its dimensions, its limits? Clearly, the very order of understanding must be re-established.

It is helpful to distinguish two progressive stages that replace the disengaged spectator of the traditional view with a multi-sensory, actively involved perceiver who is a contributing part of the aesthetic environment. Let us call the first the *active* model. Unlike the spectator paradigm, which reflects its origin in the contemplative ideal of knowledge, the active orientation centers on action and function. Although its recent sources may be found in the American pragmatic tradition and in continental existential–phenomenological philosophy, the origins of the active model go back much further to the identification of practical modes of knowing and the development of craft technology in the West. This sense of environment considers people to be embedded in their world, implicated in a constant process of action and response. There is no way here in which one can stand apart. A physical interaction of body and setting, a psychological interconnection of consciousness and culture, a dynamic harmony of sensory awareness all make a person inseparable from his or her environmental situation. Traditional dualisms, such as those separating idea and object, self and others, inner consciousness and external world, dissolve in the integration of person and place.

What is common to the various expressions of the active model is the recognition that the objective world of classical science is not the experiential world of the human perceiver. We have already noted the sharp difference between space as it is presumably considered to be actually and objectively, and the perception of that space.

The active conception of environment derives from the latter rather than the former, from the manner in which we are involved in spatial experience rather than from the way in which we objectify and conceptualize such experience. Environment is not outside us to be experienced in consciousness or feeling, nor can it even be construed as surroundings: As actors in the world, we are inseparable from it and fully implicated in its dynamic processes.[12]

Philosophical attempts to articulate this conception of experience have become increasingly influential. John Dewey's conception of the human organism in the environment is a picture of people doing and undergoing things, actively engaged in responding to conditions that impinge upon them. There is no standing apart from the course of events in such a world. In art the organism takes an active role, for "art, in its form, unites the very same relation of doing and undergoing, outgoing and incoming energy, that makes an experience to be *an* experience." Perception is not purely visual but rather somatic: It is the body that energizes space.[13]

For Maurice Merleau-Ponty, too, perception starts with the body; the presence of the body as *here* is the primary reference point from which all spatial coordinates must be derived. This leads to grasping the perceived object, not as a discrete material thing, but in relation to the space of the perceiver. I am *in* space; I live it from within. Space is continuous with my body, grasped from me as the starting point, the degree zero of spatiality. "After all, the world is all around me, not in front of me."[14]

Extending Merleau-Ponty's spatial concept, O. F. Bollnow uses the notion of *lived-space*, in which space becomes the medium of action. Here the human body is the originating point of an axial system of vertical and horizontal planes. Yet Bollnow reverts to a position closer to the traditional division between person and environment. For, he claims, the natural zero point of that system is not necessarily where the concrete living person happens to be: It is the "natural place" to which he belongs. His house is "the reference point from which he builds his spatial world," while space outside becomes a space of vulnerability, a place of danger and abandonment. Only in the inner space of the house can one be safely hidden.[15]

By taking the body as the vital center of our spatial experience, Calvin Schrag explains how we view existential space from the body, determining its directional axes and measuring existential distance. "The proper and improper places of utensils, objects, and persons are defined within the context of these regions and territories." The body's field of action, moreover, must recognize and take account of the presence of the other. Yet the egocentricity of this conception remains, for the space around the body is territorial, an enclosed space that is limited by the space of others.[16]

These phenomenological views treat space in its association with the body and its environment, then, not as an independent quantity but as an intentional object related to the perceiving body. Landscape is infused by that body with its meanings, force, and feelings. This kind of awareness has led to the characterization of architecture as "a matter of extending the inner landscape of human beings into the world in ways that are comprehensible, experiential, and inhabitable."[17]

The conception of environmental experience as active relates to architectural form that joins structures to their environmental settings, as in the organic and ecological models of building. It occurs in efforts to penetrate and dissolve the barrier wall by encouraging the fluidity and continuity of interior and exterior space, long recognized in the sliding walls of Japanese vernacular architecture. Glass windows, walls, and doors; floor plans continuous with an outside patio; interior gardens and atriums—all these contribute to the interconnection of building with environment. So, too, do building materials and shapes that both use and reflect the characteristics of the site, especially when joined with landscape design that employs native plantings to embrace a structure and naturalize its surroundings. The active environment also encourages people's responsiveness to building and design through congenial forms, comfortable lines of movement, and sensory involvement which, while recognizing the predominance of kinesthetic perception, fully assimilates the visual, tactile, and other senses as part of a single, integrated sensorium. Both in the building and in the neighborhood, efforts are made to replace the inorganic outline of the simple rectangle with biomorphic forms and surprising angles and juxtapositions. Environmental experience as an active process explains, too, how the inhabitant of the city may be understood as a moving part of the urban structure, a dynamic element whose involvement is exemplified in Lawrence Halprin's vivid description of experiencing the street:

The beautiful street is beautiful—not only because of the fixed objects which line it—but also because of the meaningful relationships it generates for the person-in-motion. His movement is the purpose for the space, and it should function to activate his kinesthetic experience in a series of interesting rhythms and variations in speed and force. The qualities of moving up and down on ramps and steps, of passing under arches and through buildings, of narrowing and widening of spaces, of long and closed views, of stopping and starting are qualities which make a vital urban experience for the walker and his mobile point of view.[18]

The active body has been transmuted through twentieth-century engineering into the automobile driver who, strapped inside a powerful machine, hurls purposefully down the highway, penetrating the reaches of visual space and turning the landscape into a playground. Water skiing is another forceful intrusion of the active, even dominating environmental perceiver. The growing popularity of hiking, camping, and other low technology outdoor activities suggests more gentle ways in which a person may move in the natural environment with care and respect, as kinesthetic, tactile, and other sensory dimensions join in equal balance with the visual. In all such cases, the environment has become the stage on which the beholder has metamorphosed into the actor.[19]

The active penetration of space by the body is not enough, however. Environment does not depend entirely on the perceiving subject; the surrounding world also imposes itself in significant ways, engaging the human person in a relationship of mutual influence. Not only is it impossible to objectify environment; we also cannot take it simply as a reflection of the perceiver or as the ground on which people carry out their activities. At the same time as we move actively in space, our surroundings exercise a creative influence in shaping our gestures and actions. By recognizing that specific features in the ambient space affect the ways we behave, it becomes necessary to extend the active model of experience to include such influences. We must balance the idea of the lived body and of lived space, of the self as initiating action and generating space, by including in the idea of environment the influences that are exerted on the body, the features and forces that guide our spatial sense and mobility and make an essential contribution to the definition of our lived space.

While the representatives of the active model would freely acknowledge the interchange between body and surroundings, they tend to give greater weight to the first. Yet the body is more than active, shaping the contours of space through its dynamic force. There is a reciprocity, an intimate engagement with the conditions of life that joins person with place in a bond that is not only mutually complementary but genuinely unified. How is it possible to represent such a pervasive field of experience and action from which the human participant cannot be separated? The usual tactic of removal and distance is unavailable, since the environmental reality that we live becomes our very world, and to presume to stand outside it ignores both the fact and the authenticity of its participatory properties. To attempt to stand *in* it implies that we are a heterogeneous element. One tactic would be to construct a conceptual frame that would identify the experiential features of various environmental orders.[20] However, environment does not lend itself to preconstructed models, largely because such structures are based on distinctions and divisions and not on continuities.

For all its intimacy, the active model still retains at bottom the discreteness of person and setting. It is an anthropocentric environment in which, no matter how close the exchange may be, there remains a residual, ineradicable difference. By contrast, the most complete development of environmental experience transcends all division. It is a condition in which every vestige of subjectivity disappears and the irreducible continuity of person and place becomes the fundamental term in grasping the meaning of environment. This is the participatory environment, a sense of the world both most ancient and most recent. To discover where it is recognized we must look to other cultures than those of the West and to other times than the Renaissance through the eighteenth century. For we are seeking a different conception of the experience of environment, one that Western industrial cultures have difficulty in grasping. It is a sense of environment as a field of forces continuous with the organism, a condition where organism acts on surroundings and surroundings on organism and where, in fact, no real demarcation divides them. This is a *participatory* model of environmental experience. No longer a spectator, no longer even an agent, we join in the movement of things very much as a performer does in theater or dance, activating the conditions with which we live, integrating them with our bodies,

and leading them to our own ends by a sensitivity to their requirements. We recognize here the human environment as a continuity of
person and place, as a unity of action and reception that is mutual
and reciprocal. Environment becomes a dynamic field of mutually
determining forces.

Psychologists more than philosophers have developed theoretical accounts of the human interplay with forces emanating from
environmental features, although they are prone to regard these as
external influences and as a matter of individual psychology that
depends on a personal response. Kurt Lewin's field theory provides a
representation of the dynamic framework in which events occur in a
life space. Situations possess dynamic properties, and Lewin identified those psychological forces in a perceptual region that directly
produce a reaction in a person. More recently, the perceptual psychologist James J. Gibson worked out a theory of perception as an
activity of the moving body in which the perceiver is an active
participant with a sensory involvement in the world. Gibson identified what he called "affordances for behavior," features and arrangements of the environment that offer or provide for us, and in relation
to which we behave in certain ways. When we perceive them, we
grasp their meanings and values directly. "Affordance cuts across the
dichotomy of subjective–objective. . . . It is equally a fact of the
environment and a fact of behavior." In recognizing the subtle influences of the forces and properties of environmental configurations
on human perception and action, researchers like Lewin and Gibson
have worked beneath the conventional divisions between person
and object to identify the reciprocities and continuities that join
them.[21]

It may be easier to understand the forces emanating from the
body as it thrusts itself into the surrounding world than it is to grasp
the magnetism of ambient configurations exerting a subtle influence
on the body. We are able to sense our own vitality more directly than
we can apprehend the pressure of spaces and masses. It is even more
difficult for us to grasp perceptually the unity of conscious body and
environment. Although both the active and the participatory models
of environment recognize the mutual interplay of body and surroundings, two factors distinguish the participatory pattern of environmental engagement: its recognition of the way in which ambient features reach out to affect and respond to the perceiver and,

more important still, the unitary experiential field that results from this reciprocal exchange. For a homogeneity of experience binds perceiver and environment in the same continuous medium.

Attempts to overcome a persistent ontology of separation display a difficult history. Aristotle had his multiple celestial spheres, and although they coalesced into two in the celestial space of Copernicus and the earthly space of Galileo, it took Newton to unify them by demonstrating that both observe the same laws of motion. In our own day, Einstein and Planck extended the Newtonian order to include the knowing observer as an essential factor. The same unity of body and field comes here to perceptual space, and it is in the aesthetic perception of environment that perceiver and proximal objects join most dramatically in the continuity of experience. The revolution in understanding nature has finally permeated the human world.

This continuity of person and environment, this integration through perception of conscious body and world, is the keynote of the participatory environment. Although not usually formulated theoretically, such a sense of environmental participation often appears in research areas such as the ecological sciences and cognitive science, in applied fields like urban planning and agriculture, and in activities such as hiking, camping, small boat cruising, and wilderness travel. We find it as well in some Eastern religions and in animistic religion, and it becomes a condition of those early rituals celebrating celestial events and seasonal change in which there is renewed interest.[22] Indeed, our primary experience of environment is participatory before we adopt special modes for special purposes: cognitive, scientific, organizational, political and, in conventional ways, aesthetic. The fundamental participatory character of such experience is being rediscovered now by people following many routes—among them phenomenological, hermeneutic, psychological, religious, environmental, artistic. Environmental engagement, moreover, can not only form the basis for an aesthetics of environment but can also stand as a model for aesthetic theory itself.[23]

Environmental participation alone, however, is not sufficient to identify an experience as aesthetic. Nor is it enough to add that participation is necessary for such experience to take place. What makes this field experience aesthetic is the central place of its perceptual qualities. These refer not so much to the sensory surface of things as to the acuteness of attention, the refined discrimination of qualities, and the multifaceted resonances of memory and imagination, which join in the rich awareness of activity and passage.[24] Actually, there are no surfaces but only perceptual situations. Surfaces require something beyond, the metaphysics of a *Ding an sich*, and they imply, therefore, the very division of reality that engagement abjures. Nor is there pure perception in the sense of sensation untouched by our past experiences, our education and training, and our ideas and other kinds of knowledge. The profound influence of culture on perception, for example, has been heavily documented by social psychologists, cultural geographers, and anthropologists. Yet at the same time, aesthetic perception is foundational, continually reappraising cultural experience by digging beneath the layers of accrued meanings and cognitive habits for its authenticity in the directness and immediacy of experience. The aesthetic character of experience lies ultimately in *direct* rather than pure perception, in perception apprehended immediately and unreflectively. It is in this sense that we engage aesthetically with environment and other modes of art. Perceptual engagement is the catalyzing and unifying force of the aesthetic field.

Aesthetic engagement with environment is not new; architecture and design have always provided occasions for such experience. Nor, as we have just seen, is the participatory environment peculiar to architecture or, more generally, to the aesthetic dimension of the human world. We are also led to it through our attempts at environmental understanding in general. What has been missing, however, is a theoretical articulation of such environmental activity and its elaboration within the conceptual frame of aesthetics. What are the contours of such an environmental aesthetic?

We must begin with the emergence of a new conception of the human being as an organic, conscious, social organism, an experiential node that is both the product and the generator of environmental forces. These forces are not only physical objects and conditions, in the usual sense of environment; they include somatic, cultural, psychological, and historical conditions, as well. Environment is the matrix of all such forces. As part of an environmental field, we both shape and are formed by the experiential qualities of the universe we inhabit. These qualities constitute the perceptual domain in which we engage in aesthetic experience.

As participants embedded in an experiential field, we act always within the fluidity of a spatial medium populated by dynamic configurations of mass. And in the continuing formation of space and time in movement and in our reciprocal involvement with the objects and circumstances to which we are joined, we generate our human world. The continuity of conscious body and environment attains its most complex and profound fulfillment in aesthetic experience. In describing this continuity in the experience of painting, Bernard Berenson expressed what is actually a rather frequent occurrence: "When the spectator is at one with the work of art, . . . he ceases to be his ordinary self and the . . . aesthetic quality is no longer outside himself. The two become one entity: time and space are abolished and the spectator is possessed by one awareness."[25]

Berenson is referring here, of course, to our usual idea of physical space and time. Consider, however, the experience of space in a participatory environment. Unlike the panoramic landscape and the contemplative environment, products more of intellectual history than of perceptual experience, the participatory environment develops a spatial continuity with the viewer. Landscape becomes environment and environment becomes humanized.[26] One can no longer stand apart as a disinterested spectator and the appeal of landscape is not exclusively visual. In fact, the sense of sight loses its privileged role as a sensory channel, since the participatory environment exerts an appeal that far exceeds the visual. Spatial awareness draws most heavily on kinesthetic responses—the body's apprehension of mass, density, texture, and of the various sense qualities that constitute the richly complex perceptual experience of environment. Furthermore, movement and time are essential components of such experience, and the homogeneity of experience renders them inseparable from space. There is a continuum here of the conscious human body and its perceptual world.

The continuity of the organism with its habitat is a central tenet of the new science of ecology. Yet this continuity is more than a biological fact; it is also true of the perceptual environment of the conscious human organism. Merleau-Ponty claimed that these two must ultimately be joined, for even physical concepts have their origins in perceptual experience: "Either what I call depth is nothing or else it is my participation in a Being without restriction, a participation primarily in the being of space beyond every [particular] point of view."[27]

The perceptual awareness of environment has become central here. Space floods our awareness kinesthetically through muscle tension and movement, as in walking or driving, for, in part, our "spatial concepts are internalized action."[28] We grasp space tactually as well, from its subtle presence to the skin over the entire body. At times we detect spatial regions through sounds heard and uttered. There is even olfactory space when smells such as cigar smoke, the aroma of a bakery, or the fragrance of a woman's perfume announce their areas. Sensory modalities may combine in the awareness of space. Like the Aivilik Eskimos, we may live in acoustic–olfactory space, or we may inhabit tactile–kinesthetic space during snow or dust storms, under water, or in dense fog.[29] But these various sensory channels to spatial awareness are never singular or even plural; they can be isolated and identified only later on reflection. "Both pure tactile and pure visual experience, with its space of juxtaposition and its represented spaces, are products of analysis. There is a concrete manipulation of space in which all senses collaborate in an undifferentiated unity."[30] Our spatial world emerges, then, from an environmental sensibility that blends sensory modalities, just as it fuses person and environment.[31]

This is a phenomenological aesthetic of space, and it defines a world vastly different from the traditional scientific ideal of physics. Space has no precise boundaries; it is not quantitative and mathematically measurable; it is not universal and homogeneous. Most of all, it is not objective, distinct, and separate from the person inhabiting it. Perceptual space is instead qualitative, not uniformly measurable but with fluid, hazy boundaries, rather like the *en* space of Japanese architecture, the intermediate space between inside and outside, as in the *engawa*, the space surrounding a Japanese house that is created by the continuation of the floor beyond the exterior walls. Perhaps the Japanese concept of *ma*, usually translated as "space–time," incorporates this aesthetic most completely. Here object, space, movement, and change are joined in subtle continuity: Space is perceived as identical with the events occurring there, and time is recognized only in relation to movements and spaces.[32] Space, then, is human space, personal space, space relative to the perceiver, and as heterogeneous as the infinitely varied times and conditions of human life. It is the space in which we live, the space which we inhabit. Thus Heidegger:

Space is not something that faces man. It is neither an external object nor an inner experience. . . . Spaces, and with them space as such—"space"—are always provided for already within the stay of mortals. Spaces open up by the fact that they are let into the dwelling of man.[33]

We come to understand space, then, not as something outside of and opposed to an observer but as reaching out to encompass the person as a participant. As the space we live in becomes localized and personal, smoothed by long activity and infused with memories and meanings, it assumes the identity and affection of place. This is our earliest acquaintance with space and with the sense of personal space for which we strive. Through architectural and environmental design we can recognize, extend, and develop the possibilities of such experience. As with space, so with mass, time, and movement. Later chapters will pursue the last two in other contexts, but it will be useful here to examine mass, which may appear at first to be the antithesis of space.

Mass usually epitomizes the environmental forces that oppose the body: obstruction—obstinate and undeniable. Yet here too we tend to construct a difference in kind where there are only changes in degree. Approaching mass perceptually *through* the body, we discover that its firmness and regularity begin to disappear. The perception of mass, for example, is affected more by the degree of opacity than by physical density. Clear glass confronts us less than dense fog or smoke, while reflective surfaces cause physical objects to disappear, a salvation for much contemporary architecture when dull boxes disappear behind mirror-glass sheathing. Mass is also correlated with light: Shadows are heavier and thicker than bright light, darkness than daylight, and all carry intervening degrees. The fusion of mass with the human body is not found in Le Corbusier's "modulor," however, where the human form is taken as the germinal unit, the design module from which the proportions of a building are derived. This is physical mass, not perceptual: It translates the experiential body into a material object instead of transforming mass into the perceptual space of body experience.

Our perceptions occur, for the most part, however, independently of physical attributes. The contrast between space and mass fades as mass dissolves into space and space condenses into mass. We can regard space, for example, as rarified or liquid mass, a medium through which we move much as fish swim through water. Objects, then, are not solids opposed to empty space; they are part of that space, concentrations of it, so to speak. Thus, in Japan, a rock, in representing the *mononoke* that permeates a locality, acquires the quality of the space it inhabits, condensing that space rather than opposing it.[34] A continuum of space and mass thus emerges in which space is diffused mass and mass concentrated space.

In its broadest outlines, then, the perceptual experience of environment is made up of features and configurations given shape by human agency and, in turn, shaping those who perceive them. To understand how this happens requires us to enter the environment as participants and not to regard it as observers. Yet this is difficult to talk about, in part because we have few concepts and techniques in our tradition to assist us. The stratagems used by architects and planners are the devices of spectators rather than of inhabitants. The site or building plan, the elevation, the isometric projection, the model, the aerial view—we have seen how all these exemplify the disinterested viewer's relation to an external environment. They describe the fixed structures and enclosed spaces of the environment as seen from without. Even landscape architecture tends to concentrate on the masonry of structures and to treat plantings as static objects rather than as masses of varying densities changing over time.[35] We have few conceptual tools by which to approach the design of movement and change—of people, light, seasons, of time itself. Nor do we stress the need to shape environment from within as participants.[36] Yet the human environment is lived and must be formulated to reflect this in theoretical terms as continuous, vital, and inseparable from the people who inhabit it. Not only is it important to understand environment in this fashion; we must also develop a fuller somatic consciousness of these perceptual properties so that we become more responsive to its dynamic workings and at the same time more deliberate in determining its shapes.

The arts can assist us in this, for here perceptual experience finds its richest domain. The sensory world of qualitative perception has always flourished in the arts, where visual, auditory, tactile, and kinesthetic awareness elaborate its possibilities with subtlety and power for those who have developed a discerning appreciation. Moreover, we can also discover in the arts a particular sensitivity to environmental perception and it is here that we encounter the qualities of human space most directly. Marin's active sea and mountain-scapes, Kokoshka's dynamic urban landscapes, the compositions of de Stael and Rothko that shape orders of varying masses and spaces, Merce Cunningham's exploitation in dance of ordinary movement and space, Grotowski's return in theater to sacred space and ritual—these are but random instances of an endlessly varied exploration by twentieth-century artists of the perceptual possibilities of the human realm. Art here functions as a cultural vanguard, leading us to discover features of environmental experience that come to emerge as vital aspects of the contemporary world.

Nowhere is this more significant than in those arts whose very nature bridges the cultural chasm between the aesthetic and the practical. The environmental arts of architecture, design, landscape architecture, and city and regional planning offer unmatched opportunities for recognizing and realizing human values by enlarging the capacity and scope of our experience. These arts of environmental design do more than give shape to space: They create the human realm, the possibilities of vision, audition, and movement, the scope of actual perception. In establishing the perceptual conditions for life, the environmental arts help determine human culture. With such a role and such an influence, these arts are the equal of any.

We find ourselves, then, inhabiting an aesthetic environment, a contributing part of its dynamic continuity.[37] Architecture has become environmental design, and environment has turned into a performative activity of persons and places. Once we recognize this, the many subtle ways in which environmental engagement occurs begin to emerge. Engagement relies on sensory involvement, certainly, but perception always bears a mnemonic component, for past perception and expectation join in the conscious present. Perceptual recall is a key factor, for example, in experiencing the stone garden of the fifteenth-century Zen monastery of Ryoanji, near Kyoto. Here fifteen rocks are set in an ocean of raked gravel, yet from wherever we sit one of the rocks is obscured. Only memory and anticipation bring it into conscious play with the others. An expanded perceptual consciousness occurs where architectural design encourages the connection between the outside and inside of a structure so that our awareness of the one persists as we perceive the other. In cases like these, sensory imagination continually supplements our direct sensory awareness. Some people hang photographs of their house on an inside wall and of their boat on an interior bulkhead. As with our home or our boat, we retain the exterior image of our car when we are inside it and the sense of its interior when we stand without. Similarly with a building. Rather than being dismayed at the fact that one cannot *see* at the same time both inside and outside or all sides of a building, we must recognize that architectural experience is not primarily visual, at all. It is rather an experience of the body moving in space, creating through a developed capacity for awareness a functional unity of sensation and action as we enter into a temporal relation with the structure. Eventually a total physical and conscious sense of coherence of person, structure, and setting may develop.[38]

This notion of participatory engagement with environment, however, may yet seem evocative but insubstantial. The dynamic continuity of space and mass, of person and place, of nature and perception, of the aesthetic and the practical, of sensation and imagination, of presence and recollection—all these may appear to be but fanciful constructions with little bearing on the specific demands of the environmental arts. Nothing could be more mistaken. The most compelling argument in favor of engagement is an argument from experience, and it will help make these ideas about environment more definite and their force more direct by translating the notion of participation into the language of environmental design. For the implications of an aesthetics of engagement, as well as the evidence in its support, extend to the full range of human environments, from the museum to the highway, from domestic architecture to city planning, from park design to wilderness management. Let me offer, then, some illustrations and some possible applications of this aesthetic.

Consider the museum. Museums are ordinarily thought of as repositories of great art, places where these works can be kept safely and exhibited as rare and precious objects to a deferential public. Yet the discussion of pictorial space in landscape painting in the preceding chapter has direct consequences for museums. A participatory aesthetic implies that we experience art objects from the best position for engaging in the space of the paintings. For example, in his paintings of Mount Sainte–Victoire Cézanne obtained his distinctive grasp of space by situating himself far across the valley. Those paintings also require the viewer to stand at a considerable distance in order to project into the pictorial space. Monet often demands middle distance, although sometimes, especially in the many *Nymphées* and other late works, the optimum distance is very great. Without sufficient distance, the brushstrokes do not have the room to resolve into richly evocative blossoms and so remain unrealized abstractions. It is more usual, however, for landscapes, portraits, and still lifes to need a surprising degree of intimacy. If we stand close to the pictorial surface, we can no longer regard the object as a whole but look into the painting and merge with its space. Museums and galleries could be designed to lead the viewer into the most effective position and relationship to particular art objects, giving perceptual shape to the sequence of art experiences.[39]

Buildings also offer opportunities for participation in ways that contrast with their usual treatment as visual objects. The buildings that engage us most are not isolated structures that oppose the perceiver; rather they possess human scale, joining with the people who complete them. The Katsura Imperial Villa in Kyoto and the Calgary Airport in Canada, two vastly different structures, have the common effect of evoking our active interest by reaching out to us with embracing configurations that welcome our approach and invite access. This invitation to take part in architecture is nowhere more pronounced than in the case of entrances and doorways. When effective, these draw one in rather than put one off. They do not interpose obstacles or ambiguous shapes, nor do they present indiscernible or intimidating ways of passing into a place or a building. A participatory entrance is easily and clearly recognized. It is appropriate to the body, perceptually inclusive, and welcoming in its affective qualities, such as the stairway to the church in Šibenik, Yugoslavia (*see illustration*). Gateways function differently, marking openings in a boundary or a barrier. They may be designed, like the Arc de Triomphe, as symbolic monuments to impress the spectator visually and intimidate one physically. At their humanized best, however, they provide physical evidence of the transition from one space to another and an invitation to pass through.

Paths are environmental features with rich significance. They are not experienced as cognitive symbols but, if one insists on using that term, as living symbols that embody their meaning, symbols that make us act, make us commit our bodies, our selves, to choices. Malcolm Lowry conjectured that "there has always been something preternatural about paths . . . for not only poetry but folklore abounds with symbolic stories about them: paths that divide and become two paths, paths that lead to a golden kingdom, . . . paths that not merely divide but become the twenty-one paths that lead back to Eden."[40] But what is most striking is the way in which paths, as features of environment, act upon us. In describing the hiking path, Bollnow comments that "the path does not shoot for a destination but rests in itself. It invites loitering. Here a man is *in* the landscape, taken up and dissolved into it, a part of it. He must have time when he abandons himself to such a path. He must stop to enjoy the view."[41] The pedestrian streets of Venice are a well-known example of paths that lead one onward. Others, such as La Grande Rue in Geneva and even the path atop the city walls of Dubrovnik, also possess this quality, common in towns and cities whose streets originated as foot trails. More recently, linear parks that are built around pathways, like San Antonio's Riverwalk, may succeed in creating that invitational quality. So may a boardwalk that crosses a marsh, such as the one in Plitvice Lakes National Park, Yugoslavia (*see illustration*). Even college campuses may have paths that exert a similar attraction on the pedestrian.

Roads, like paths, act on us in diverse ways, inviting us to move down them or putting us off. This may explain why routes are often more appealing in one direction than in the other, so that on a routine trip we are likely to follow one course going and a different one returning. A road that engages the traveler will reflect the geological and topographical features of the countryside, conveying its contours to the driver and encouraging a response to the rhythms of the landscape. When a path or road curves, for example, its appeal is kinesthetic as much as visual: It beckons one to move down it and around the bend. The Taconic State Parkway north of New York City is an outstanding instance of environmental sympathy, a divided highway that moves through the hills of farms and woodland and shapes its path to the rising and falling terrain. At the same time as the road responds to the land, the driver responds to the road, for the Taconic leads us on, offering a constantly changing rural panorama to the participating perceiver.

Guided by an aesthetics of engagement, housing would bind people to a place of domestic architecture that reflects its physical, historical, and regional traits, rather than the impersonal imposition of stock patterns on an anonymous tract of land. The use of local materials and regional designs and of site plans that are sensitive to the geomorphic characteristics of the area, and the modification of standard architectural features to fit individual personalities and needs—steps such as these would help achieve communities with a magnetism that would provide a sense of place and personal belonging.[42] Cities, too, can offer opportunities for embodying the distinctive spatial and cultural experiences of different social and cultural groups and traditions and not be mainly economic arrangements shaped by a politics of expediency, cost, and profit. An engaged urban environment joins built structures to the moving body instead of distributing urban spaces as if they were viewed in perspective from a fixed point. As there are few straight lines or flat planes in the natural environment before the visually guided human hand has had its way, so urban space can be shaped for the dynamic body and not just for the eye. One of the city's strongest aesthetic appeals is to the person as pedestrian, and this appeal rests very much on its attraction to the moving body, its ability to entice one to follow along a street in relaxed and irregular rhythms.

Open space has many shapes in addition to the street. Plazas and squares may be inviting and discouraging in much the same way. They need not present us with simple geometrical forms that require distance to be observed, for these tend to oppose the person: A square need not be square, and it need not be grand. Participatory spaces encourage entry; they evoke our interest and pull us in. The shape of a public place can reflect both its function and its larger setting. A rectangular village green or campus quad spaced about with lofty trees may create an air of tranquility and an equanimity of spirit. Less formal shapes and smaller and more intimate spaces are more likely to engage the body as a dynamic inhabitant. A public square can engage us by comfortable irregularities, dividing great open spaces into smaller protective ones in which enclosure replaces exposure, and providing an easy habitation for the body and opportunities for social exchange. The main plaza in the Colombian town of Giron is home to a great spreading tree, offering shade and shelter from the brutal sun and open, barren ground. A pedestrian mall in Sacramento breaks up the rectangular space between large apartment buildings with plantings, walks, lampposts, and benches. These instances differ sharply from the overpowering forms and intimidating spaces of the federal area in Washington, City Hall Plaza in Boston, and of Brasília, urban areas that swallow the body and diminish the person.[43]

Urban experience can extend beyond the functional to offer opportunities for tapping a variety of wider connections: the distinctive physical and cultural traits of a city's geographical and historical features; the play of fantasy and imagination in the color, surprise, and unexpected richness of the urban setting; the metaphysical roots of human existence through occasions for encountering the sacred and the artistic; the cosmological bonds with the universe by the association of a city's site and plan with the constant and inevitable transition of the seasons and the changes in position and light of the sun and moon.[44]

All these instances suggest how aesthetic engagement can be a guiding principle in experiencing environment. Entire participatory environments, however, are unfortunately no longer common, particularly as we enter the industrialized world, with its rationale of regimentation, uniformity, and mechanical efficiency. One thinks, perhaps with romantic nostalgia, of the New England farmstead, whose house and outbuildings seem to emerge organically out of the landscape, while they are enclosed protectively by the surrounding hills, and whose drives and paths follow the contours of the land, the physical evidence of long and regular activity. Here is the reciprocity of the human and the natural made tangible. Yet it is possible to attain today, in a conscious, deliberate way, what was achieved intuitively through ages of use and custom. To accomplish this, however, requires recognizing the processes of environmental participation and applying them with artistic sensitivity to particular situations.

Environment, then, is no foreign territory surrounding the self. Understanding environment involves recognizing that human life is lived as an integral part of a physical and cultural medium, under conditions through which people and places join together to achieve shape and identity. Within this environmental medium occur the activating forces of mind, eye, hand, climate, and the other processes of nature, along with the perceptual features and structural conditions that engage these forces and evoke their reactions. To grasp environment, every vestige of dualism must be discarded. There is no inside and outside, human being and external world, even, in the final reckoning, no discrete self and separate other. Marcel urges us to say, not that I have a body but that "I am my body."[45] So we can say, similarly, not that I live in my environment but that I am my environment. The conscious body moving as part of a spatiotemporal environmental medium becomes the domain of human experience, the human world, the ground of human reality within and from which discriminations and distinctions are made. The traditional notion of the environment as an external setting is a false abstraction from the unity of the human world. We live rather as a contributing and responding part of a dynamic nexus of interpenetrating forces.

An environmental aesthetic becomes at the same time, then, a cultural aesthetic, the analogue of the cultural landscape of which anthropologists and geographers speak. It comprises not only a study of the perceptual features of the environmental medium that participate reciprocally with people but includes as well a correlative study of the influences of social institutions, belief systems, and patterns of association and action that shape the life of the human social animal and give it meaning and significance. The cultural aesthetic is the characteristic sensory, conceptual, and ideational matrix that constitutes the perceptual environment of a culture. This includes the typical qualities and configurations of color, sound, texture, light, movement, smell, taste, perceptual pattern, space, temporal sensibility, and size in juxtaposition with the human body, and the influence of traditional patterns of belief and practice on the creation and apprehension of these qualities. The human environment is always historico-cultural, and formulating a cultural aesthetic requires us to identify the configuration of perceptual features that is characteristic of a particular human culture at a given time. Certain places exemplify such an aesthetic: In a medieval Gothic cathedral appreciative perception through distancing does not occur. Here light filtered through stained glass windows, linear masses and volumes, the reverberations of chanting voices and organ, the smell of incense, and the taste of wine and wafer combine to absorb the believer into a multi-sensory, multi-media environment. Another example is the Chinese scholar's garden of the eleventh to nineteenth centuries, which creates a harmony of spirit and place, man and nature. Studies in cultural aesthetics are an important way in which aesthetics can enter the social sciences.[46]

We arrive, then, at a conception of environment as a dynamic perceptual–cultural system that assimilates person and place. Heidegger writes of a bridge creating an environment by bringing "stream, banks, and land into each other's neighborhood." The bridge actually "gathers the earth as landscape around the stream." More than this, it "gathers to itself . . . earth and sky, divinities and mortals."[47] We must, then, dispense with the notion of space and consider place, instead, for it is through dwelling, belonging in a place, that the human relation appears. Like the idea of a painting as an object, the environment as external surroundings has been transformed. By exploring the architecture of environment, we can begin to grasp how structure is transmuted into environment and environment into a medium of engagement. Environment has become a realm of dynamic powers, a field of forces that engage both perceiver and perceived in a unity of experience, turning the world we inhabit into a truly human habitation.

CHAPTER FIVE

The
reader's
word

IT IS ONE OF THE DISCOVERIES OF RECENT LITERARY CRITICISM, perhaps its most far-reaching claim, that a text does not stand alone. A text requires a cohort of critics and readers, a literary public, a linguistic system, all surrounded by a larger society with its conventions and beliefs, and all placed in an ordered historical perspective to be interpreted and understood. Gone is the illusion, now known to be naive, that a literary text possesses a self-sufficient integrity, an integrity that imposes its own demands on anyone who comes to it, whether as innocent reader or deferential student. Moreover for the semioticians, at least, the text has expanded indiscriminately to subsume every object, practice, and event that holds meaning, and meaning has likewise enlarged to accommodate every presumably cogent interpretation from any direction—linguistic, semiotic, Freudian, Marxist, formalist, feminist, political, until under the deconstructionists the text surrenders any claim to authority.

What, then, remains of literature? The celebrated autonomy of the work of art, the regality of the masterwork have fallen before their interpreters and critics. With the expansion of the text and the multiplication of interpretations, we may yearn for Calvino's solution where, "putting behind you pages lacerated by intellectual analyses, you dream of rediscovering a condition of natural reading, innocent, primitive."[1] Literature, moreover, is not unique in this fall from grace. We have already seen that its fate is shared by painting and architecture, a loss of self-sufficiency that we shall find in other arts as well. Yet what is in question is whether the arts ever possessed the autonomy with which we have been so accustomed to invest them and, in fact, whether this change in status might not signify their resurrection into a new and more vital life, recognizing a power and importance that had remained partially hidden under the protection of a mistaken self-sufficiency. Perhaps the salvation of literature does not lie in preserving the purity of the autonomous text but in identifying the locus of literature. But what is literature, if not a text?

The identity of literature is no easy question in this age of competing scholarships. Nor are the alternatives simple ones, for their subtle elaborations extend the focus beyond the apparent boundaries of author, text, and reader. Edges blur and domains merge in the different efforts of formalists, structuralists, subjectivists, reader-response theorists, and deconstructionists to locate and comprehend literature. Yet the centers of these views are clear enough and the alternatives they offer sufficiently different to make it important to identify them and attempt to place them within a somewhat more inclusive perspective, for it is easy to mistake one domain for the world. Let us focus first, then, on some of these alternatives, not representing them fully but rather identifying their central points as poles of a larger conceptual structure. This will lead to the main purpose: pursuing the assimilation of the reader into the literary process.

Centering the understanding of literature on the text alone is the clearest and most direct strategy. It has had a powerful appeal in this century because it offered a means of applying the presumably objective procedures of scientific inquiry to the intangible and elusive art of literature. From different directions the New Critics, structuralists, linguists, and other formalists have taken the text as the object of inquiry, an object to be analyzed, divided, and unraveled, and then its meaning reconstructed in the clear daylight of reason.

Among the most influential exemplars of this approach was the Russian formalist Roman Jakobson. Jakobson proposed a formula that identified two basic principles that organize speech: selection and combination. Selection rests on the capacity of language for metaphoric equivalence, either by similarity or dissimilarity. Thus the speaker chooses a subject for discussion from among possible synonymous alternatives, and this becomes the subject of the sentence. The speaker then selects what to say about it from other synonymous terms to establish the predicate. As an act of verbal communication, poetry employs the same scheme as every other function of language, but it uses rhythmic, phonetic, and other forms of equivalence along with structural ones in combining words as well as in selecting them. Furthermore, the focus in poetry is on the message for its own sake. The two principles of selection and combination form complementary axes here, leading Jakobson to define a poetic structure as a structure "characterized by the projection of the principle of equivalence from the axis of selection to the axis of combination." Words combined by their phonological equivalence, as in alliteration, rhyme, or rhythm, produce semantic relations between those perceived to be similar, such as simile or metaphor, or dissimilar, such as antithesis. Parallelism, or the recurrent use of the same forms, provides poetry with a language that may occur simultaneously or successively on any of the several levels: semantic, syntactic, phonological, or phonetic.[2]

We have, then, a structure that comprises a number of interrelated parts. While this is an invariant system, it is capable of internal transformations, so that a set of variants may occur, all of which are of the same type. This leads Lévi-Strauss to hold that "a poem is a structure containing within itself its variants ordered on the vertical axis of the different linguistic levels." The same structure, then, embraces any number of variants; within this structural frame we can analyze a poetic text at any linguistic level.[3]

Procedures such as this rest on the premise that language is entirely a system of signs. For Ferdinand de Saussure, who established the study of structural linguistics early in this century, words have no meaning in themselves nor do they refer directly to things themselves. Within its system, a sign contains a sound or graphic image, called a signifier, and its meaning, called a signified; and it refers to an object, called the referent. Only within the objective structure of its system does a sign possess meaning, and the system, moreover, is entirely conventional. Meaning is a function, then, of signs and not of people's speech or the things we talk about. "Words do not 'refer' to things themselves. Rather they have meaning as points within the entire system that is a language."[4]

The coherence of this order masks an underlying difficulty,

however: the pervasive arbitrariness of its elements. There is no meaning inherent in any particular signifier, signified, or referent. They acquire their meaning from their differences within the functional order of a linguistic system. In Saussure's words, "In the linguistic system, there are only differences."[5] An even more compelling question, however, is what the analysis of linguistic structures tells us about poetry. As Riffaterre notes, "There is no doubt that a linguistic actualization does take place, but the question remains: are the linguistic and poetic actualizations coextensive?"[6]

Both sign and referent, then, carry a certain arbitrariness. Together they acquire an identity, fluid but cohesive. Yet the closed system of signs is essentially incomplete. The arbitrariness of language as a formal structure can be overcome only by turning outside the system to an act of stipulation. Words themselves do not refer; people use words to refer, and it is the user who creates the bond between sign and referent. The human contribution provides the ontology that unifies word and object. Similarly, it does not follow that a satisfactory linguistic analysis can adequately reach the poetic or literary condition of a text. To decide this requires a turn to experience to judge the accuracy of its findings. In either case we must escape from the system of signs into the larger conditions of their use.

A text, then, cannot stand alone: The essential incompleteness of the formalist approach to literature forces us to break out of the limits of the text. The study of language in literature directs us beyond the written word, even beyond its author, to the reader who actualizes language at any given moment. In more recent structural linguistics, the reader becomes the subject who is produced by the structural features of language. These features establish the relation between the text and its reader by the use of pronouns, voice, point of view, tense, and forms of address. Moreover, it is the reader who re-invents the sign, locates its referent, and joins them into a unity by the act of reading. Only in reading do sign and referent function as such, yet in functioning they lose their separate identity to assume a new one. The sign is no longer a sign, because it is not a linguistic object that possesses a definite meaning that can be attached to the sign itself. It becomes "palpable," to use Jakobson's term; its material qualities form in the mouth, resonate in the ear, and are given body by the breath.[7] In conjunction with other signs, it contributes to the formation of meaning. And the referent, too, never stands alone but is selected and focused by the reader.

Reading, then, transforms literature from an object into an event, and an event cannot be objectified, grasped, and held at arm's length. It is something more elusive, more intangible. Moreover, it assumes a life of its own. Calvino has one of his fictional authors admit that "in reading, something happens over which I have no power."[8] And Barthes, in writing of the "death of the author," comments that "it is language which speaks in literature, in all its 'polysemic' plurality, not the author himself. If there is any place where this seething multiplicity of the text is momentarily focused, it is not the author but the *reader*."[9] Here, perhaps, lies the necessary counterweight to the text. Even some critics whose formalist credentials are unimpeachable appear to have been led to the same conclusion. William Empson was one. His study of ambiguity, by which he meant "any verbal nuance, however slight, which gives room for alternative reactions to the same piece of language," led him to acknowledge that ambiguity depends on the reader, who supplies the social context of discourse, the conventional meanings and unspoken assumptions one brings to the reading of literature.[10]

Many paths, then, lead from the text to its reader. Yet the present popularity of attempts to identify the reader's contribution as an antidote to the formalists' objectification of the literary text may lead one to overlook the fact that literature has long been recognized as an art of speaking and reading. The passive model of appreciation never did hold well here, because literature is a language experience. What sort of experience, then, does such language provoke?

One time-honored answer is Aristotle's. His study of tragedy involved a careful analysis of the factors in plot, action, and character that evoke pity and fear. Somewhere in that connection lies the force of drama, for Aristotle combined a concern for the audience's response with attention to the kinds of potentially dramatic human happenings that take place.[11] One could interpret this approach to tragedy as an attempt to develop, not a theory of imitation or of emotion, but the rudiments of a theory of aesthetic experience.

The idea that the literary audience takes an active role, then, has early origins. It reappeared during the eighteenth century in the importance given imagination, as when Laurence Sterne observed in *Tristram Shandy* that no author, who understands the just boundaries of decorum and good-breeding, would presume to think all: The truest respect which you can pay to the reader's understanding, is to halve this matter amicably, and leave him something to imagine, in his turn, as well as yourself. For my own part, I am eternally paying him compliments of this kind and do all that lies in my power to keep his imagination as busy as my own.[12]

While giving imagination its due, that century, however, was more taken with the analytic process of identifying differences, in this case the distinctiveness of the art object, than with drawing the interrelations and connections among things. The fascination of the romantic movement with the domains of feeling and the recognition of a kinship with nature through art brought art and its appreciator closer together. For Thoreau this was a kinship closest to life. Literature "is the work of art nearest to life itself. It may be translated into every language, and not only be read but actually breathed from all human lips;—not be represented on canvas or in marble only, but be carved out of the breath of life itself."[13]

Language not only conveys feeling and commands the breath, but it engages the senses as well. What Ben Jonson asked of literature, "Speake, that I may see thee," and Robert Frost called "the sound of sense," Joseph Conrad articulated as theory. The primary appeal of all art, he claimed, is to the senses. This is the artistic aim of the written word if it wishes to touch the source of emotional responsiveness. Through ceaseless care "for the shape and ring of sentences," they may evoke for a passing moment the magical suggestiveness of words over the commonplace dullness of habit.[14] In speaker, in listener, in reader, then, language realizes its special power.

The central importance of their interdependence emerged, however, in our own century, and it has grown increasingly significant. Jean-Paul Sartre, for example, assigned an essential, creative role to the reader, recognizing that literature not only requires the powers of imagination but possesses an important social function as well. In "What Is Literature?" he insisted that the prose writer is engaged in his society and, through disclosing aspects of the social world, performs actions by his words that contribute to changing it. There is, in fact, a "pact" between author and reader, Sartre holds, in which the latter makes a contribution essential for the completion of the writing:

> When a work is produced, the creative act is only an incomplete, abstract impulse; if the author existed all on his own, he could write as much as he liked, but his work would never see the light of day as an object, and he would have to lay down his pen or despair. The process of writing, however, includes as a dialectical correlative the process of reading, and these two interdependent acts require two people who are active in different ways. The combined efforts of author and reader bring into being the concrete and imaginary object which is the work of the mind. Art exists only for and through other people.[15]

A literary text, then, cannot be taken alone. It has become increasingly clear, moreover, that different texts imply different kinds of readers, that readers take an essential part in determining literary meanings, that conventions in reading affect the interpretation of texts, that the unfolding of meaning in reading is a temporal process involving the arousal of expectations and their satisfaction or frustration, and that a person's self-identity and self-processes influence the ways in which he or she will engage in textual interpretation. In current philosophy and criticism, elements that suggest the interdependence of text and reader enter into the germinal center of literary theory from many theoretical orientations, among them phenomenology, semiotics, psychoanalysis and, as we have seen, sometimes even formalism and structuralism. However, these elements have coalesced to form the main theme of the movement in literary theory known variously as reader–response criticism, or reception theory.[16]

Stanley Fish moves the discussion of literature from the text with its objective meaning to the reader. Literature is no independent body of special texts culled from the vast ocean of print by standard canons of normative judgment. In place of the formal structure of the written word, Fish looks to the structure of the reader's experience. Language is not the embodiment of meaning but the utterances we make and hear, and their meanings lie in those experiences. The reader, then, does not discern the meaning hidden in a text: Apart from the reader, the text has none. It is merely the medium through which the meaning enters the reader. There can be, in fact, no literary text without a reader who activates the word, transforming it from a black mark against the purity of a white ground into living meaning. Nor does reading defer to the integrity of the text. Formalism is mistaken in supposing not only that there is a self-sufficient text, with its inherent structures and meanings, but that the text can be described in itself. Description presupposes an independent text that we can depict impartially. Fish claims, contrariwise, that this is impossible and that the very identification of formal units is the result of the reader's interpretive model. Formal patterns "do not lie innocently in the world" but are constituted in the act of interpretation. We do not first read a text and then proceed to interpret it; interpretive strategies shape our reading, deciding not just *how* we read but *what* it is we are reading. No description is possible, only interpretation.[17]

Placing the weight of literature so heavily on its reader does not necessarily rest it on the soft ground of subjectivity. Even though there are no "true," objective meanings embedded in literature, there is the obvious fact that readers agree widely on meanings, formal units, and even interpretations and judgments. This is because readers never act and think in isolation but share a body of experience, attaining a common base, much like Saussure's concept of *parole* and Chomsky's notion of "linguistic competence." Moreover, as people engaged in any activity do, we develop ways of thinking, experiencing, and responding through our exposure to literature in the course of education and under common social and historical influences. As readers, we are never independent but members all of interpretive communities, who will agree with others in the same group because we see everything according to similar purposes and goals. Meanings reside not in a stable text or in the independent reader; they emerge from features of the text that direct the reader and shape the literary experience.

Phenomenologically oriented theorists vary in the extent to which they bring together reader and text. Ingarden represents one extreme, regarding literary works as integral wholes whose indeterminacies the reader must complete in a "proper" manner as prescribed by the text.[18] Dufrenne expresses the other when he claims that in aesthetic experience there is no longer any separation between the object perceived and the experiencer.[19] Wolfgang Iser has developed an intermediate position, a phenomenological theory of literature in which the constitutive response of the reader forms the cornerstone. Because of the detail with which Iser has developed his theory, let us consider it as representing this approach.[20]

For Iser neither text nor reader can be understood separately. In fact, the very designation "fiction" misdirects our understanding of literature, for it suggests that a text stands independent of any outside reality and can therefore be analyzed in itself. Fiction does not rest in opposition to reality but has an obvious connection with it; in fact, fiction tells us something *about* reality. That connection, however, cannot be grasped by searching for what literature *means:* The link between fiction and reality lies in what literature *does.* Only when we examine what it does in the dynamic interaction of text and reader will we begin to discern how fiction acts in exposing reality.

The text thus carries potentials that are realized only in the process of reading. This is the kind of event that takes place as the reader constantly adds reactions to new information in an unresolved situation, as part of a continuing process of realization. Speaking more abstractly, a dialectical relation develops between the textual structure and the structured act of the reader through which a literary work is actualized, and it is this relation that defines the role of the reader. Its explanation requires what Iser calls a theory of aesthetic response (*Wirkungstheorie*) and not one of the aesthetics of reception (*Rezeptionstheorie*), that is, a theory of interaction and not of reaction. Instead of looking for the meaning of literature, then, we must look for its effect. Here is where we can discover the function of literature.

A text, then, cannot be grasped as a whole; it is rather a process of changing perspectives from which the reader constructs a total situation. It offers a literary repertoire that provides materials for the interplay between text and reader. Using Mukaroвský's sense of the term *structure,* which stresses its energetic and dynamic character, Iser holds that the repertoire of a text—references to social and historical norms, to literary works, or to an entire cultural tradition— "forms an organizational structure of meaning which must be optimized through the reading of the text." The strategies of the text organize these materials and the conditions for their communication. This is a process of forming a gestalt out of the network of possible connections from which the reader selects those to actualize and guide the shape of the aesthetic object. A complex imaginative process takes place, in which the reader tries out and develops gestalten that organize the intricacies of a text, bringing in past experiences and becoming entangled in the text, while at the same time, making it into a personal presence. An interaction occurs, then, between familiar experiences and new ones, and the reader's response to the text develops out of this interplay. These attempts to form gestalten produce textual ambiguities that press us further into trying to resolve their confusions and contradictions.

There are, moreover, indeterminacies in a text or gaps in its sequences: *blanks*, Iser calls them. These are the pivots around which text and reader turn and which the reader fulfills by completing the aesthetic object. "The asymmetry between text and reader stimulates a constitutive activity on the part of the reader," which acquires its specific structure from the blanks and the negations that the text generates. Here is the structure that controls the process of interaction. Added to all this are protension and retention, as expectation and memory project themselves on one another in the experience of reading. This requires syntheses that are produced by the reader's imagination, not working alone, but guided by signals from the text "which project themselves into him." The two cannot be separated.[21]

In being led to this interpenetration of subject and object, of reader and text, Iser enters a terrain difficult to map, since our conceptual key contains no simple sign for such a concept. Literary theory reflects gropings in this direction from other sources. Working from a psychoanalytical orientation, Jacques Lacan followed Freud in holding that early in its development the infant has no clear sense of the difference between itself and other things. To explain this, Lacan developed the notion of the *imaginary*, a condition in which there is no clear sense of self. In this state there is a continuous exchange between our self and objects, a continuity between subject and object in which our self seems to merge with objects, to pass into objects, and objects seem to enter into the self. As accumulating experiences make our separateness increasingly inevitable, we begin to construct a unified self-image through what Lacan called "the mirror stage." The child sees its integrated image reflected in a mirror and thus begins to attain a sense of an integrated self, a self that is both like and unlike the image. In a similar way, other objects and people reflect us back to ourselves, and we identify with those reflections in the same way we do with the image in the mirror.

Lacan believed that identifying with things in the world is essentially a narcissistic process for attaining a unified sense of the self. The process of maturation requires us to develop an awareness of the difference between our own self and other people and other things, a sense quite different from the unified realm of the imaginary. Language is the principal vehicle for this process. It offers symbolic expression of what is not present, a sign that replaces the real object and that acquires meaning from its differences from other signs. Desire originates in this consciousness of difference and absence, a lack embodied in language. These forms of divisiveness sever us from what is truly "real," from a condition of unity that lies beyond language and to which we hopelessly endeavor to return.[22]

Among the reader–response theorists, Norman N. Holland goes perhaps as far as anyone toward assimilating the text to the reader. He distinguishes three theories of reading: active, in which there is a proper, standard response to the text; biactive, in which a text and its reader, separate from each other, join together in the response; and transactive, in which there is a continuous transaction in the process of reading, which creates meaning and feeling and in which the contributions of both reader and text are indistinguishable. Holland argues for the last of these, describing the process as a feedback loop which I, as reader, start, sustain, and interpret through a personal process, transforming the text into an occasion for achieving identity. "All of us, as we read, use the literary work to symbolize and finally to replicate ourselves." In his search for an integral self, Holland argues that the goal of literary criticism is the merging of self and other, that is, a coalescence of self with author or text. He proposes a transactive model in which the reader emulates the writer's creative ability to overcome, in Freud's words, "the barriers that rise between each single ego and the others." Yet this remains a suggestive goal, not a developed proposal, and it is obscured by Holland's own concern with the psychology of identity formation.[23]

We have a continuum, then, that moves from the formalist objectification of the text through stages to an emphasis on the reader who transmutes the text into a psychological process of self-discovery. Is there any alternative to this opposition of forces in literary experience? Let us turn briefly to two commentators on the poetic who carry the subjective process of literature in surprising directions.

In drifting along the reveries of the reader, Gaston Bachelard appears to represent the opposing pole to the formalist's structuring of the poetic world. As he sees it, there are two antithetical and untranslatable orientations, knowledge and poetry, the one centering around concepts, the other on images. "Images and concepts take form at those two opposite poles of psychic activity which are imagination and reason. Between them there is a polarity of exclusion at work. They have nothing in common with the poles of magnetism. Here, the opposing poles do not attract; they repel." For Bachelard, poetry takes us on a voyage into the domain of the imagination, a movement we feel within ourselves. In poetic language, we go beyond ideas and sensations to what is new and unknown. Rather than deriving from speech that is already familiar, the poetic image "opens a future to language." We must take such images in their directness but only for ourselves. A poetic image can, in fact, be the seed of a universe that the poet creates in reverie and with which we must actively join. Such reverie through poetic imagery leads a soul to discover its world: Poetry is the language of souls. The poet not only leads us into the realm of imagination; the true poet invites us to embark on a voyage, setting in motion a dynamic reverie. Through a sequence of images we pursue a dream, not just to the realm of the imaginary but to its immanence in the real. There is a "continuous passage from the real to the imaginary."[24]

The Swiss critic Georges Poulet also subjectifies the literary work. In the act of reading one enters the book; the book disappears as an object to become "a series of words, of images, of ideas which begin to exist . . . [in] my innermost self." The text is no object opposed to the reader; language enables everything to become part of the reader's mind. It is as if reading enabled a thought alien to me to become part of me. Indeed, reading places my own subjectivity in question as I lose myself to another, relinquishing my own identity to the work, the work that has now come to define my consciousness.

This sounds like an abandonment to the text, an assimilation of the reader by the work. Is this an inverse subjectivism, one in which the loss of self to the work is actually an ingestion of the work by the reader? Poulet writes about the experience of interiority, however, in a way that seems to transgress the boundaries of reader and book. A book, he holds, is not walled up like a fortress but wants to exist outside itself or, to say the same thing, wants to let the reader exist in it. The barriers between both melt away. "You are inside it; it is inside you; there is no longer either outside or inside." Yet there still seems to be a mutual subjectification at work here. The book has turned into words, images, and ideas, subjectified objects that have become part of my mind. Yet at the same time these words are not myself, they are foreign to me and appropriate my consciousness by becoming the "I," not only defining but assimilating my consciousness.[25]

There is subtle irony here in this return to the dominance of the text, a dominance not as external object but as internal consciousness. Poulet appears to complete the circle from formalism and structuralism to subjectivism by returning to the work as an object, but as an object of consciousness that takes over and defines my identity. The work does not displace me. A common consciousness develops, but the work and the reader do not have equal importance. In the foreground stands "the consciousness inherent in the work," which relates to its own world and its own objects. As reader I have a much more modest place, passively recording what I am experiencing. This is "a subjectivity without objectivity," that is, a subjectivity that stands apart from the objective, formal elements of the work, revealing itself in the work in an ineffable and fundamental indeterminacy to which I, as the reader, must abandon myself.[26] Is this a return to the plight of Ion, who acknowledges not being in his right mind when he is carried out of himself and overcome by emotions appropriate to the situation in the poem he is reciting?[27]

This spectrum of views reflects the main ways in which reader and text can be related. Although there are other major directions in contemporary literary criticism, such as semiotics, poststructuralism, hermeneutics, deconstruction, and postmodernism, they add only variations to the particular theme we have been pursuing here. For in spite of the radical transfer of attention from the text to its reader, the intent of criticism has remained virtually unchanged. Although Bachelard and Poulet are exceptions to this, more recent criticism continues to occupy itself with interpretation, and this centers the discussion of literature around questions of meaning. What has changed is not the function of criticism but its locus, which has now been displaced from the text to the reader. In fact, formalism, reader–response theory, and subjectivism are themselves interpretive strategies: All propose to explain how to determine what literature means. Each seizes upon a different feature of the aesthetic field around which to develop its account—the text, the author's perception, the psychology of the reader, or the mutual contribution each makes to the work's meaning.

While reader–response theories appear to offer an account of reading in addition to a theory of interpretation and a support for the critical discussion of a text,[28] these theories rest their collective weight on a single premise, that understanding what happens in reading provides the proper basis for determining meaning. Although a deep division lies between the experience of literature in reading and reading as the grounding of literary theory, the critical assumption is that there is no difference between the two, indeed, that they need not be distinguished: The theory of reading stands as a clear and accurate reflection of the activity of reading. Yet these are profoundly different matters, for the theory imports a structural division of the field of analysis into reader and text, while reading presumes their connection. More distressing still is the fact that people continue to practice criticism as usual. As Tompkins observes, "Only the vocabulary with which they perform their analyses has altered." Interpretation remains the goal of critical inquiry, and the text is still its source. The literary text is not an independent event or experience; it remains an object whose concealed meaning needs to be unearthed. Critics continue to work within an institutional context dominated by formalist doctrine, which dictates that interpretation is the only legitimate function of criticism.[29]

One might argue, however, that the search for meaning is an unexceptionable premise of criticism: It is meaning that guides the discussion and demands explication. What else could reading be about, where else should a theory of interpretation be directed? Isn't meaning the end of literature, as it is of every other intellectual endeavor? Yet meaning can itself be placed in question. If meaning is to guide the critical discussion of literature, doesn't *this* require explanation and justification?

These questions suggest several points, the first of which is to make explicit this assumption of the priority of meaning. If meaning *is* the end of criticism, or if its explication has pedagogical utility, we should see that as our clear program and acknowledge its central place. However, at the same time we must recognize that specifying meaning as the purpose of criticism or a convenient aid in teaching literature does not thereby turn it also into the goal of reading. In fact, to maintain this is to reverse the logical order, to confuse the tail of the beast with its head. Joyce Cary once observed that

> we have to have conceptual knowledge to organise our societies, to save our own lives, to lay down general ends for conduct, to engage in any activity at all, but that knowledge, like the walls we put up to keep out the weather, shuts out the real world and the sky. It is a narrow little house which becomes a prison to those who can't get out of it. The artist, the writer, simply in order to give his realization, his truth, has to break these walls, the conceptual crust.[30]

Have we, as readers, forsaken the writer and surrendered the art in literature for knowledge in literature?

Yet meaning is not the entire matter, for all meaning and each theory of how it emerges rest on some account of the experience of literature. It is, in fact, crucial to recognize the difference between the experience of literature and the analysis and theory of that experience. Most accounts of literature invert the order, starting with some theoretical presupposition and then dictating what that experience must be. Whether literature be an experience of sounds, syntactic orders, images, personal associations, responses to verbal stimuli, or psychodynamic processes, any account of *how* these incorporate, display, present, or transmit meaning is quite distinct from how we *experience* meaning and, more generally, from how we experience *literature*. For literature is more than a vehicle for embodying and transmitting meanings. It has sensuous dimensions; it requires somatic involvement; it stimulates psychological processes of imaging, of imagination, of association, and of the abandonment to memory, which are distinct from the cognitive one of locating meaning. These processes are often mixed with the interpretive enterprise, but they are different enough that a primary concern with interpretation obscures their operation and neglects their importance.

There are, then, theories of how meaning occurs in literature, and theories of how other experiential factors join in the literary process. Moreover, we must not forget that every theory, whatever its province, is theory, not literary experience. As such, it is a cognitive activity, not an appreciative one, yet it is the latter that is the heart of the matter. Our engagement with literature comes first, and how we interpret it or otherwise explain that experience is, in the final analysis, derivative. Confounding theory with experience is the great danger of the scholarly process, and nowhere is this more subtly poised to entrap the reader than in the art that uses the very medium of cognition, language.

Not only can one question the stand that the interpretation of meaning is the single legitimate function of criticism; one can also question its essentialist assumption that literature possesses a fundamental function. For this directs the critic either to identify the meanings associated with a text or to discern some other central role, such as regarding a text as a means for the exercise of political power, as Foucault interprets it in *The Archaeology of Knowledge*. Yet these are but two possible functions of criticism, and they may both be present at the same time in different degrees. How can one deal with a work like *Kubla Khan*, for which neither of these functions seems to hold? Why, indeed, restrict ourselves to but two alternatives? Aren't there still other possibilities for literature that criticism can elucidate? Literature may be a socializing force, acquainting the reader with the belief system, conventions, attitudes, values, and traditions of a culture, with its mind-set, and giving these an aura of rightness, of authority, even of sanctity. Perhaps this is another name for Foucault's power, but that dismissal does not apply to those cases in which the tradition is one of pluralism, the values are of tolerance, the attitude is of dissent. Nor does it hold for that time-honored way of crossing over into the ambience of another culture through the study of its language and literature. There are, moreover, still other ways in which literature may work: It may offer a fantasy life of adventure, intrigue, excitement. It may have psychotherapeutic value, offering opportunities for wish fulfillment, sublimation, or projection. It may provide an occasion for daydreaming, for reverie, Bachelard's beloved oneiric activity.

Criticism may reveal and clarify, then, all these uses of literature. Restricting its function exclusively to interpretation rests on the narrow assumption that the cognitive role of language is the legitimate one, all others being dismissed as intellectually disreputable. Nonetheless, alternative places for literature have equal claim before an impartial judge: conative (instrumental or goal-directed), connotative, presentational or exhibitive (to use Buchler's term) are still others. In fact, Buchler's principle of ontological parity, which would afford equal standing to each function, is a less presumptive premise for criticism.[31] Furthermore, a democracy of critical functions allows us to adopt new forms of organizing the conceptual and social framework within which criticism itself takes place.

There is still a more disquieting difficulty with criticism than an exclusivity of function. Most of these discussions of the reader's contribution remain bound in obscure but no less powerful ways to accounting for the complexities in the relationship between reader and text as two connected but separate factors. It is exceedingly hard to evade the pervasive dualisms of Western culture. "The doctrines of the unified self and the closed text surreptitiously underlie the apparent open-endedness of much reception theory,"[32] Eagleton notes, an observation that holds equally true of most of the other attempts to relate reader to text. Bachelard and Poulet begin to suggest something different only to become engulfed by the quicksand of subjectivity.

Transactional theory offers a significantly different direction for moving beyond this deep division of reader and text. Applying a relational model developed in theory of knowledge and psychology to the study of literary experience, Louise M. Rosenblatt regards an aesthetic encounter with literature as a temporal event, to which a reader and a text make an equal contribution. This is not, however, an equal exchange; in fact it is not an exchange at all. Rather, both reader and text join in a unified occasion: The poem is not an object but an experience, one in which reader and text join. It is an event that occurs in the time of experience, to which the reader brings knowledge, background, personality, and the skills of perception and comprehension to activate the ordered symbols of the text. This is probably the fullest development of the reader–response direction, one that comes closest to a complete integration of text and reader.[33]

There may be good reason for moving beyond the cognitive and other functions of literature, important though they be in their place. For, Calvino remarks,

> just when you are convinced that for the professor philology and erudition mean more than what the story is telling, you realize the opposite is true: that academic envelope serves only to protect everything the story says and does not say, an inner afflatus always on the verge of being dispersed at contact with the air, the echo of a vanished knowledge revealed in the penumbra and in tacit allusions.[34]

What happens when the text disappears as a real or even as an ideal entity, when it cannot be located or spoken of as a discrete object, when the boundaries of literature are redrawn the way we now shape terrestrial space into an ecosystem and astral space into galaxies? What happens when the reader vanishes as an identity, as an integral self the way the citizen has changed from a private individual with personal rights into a social being who embodies the belief system, values, customs, and movement patterns of his or her cultural group? To move beyond the dualism of text and reader in dealing with the literary experience seems to leave us without a vocabulary to describe it.

Perhaps it would be best to set aside the cognitive and other functions to which criticism has been beholden and shift more directly into literature as a word experience. This takes us beyond the capacity of a text to place the reader in contact with the author. For the author becomes not only a persona but also a personality, a consciousness, a mentality inseparable from the text, which embodies the author's characteristics and with whom the reader joins in a kind of experiential identity. This turns us toward the ontology of literature, a domain more elusive, more subtle and, to my mind, more intriguing than any of the other regions in which literature has been explored. The experience of literature may then be characterized best as a *condition:* the grasp of a social situation, of a state of mind or a relationship, of the sense of a particular place or a perception of the world, of the very order of things. This is not just a form of escape or free imagination; it is the irrepressible intuition of what is real, a sense gained *in* literature, not *through* literature.

Indeed, what happens in the experience of literature is not first and foremost a cognitive act; it is an ontological event, one which both constitutes and joins a realm of being, a world of the word into which the reader enters, a world that possesses its own order of reality.[35] "First and foremost" is a misleading locator, for we are speaking here not of an invariable temporal order but of an appreciative one. We may travel far through a maze of interpretations before we arrive at that primary state, but when we do, it is like that stage in the education of the guardians in *The Republic,* when they are finally able to behold the Forms that they could not be shown by others, or like Wittgenstein's throwing away the ladder by which he raised himself to a vision of the order of things. There is a self-sufficiency here in an elusive condition beyond, or perhaps before, our attempt to grasp and subdue the world through the variable concepts by which we order it.

What is this condition that literature leads us into, and how does literature accomplish it? How can one characterize that merging of reader and text, that world of literary experience? We face the difficulty of describing the language *of* experience by a language *about* experience. This is the primary, underlying problem of all criticism. It is really an act of translation to render the experience of literature, a language experience, into critical, that is, theoretical terms. The result is almost invariably misleading, for it transposes the direct qualitative apprehension that is literature into a critical frame that fixes it in an order foreign to the experience, an order that is not only falsely structured but also falsely stable. What is an experiential unity becomes divided by criticism. If reading is "an operation without object" whose "true object is itself" and "the book is an accessory aid, or even a pretext," as Calvino has one of his characters claim,[36] how then can one talk about it? Are Bachelard's reveries on images, reveries that follow the mobility of thought, the way to proceed? For him poetry consists of living images, images in motion that pulsate as they are reimagined and experienced in consciousness. There they "reverberate" and so lead one, at the same time, both in new directions and in communication with the poet. Poetry lives in new images, images so fragile that any explanation can destroy them.[37]

Speaking of Dickens's descriptions of London, V. S. Naipaul characterizes the way in which the Victorian novelist was able to give his reader a sense of that city: "using . . . only simple words, simple concepts, to create simple volumes and surfaces and lights and shadows: creating thereby a city or fantasy which everyone could reconstruct out of his own materials, using the things he knew to recreate the described things he didn't know."[38] In much the same way Sartre described Guardi's paintings of Venice, which presented the city "as it has been experienced by everyone and seen by no one," and Calvino depicted his cities of the imagination, fantasy cities, cities that have the locus of myth and yet which we somehow have the sense of having visited. For Gadamer, all writing has this ability to transcend time and place and achieve "sheer presence."[39] The novel has this ability to make a world present, to "become the means whereby readers immerse themselves in human experiences." In a great novel the characters achieve an extraordinary reality, so that we come to know them and to share their experiences, much as we share the experiences of an intimate friend. The novel, James Farrell has remarked, is, in fact, "a means of 'shared experience'."[40]

How does literature accomplish this? How does the poet or novelist engage the senses? The means are as varied as the modalities, techniques, and styles of that art. Consider the "New Novel." Alain Robbe-Grillet maintains that here descriptions no longer provide us with a setting to fit a story, a setting external to the plot. The novel now comes to treat people's experience *through* description, indeed as the very substance of description. Like the camera, the novel can explore the subjective and imaginary, *becoming* real in the process rather than offering us reflections on an already formed reality: It destroys realism to achieve reality. Similarly with time. The novel is no longer concerned with the passage of time but with our present awareness of it. The sense of time is always historical. When it is lived, however, time is only in the present tense; that is to say, it does not yet exist. The new place of such factors as time and description changes the novel from a narrative account into an experience of awareness in which the reader joins the author in the creation of his own life. What the writer asks of the reader "is no longer to receive ready-made a world completed, full, closed upon itself, but on the contrary to participate in a creation, to invent in his turn the work— and the world—and thus to learn to invent his own life."[41]

Of course each movement, each style, each period in literature invents its own ways of creating its world. Some demand the reader's collaboration more explicitly than others; none, however, can proceed without it. Grammatical devices like periodic sentences, serial predications, and complex subordinating constructions require reading to achieve their effect.[42] But so indeed does every sentence of whatever construction need its reader to balance and combine its words, phrases, and clauses into coherence. What is true of grammar is, *a fortiori*, the case with literature, and with far greater scope and complexity. Narration, character portrayal and development, the dynamic of dramatic progress, plot, metaphor—every technical device and analytical feature of literature requires and, in fact, is devised precisely for the reader to activate it, to turn language into experience through such activities as remembering, imagining, relating, and ordering.

Thus a writer's style is not a peculiarity of skill but rather a mirror of that individual's sense of reality. The choice of person in narrative, for example, does not decide among stylistic alternatives that clothe the same thought with one or another convention; it shapes the very quality and character of the narrative. Except for those who believe mistakenly that cognitive content is the matter of literary discourse, that the statement, proof, and communication of assertions are all that is significant, it is clear that a particular stylistic character shapes the very nature of a literary experience.

More forceful yet than the adoption of stylistic devices and other technical features is the power of the vital image and the metaphor. Thus Nietzsche: "For the true poet a metaphor is not a figure of speech but a vicarious image which actually hovers before him in place of a concept. To him a character is not an aggregate composed of a number of particular traits, but an organic person pressing himself upon his attention."[43] The strong metaphor can overcome the reader, as it overpowers the protagonist in Takeshi Kaiko's *Darkness in Summer:*

> As in the days when I was waiting for her in the room with the worn-out red curtains, passing the time sleeping and waking, a strange flaccid thing is beginning to grow out of my body. It is taking root, extending its stems, spreading leaves, and waving tendrils. It has entrapped me, forcing me down onto the couch so that I cannot move, and then has overflowed onto the floor, creeping over the carpet, slowly proliferating, covering the yak hide, and now it is trying to cover the entire wall. Rustling and breathing heavily, it is about to pin me down to the sofa and cover my entire body. If I sit up, it hesitates and vanishes momentarily, but as I cross the room, go to the bathroom, and turn the shower handle, it is already encroaching there too. It starts to envelop me from my head down, spreads silently around my shoulders and my belly, and, then, rustling, it starts to crawl up the shinbones to the thigh. When the cold water spurts over my head, it retreats briefly; but as the liquid warms and flows down my head, shoulders, chest, abdomen, testicles, and things, it gets more and more of a hold, trying to imprison me. I am a room; a hollow room. There is no man, no light, and yet luxuriant vines cover the wall.[44]

We could, in traditional fashion, ask what this metaphor means, what it symbolizes, and surely all sorts of imaginative answers might be devised. But the force of the metaphor does not lie principally in what it means but in what it does. The figure works differently if one does not just picture this thing growing out of the narrator's body but senses it growing out of one's own body, feeling this fecund parasite grip the flesh, surround it, and spread to imprison one in its luxuriant growth. It is, so to speak, a living metaphor.

A living metaphor has the power to engage our senses, our body. In the same spirit in which Henry James considered the novel to be "felt life," Joseph Conrad spoke of the sensory attraction of the arts. The senses are "the sacred spring of responsive emotions" to which language must strive, aspiring to "the plasticity of sculpture, to the color of painting, and to the magic suggestiveness of music."[45] Why the senses, if not because of their direct channel to consciousness, to feeling, to the responsive action of the body? Here is the true region of metaphor, of language.[46]

While metaphor has the power to engage us and not become but another trope that stands as an enigma to be deciphered, its vitality is concentrated in the image itself, and nowhere more forcefully than in poetry proper. Bachelard is mistaken when he relegates metaphor to understanding, even though it is usually taken as part of the intellectual substance of criticism. But he possesses a rare sensitivity to the supervening power of the image. Images, he declares, must be "lived directly, . . . taken as sudden events in life. When the image is new, the world is new."[47] What is a living image? How does one live an image, as Bachelard would have us do?

Images alone in vivid concentration or in their more extended, complex occurrence in metaphor and symbol impose a demand on the reader for participation. But it is in poetry that the power of the image is most focused. This *waka* of Saigyō turns the rather commonplace observation of the first lines into unutterable poignancy in the images of the last:

Even a person who has forsaken common feelings
Can grasp the anguish of life.
A shrike rises out of the marsh.
Dusk in autumn.[48]

There are many who know the truth of the initial couplet: the Chinese literati of the seventeenth century, the Tibetan monk, the Indian yogi, the Catholic nun, the recluse, the druggie, the disillusioned. Yet not just such a person but anyone on whom perception is not lost can be penetrated by the landscape described in the final lines. Of course the reader cannot be mindless or ignorant. Resonances of significance surround each component image of the complex: the shrike, a small but aggressive bird, which impales its prey on thorns; the marsh, an undramatic landscape, flat, low, open, utterly exposed under a great expanse of sky; autumn; and dusk: common images that convey a sense of decline, dimness, impending finality, yet all of these in an unending cyclical process. But the forcefulness of this cluster of images lies in the interpenetration of all three features, which combine exposure, violence, and inevitability in a somber scene. This is capable of breaking through a person's protective layers to impale one's own being in that place.

The last line of Dylan Thomas's "A Refusal to Mourn the Death, by Fire, of a Child in London" acquires substance and profundity only after the rich course of images that tumble in a breathless wail from the poet's tongue:

> Never until the mankind making
> Bird beast and flower
> Fathering and all humbling darkness
> Tells with silence the last light breaking
> And the still hour
> Is come of the sea tumbling in harness
>
> And I must enter again the round
> Zion of the water bead
> And the synagogue of the ear of corn
> Shall I let pray the shadow of a sound
> Or sow my salt seed
> In the least valley of sackcloth to mourn
>
> The majesty and burning of the child's death.
> I shall not murder
> The mankind of her going with a grave truth
> Nor blaspheme down the stations of the breath
> With any further
> Elegy of innocence and youth.
>
> Deep with the first dead lies London's daughter,
> Robed in the long friends,
> The grains beyond age, the dark veins of her mother,
> Secret by the unmourning water
> Of the riding Thames.
> After the first death, there is no other.[49]

Taken as an assertion of fact, the final line is clearly false. Yet while deeply ambiguous, it is a powerful statement. If we ask what it means, we are led into the usual critical exercise, not without its value, to be sure. Let us proceed on this course for the moment, if only to abandon it later.

As a philosophical comment, the line states a profound truth: Human life is unquantifiable and each death is final. Understood symbolically, this life, like every life, is an ultimate value. Taking this death as a metaphor for one's own death, it conveys the understanding that my death is the first death, that after my death nothing else is real and nothing more can happen. Interpreted as a social comment, the line is a criticism of the expendability of human life in a mass urban population. It rescues this death from the anonymity of a statistic since, unlike the practice in earlier romantic elegies, the girl is not named. Finally, the line stands as an existential observation on the fragility of life, the difficulty and yet the necessity of living in a world of holocausts, mass exterminations, official megadeath scenarios, and underground refuges for the privileged and powerful.

But none of this needs the poem to say it, and all have been proclaimed many times. What does the poem do that is different? It does not *tell* us this truth, it *confronts* us with it. It more than confronts us; it clothes an unutterable realization in a succession of uttered images each of which requires the reader to grasp it. From this emerges a realization that gathers to itself a cosmic range of associations with darkness, with the refuge of religious thought and practice, and with the history and community of the dead. This lament for a girl who died in a London fire becomes a dirge for all human death, for all human life. And sung, like all Thomas's poems, it becomes the body and breath of the poet/reader, becomes that person's own lament.

Image and narrative alone do not make language into literature, but language without them is not literature. The living image in poetry, the embodied narrative in the novel are a sine qua non for the experience of literature. Grammar, style, figure—all are but categories by which we analyze and discuss the literary use of language. None, however, can have any significance for literature without the contribution of the reader. And, as this discussion has tried to show, that contribution is more than the reader's addition or completion, more than the collaboration of a discrete reader in the literary process. These features merely identify ways by which we enter the world of the word and, through the word, the condition of primary, direct experience. Literature *is* such a language experience.

There is no unified self, then, neither a transcendental ego prior to experience nor a coherent self acquired from a mirror stage. Through literature and the other arts, or rather *in* them, we can attain or perhaps return to this unified state. Language cannot *hold* meaning; it can *lead* us to encounter meaning, and nowhere more effectively than in literature. Literature as experience is the language of meaning. It is meaning embodied, not the path by which it is attained.

The relation of the reader to the text, like the more general philosophical problem of the relation of words to things, is a scholar's problem, not a problem for those who use language and experience literature. It is a problem that arises out of self-consciousness about language, not out of language experience, that is, consciousness that comes about or is directed through the use of language. The problem of the relation of reader to text is but another subtle form of psycho-physical dualism, which takes the text (body) apart from and independent of the reader (mind) and then orders that text by means of language (mind). Such an approach to literature, however, does not reflect the usual ways in which we use our language but only the ways we talk about our use of language. It may reflect how we employ unfamiliar languages when they possess a kind of artificiality, as in learning a new language. In our customary use of language, however, we observe no real division between word and thing, and this identity is especially marked in ritual, as well as in literature, when language occurs in conjunction with overt dramatic devices, objects, and symbols.

Language, then, is one with our world and embodies that world in various ways. It is an important means of acting in and on that world in a realm that is in part imaginative, in part overtly behavioral. Indeed, language maintains no sharp division between these modes. We move easily from commands to plans, from statements of fact to conjectures and possibilities. In the word lies our human world. Valéry's description of poetic experience holds true for all literature: "The poem unfolds itself in a richer sphere of our functions of movement; it exacts from us a participation that is nearer to complete action."[50] Perhaps we can call this condition of the experience of literature "transrealism," the affirmation of a bond that extends across the distance between image and reality, of a connection that binds them together so that nothing can be considered independently "real." Isn't this the difference Calvino draws between the professor of linguistics and Ludmilla, the heroine as reader? "Reading," the professor states,

> is always this: there is a thing that is there, a thing made of writing, a solid, material object, which cannot be changed, and through this thing we measure ourselves against something else that is not present, something else that belongs to the immaterial, invisible world, because it can only be thought, imagined, or because it was once and is no longer, past, lost, unattainable, in the land of the dead,

while Ludmilla says simply, "Reading is going toward something that is about to be, and no one yet knows what it will be."[51]

There are, then, many ways of understanding how the reader comes to a literary text, for no text stands in sacred isolation. For the formalists, the structure of the text is primary, yet they recognize that the reader must take the sign, select the referent, and secure them to each other in the act of reading. The sign, however, is more than a linguistic object: it is a bodily event of breath and speech. In centering literature on its audience, the reader–response theorists move toward the opposite pole. Without a reader, a text has no meaning. A text requires reading to animate it, to interpret it, to transform what are only potentials into a literary experience. In various ways the reader and the text interact and interpenetrate, each making a contribution of equal substance. Still other commentators, like Bachelard and Poulet, take literature as a vehicle of imagination, in which the text is assimilated into the mind of the reader, or the reader is absorbed by the book. Yet, for the most part, all these are theories of criticism, and questions of meaning remain central. Transactional theory goes further by integrating reader and text, moving away from a fixation on meaning and toward the sense of literature as a temporal experience.

Grasping literature as a language experience captures its full integration, engaging author, text, and reader as participants in the process of literature. Style, image, the grammar and body of literature are all assimilated into the process of literary experience, in which no part stands alone and no aspect can be viewed apart from the whole. What we have is something quite different from its components, different in kind as well as in its boundaries. In transcending the limits and divisions of our usual world, literature exceeds the claims of that world and assumes its own real place in the order of things. The activity of the reader, the contribution of the reader, and the engagement of the reader are all profoundly different. The ultimate condition of reading is not collaboration but identity.

CHAPTER SIX

Musical
generation

MUSIC SUFFERS IN DISCUSSION MORE THAN MOST ARTS. THE DIFFI-
culties of grasping the workings of an art whose materials of sound
are intangible, elusive, and ephemeral are increased by the usual
practice of employing physical and other alien metaphors to convey
the activities of musical creation and appreciation. It is common to
hear even musicians speak of constructing a composition, as if music
were an object to be structured by joining together tones, chords, or
melodic elements and arranging them in acceptable order by conformity to established metrical and formal patterns. The very word for
the creation of music, *compose,* incorporates the same mythical assumption of the musical work as a thing, a piece that is put together
out of pre-existing materials. The creative process, difficult to understand in any art, is even more recondite in the musical one.

It is tempting to parody this constructivist prejudice with a trope
which condemns that opinion by affirming its negation, and so speak
of musical creation as "de-composition." This image recalls the dark
wit of that arch iconoclast, Baudelaire, whose prognosis for love
likened the future of his beloved to a dog's decaying carcass.[1] While
the discussion of musical creation that follows may seem quite as
shocking to the traditional lore of aesthetics as the poet's song does to
that of love, let me carry the comparison no further and offer, not a

romantic apostasy of love but, following the biological metaphor, a romantic affirmation of art. In any event, my interest here is not in organic degeneration but in artistic generation, and I shall suggest that in the case of music and, *mutatis mutandis,* the other arts, some common ways of regarding the creative process are as misleading as they are misapprehended. More positively, an alternative will emerge that may grasp more successfully something of the nature of musical creation and, through extension, the performance and appreciation of music, by considering it as a process of aesthetic engagement of an exemplary directness and intimacy.

The manner in which music is made often baffles the nonmusician, probably because the materials of music and the ways they are shaped seem markedly different from those found in other arts. Moreover, they appear to have little direct connection with those activities and experiences that lie outside that art and with which we are far more familiar and easy. And so the challenge of arranging tonal materials seems incomprehensibly strange. Perhaps that is why in the Western classical tradition music is so often called the most abstract of the arts, for it rarely draws directly from the sounds of the world outside the concert hall, nor does it usually assume the fragmentary or unbounded forms in which they appear. Even when music is combined with theater as in opera, with poetry as in song, with rhetoric as in melodeclamation, or with environment as in *musique concrète,* it does not seem to possess in any direct fashion the referential character that language appears to have in literature. Nor does it carry the images and forms of the world that painting and sculpture have, until recent times, exhibited directly and with which, even in their most abstract instances, they still remain connected. Music does not fashion itself out of the social condition of human action and reflection in the manner of narrative literature, nor can it grasp the steadying hand of structure and function that are an inherent part of architecture, to which Goethe and Schopenhauer once compared it.[2]

It is true that theorists have sometimes claimed that music reflects or embodies the qualities and dynamic forms of emotional states. The respectable history of this notion can be traced back to classical philosophy. It reappeared in certain theories during the sixteenth and seventeenth centuries, emerged as a position in its own right in the *Affektenlehre* of the eighteenth-century Germans, continues in Langer's theory of the arts as symbolic of feeling in the twentieth, and remains popular still as one of the questionable truisms of aesthetics. Yet this is a connection that requires a developed theory for it to be taken seriously, and such proposals have by no means been universally convincing. Apart from the commonplace association of music with feelings, a connection that results in rather little intelligibility by balancing the intangibility of the one against the indeterminateness of the other, music remains perhaps the most arcane of the major arts, an intriguing yet incomprehensible wonder of creation. Indeed, there is surely the prospect of rest and redirection to be found in Schönberg's remark that "from the point of view of pure aesthetics, music does not express the extra-musical."[3]

This, then, is the peculiar travail and glory of the composer. By inventing and ordering sounds that have no direct tie to the world outside music and that serve no primary purpose, he becomes a Promethean challenger of the divine monopoly on original creation. Apparently beginning with no more than a self-contained history of practices and techniques, the composer brings something into being where nothing was before.

Yet at the same time that music is abstract and intangible, it is also concrete, employing the most direct qualities of audible experience. What these qualities are has often been specified by such terms as tone, pitch, timbre, duration, intensity, volume, rhythm, meter, tempo, and the like. Joined together in a musical work, these immediately perceptible qualities make music instantly accessible. There need be no intermediary for perceptual experiences that we can apprehend in their striking directness and whose force requires no explanation, even though it often tempts one.

In arranging these aural qualities lie the confusions and challenges of musical composition, and much has been proposed and denied about this process. Some have tried to characterize the outcome of such an ordering in the most general terms. Hanslick's account is the classic statement of the formalist position—*tönend bewegte Formen*, which may be translated variously as "sound and motion," "forms moving in terms of a tonal system," and "tonally moving forms," but which can be read, closest to the last of these and least assumptively as "forms of moving tones."[4] This is a position that has clear echoes in Stravinsky's observation that "the phenomenon of music is the phenomenon of speculation aimed at the elements of sound and time"[5] and in Langer's claim that the essence of music is "the creation of virtual time, and its complete determination by the movement of audible forms."[6] Yet these highly generalized characterizations, while commendable for being more literal than most, seem to help us rather little in accounting for the ways in which music is shaped from these basic materials into individual works.

Specific systems of rules are sometimes adduced here, the most famous of which is surely Schönberg's serial technique. Yet except in its most attenuated and cabalistic post-Webernian manifestations, a tone row specifies an order of pitches roughly comparable to a mode or a scale, except that the sequence in using the pitches is obligatory once the row has been decided on, and none of the twelve pitches can be repeated. This leaves an enormous range of possibilities to the composer's individual discretion, resulting in music as varied stylistically as Schönberg's *Violin Concerto*, Berg's *Lulu*, and Webern's *Symphony* op. 21, to cite some of the most famous instances. More determinate rules have often been adduced for the writing of music, from Fux's codification of contrapuntal practice and Rameau's ordering of the tertiary harmonic idiom, both early in the eighteenth century, to Goetschius's neat classification of homophonic and contrapuntal musical forms at the turn of the twentieth, and to periodic attempts to specify rules for writing four-part harmony. Yet except for serial composition, such systems of rules have most typically followed practice, not prescribed it, and have led to enshrining uninteresting conventions once the practices they specify are no longer fresh and unpredictable. The composer who does not recompose the works of others is likely to be guided, knowingly or not, by the remark of the colleague who advised, "The modern composer should know no rules of composition aside from some vague generalities." This is not a romantic disclaimer of order or another expression of contemporary iconoclasm, for it was written by Benedetto Marcello, an early eighteenth-century composer whose work reflected the conventions of the Baroque as much as any other musician of the period.[7] Apart from the technical skill and the auditory awareness that may be acquired by mastering an already petrified technique, rules have little to offer, either as a method for or an explanation of musical creation.

There is another even more common account, whose simplicity and obviousness are compelling to the amateur and musician alike.

This is to regard musical composition as a process of shaping tonal materials by the demands of some musical form. Not only does a preponderance of the musical literature—classical, folk, or popular—follow an easily identifiable formal structure, but those forms also supply the names for much of that literature. Songs, ballads, fugues, canons, sonatas, symphonies, rondos, and variations offer both titles and explanations of music simultaneously. It is clear and easy to consider a musical form much in the manner of a mold that gives shape to its contents. Musical sounds are arranged within the restrictions imposed by a form, and that shape guides the composer in elaborating and ordering the materials. Such forms are a rough analogue of the Kantian categories of the understanding and appear to function as *a priori* determinants of tonal matter which, without such ordering, would be both shapeless and incomprehensible. Even if one wisely acknowledges the arguments for literature and painting that advise against thinking we can separate form and matter, the distinction seems convenient and compelling in the case of music, and it appears to offer a plausible account of the compositional process. Indeed as we noted at the outset, the very word *compose* means, by etymology and usage, "to place together," and suggests a constructivist activity. Thus usage, convention, and intuition concur here.

As an account of how composers actually write their music, the process of shaping musical materials according to the patterns and strictures of a previously determined form is no doubt true in many cases. Production by formula has, to be sure, a long and tiresome history for the listener as well as for any artist of limited originality. Even though we are ready to admire Bach for those marvelous dissonances that stand as exceptions to the conventions of voice-leading, which were codified only after his time, and we extol Beethoven and Mahler for their daring in bursting the confines of the classical symphony, it is still true that there is a vast musical literature that seems more or less to conform to those established patterns.

Still, there are problems. For example, musical forms are not neutral structures that can be filled by any auditory material at hand. You cannot have a Dutch colonial skyscraper, Philip Johnson and postmodernism notwithstanding, just as you cannot have a monumental classical symphony. When Mozart approached this in the finale of the *Jupiter Symphony,* for instance, he had to break the bonds of the sonata–allegro form and adapt it to his own purposes, just as Beethoven did for the same reasons in the first movement of the *Eroica.* There cannot be a monochromatic still life or an epic sonnet for the same reason that the subject of a Bach fugue cannot easily serve as the theme of a symphony or a three-part song. That is because musical materials place demands on the composer; they require certain forms of elaboration and oppose others. And when a composer is more swayed by the force of convention than by the force of the musical ideas, the result shows the strain, as when Schubert bent his extraordinary genius for lyric melody into awkward and ungainly dimensions under the expansive developmental requirements of the symphony. To be able to function in a different, uncongenial form, the character of musical ideas must be modified, as when the theme in a sonata–allegro movement is used as the subject of a fugato. But the converse is equally true, for at their most successful the ideas change the form as well. At the very least, then, there is a correlation between musical materials and forms: The materials suggest what form is most suitable, and the form influences the kind of material appropriate to it. But this is an uneasy balance, probably because the terms of the equation are the wrong ones and, indeed, because there is no equation in the first place.

For there is more to be answered here than this convenient falsehood can manage. The forms we have been talking about do not appear ready-made; they have their histories. Different shapes and materials appear in musical practice, and an altered sensibility develops. Over the course of the history of the art there have been fluctuations in melodic style, different orderings of line and texture, altered and expanded harmonic structures, and fresh sounds and effects made possible by the technical capabilities of newly invented instruments, like the piano in the eighteenth century and the synthesizer in the twentieth, as well as major changes in the social conditions of musical experience, such as the public concert. These novel developments force an extension of the prevailing forms, such as the expansion of the Baroque binary form into the sonata–allegro form, the evolution of the classical symphony into the romantic one, and the replacement of individual pitches and chords as the units of musical order by patterns, textures, and agglomerations of sound. Isn't it more plausible to suppose, then, that the kinds of thematic, textural, and harmonic materials of a period influence and indeed shape the prevailing forms of that age? At the very least, composers of talent instill freshness and life into the conventions they inherit, as Bach, Brahms, and Stravinsky did. Often they develop and extend those conventions, as occurred with Haydn and Mozart, stretch them into unrecognizability, as happened with Bruckner, Mahler, and Wagner, and seize on new vehicles to carry their distinctive ideas forward, as did Chopin, Liszt, and Satie. Such composers can hardly be said to "follow the form" when their musical materials just would not abide by the strictures of those forms. To take form as "superinduced," Elliott Carter claims, "is either the death or the imprisonment of the thing."[8]

However we structure the problem of the relation between musical form and materials and attempt to resolve it by attenuating the distinction and urging the reciprocity of its terms, the issue will not settle comfortably. For the phenomena of music, complex and recalcitrant, are not packaged that way, as far as perception is concerned. The distinction between form and materials in music comes after the fact, not before it. It supplies an ordering by which we mistakenly hope to understand those phenomena better. Yet it is hard to avoid the thought that this may be yet another case of the common philosophical phenomenon of concepts and distinctions that generate more difficulties than they dispel. When it is the composer who leans on the form—materials distinction and guides the musical ideas by the demands of a form, there emerges all the tediousness of derivative art, of pat formulas with predictable products. While new tonal materials and technologies are a major cause of changing musical sensibilities, which then press in fresh directions for their embodiment, they offer but the most obvious case of what all art compels. In music, as in the other arts, the work is not a construction from elements but a growth toward an integral unity. Musical perception confirms this fulfillment of auditory sensibility.

How better to develop a theory of musical composition than from the standpoint of perceptual experience? If we are sensitive to musical sounds as they are directly heard, we may discover that they possess a dynamic, generative character.[9] A tone, for example, will not stand alone: Its very duration extends the tone and projects a tension that propels it forward. Accretions and groupings develop, and each of these contains its own aural impulses which compel it to move ahead. From the Baroque passacaglia and the opening motive of Beethoven's *Fifth Symphony* to the five-note figure that begins Bartók's *Music for Strings, Percussion, and Celeste,* the history of music is replete with works that develop out of the germinal forces inherent in their initial motivic ideas.

Yet there are many other ways in which musical forces move. Patterns of tones, of rhythm, or of harmony, for example, may set up a momentum that must be continued and carried to fulfillment. Many of the Preludes from Bach's *Well-Tempered Clavier* are uniform figurations, derived from harmonic progressions bound in sequential relation on the circle of fifths, which constitute nearly the entire piece. Recent minimal music carries out the same impulse to fulfill the dynamic pressures established by a harmonic and rhythmic pattern. Zuckerkandl's discussion of the dynamic properties of tones in the diatonic system does much to illuminate how connections among pitches are not fortuitous but are generated out of tensions inherent in their relationships. Thus melodies have a kind of logic in their fulfillment, although words like *logic* or *necessity* have connotations too rational to convey the dynamic qualities of sound that the composer shapes intuitively. A piece like Ravel's *Bolero* is a complex instance of these processes, combining a persistent rhythmic pattern with two similar melodies that are repeated endlessly, and all cast under the dynamic framework of a single great crescendo to fashion a work of obsessive force.

Repetition, in fact, may be the single most significant factor in the development of musical materials. It is important, however, not to construe repetition in a mechanical sense, for music is not built up out of identical repeated units, like a building constructed out of brick or blocks of stone or modules of pre-cast concrete, or like an internal combustion engine, which fires its cylinders ceaselessly in an unvarying order. Repeated melodic, rhythmic, or harmonic patterns breed their sequels, so to speak, because the ways in which continuity develops are not only cumulative but generative.

The chaconne and the passacaglia are instructive examples of how this may occur. Used mainly in the Baroque period but still found today in popular as well as classical idioms, these are two related modes of composition that shape a piece out of a single repeated unit. Although there is some disagreement about the exact distinction between them historically, there is reason to associate the chaconne with a repeated harmonic sequence and the passacaglia with an ostinato or repeated ground—a line that appears mainly but not always in the bass. Out of a germinal unit that is usually made up of a set of four or eight bars in slow triple meter, a series of continuous variations unfolds, carried along by their own momentum to sometimes dramatic conclusions, as in the thirty-one repetitions of the opening eight bars of the final chaconne in Bach's *Partita No. 2* for unaccompanied violin and the thirty-four variations of the first eight measures that constitute the passacaglia finale of Brahms's *Fourth Symphony.*[10] A different use of a repeated musical unit forms the basis of Schönberg's serial technique, whose structural unit, the tone row, usually made up of the twelve semi-tones within an octave, is arranged by the composer in a different and distinctive order of pitches and intervals for each individual musical work. The row is repeated always in the same order but under the varying rhythm, range, harmonic, and melodic appearances that constitute the distinctive character of that particular work.

Repetition assumes many different forms in music. At times it may center on a single note: Of the first thirteen melodic notes of Chopin's *Etude* op. 25, no. 1, eleven of them are the same E-flat. Or it may be of a simple interval, as in the prevalence of the minor second in Beethoven's *Quartets* op. 95 and op. 132 and the fifths and fourths at the opening of his *Ninth Symphony.* Fugal subjects are characteristically repeated in their entirety, and any transformations are made carefully so as not to affect the subject's integrity and recognizability. Again, signs in the musical score directing the literal repetition of each section of a binary composition were universal during the Baroque, and they continued as common practice in the exposition sections of sonata–allegro movements of sonatas and symphonies well into the nineteenth century. If these are understood as recommendations for experience and not merely as a notational convention, and if they are performed accordingly, these repetitions are no mere blind duplications but new and different experiences in their own right. Repetition then becomes regeneration rather than reiteration. One is reminded of William James's comment that

> no state once gone can recur and be identical with what it was before. . . . Does not the same piano-key, struck with the same force, make us hear in the same way? . . . It seems a piece of metaphysical sophistry to suggest that we do not; and yet a close attention to the

matter shows that there is no proof that the same bodily sensation is ever got by us twice.[11]

Since the forces and tensions inherent in musical sound occur in elusive ways, one can think of the composer as an artist who possesses a special sensitivity to their dynamic pressures. All musical materials have distinctive traits and thus generate their own individual manner of development. And because these sounds and their germinal shapes are always different, there are no formulas for realizing their possibilities in ways that carry richness and wonder, especially under repeated listening. Every original work, then, is newly made, not by constructing or building up a structure but by a process of germination and growth. In musical creation the composer engages with the tonal materials, participating in their dynamic forces and moving them to completion through the reciprocal interplay of composerly intuition and auditory perception.

Musical creation is therefore an activity of tonal engagement, a fusion of composer and sound in a dynamic process of elaboration and fulfillment. One thinks here of such striking examples as the tone poems of Liszt, whose motives emerge and expand, the music dramas of Wagner, with their ceaseless interweaving of leitmotifs, and even a work like Sibelius's *Fourth Symphony*, whose themes appear at the culmination of the movements rather than at the outset. But what is most pronounced in these cases is but a manifestation of the pervasive and central trait of musical creation. Musical generation means, then, that making music is not an act of combination but a process of producing sound sequences and structures by drawing out the expansive possibilities of the musical materials. Writing music is therefore an activity of extension rather than of retention or construction.

Just as musical materials should be thought of as germinal and not substantive, so our understanding of form in music must be transfigured along similar lines. When musical form is considered perceptually, it undergoes a metamorphosis from a structure within which figures or themes are placed and developed to become the processive shape of auditory experience. A musical form is not a container within which sounds are situated or a framework inside which they are arrayed. Form in music, and indeed in the other arts as well, is rather the order of experience, "form as proceeding,"

Carter calls it, which in music becomes the perceived succession of sounds as they are grouped, identified, and shaped sequentially. The overall dynamic continuity of *Erwartung*, for example, gives Schönberg's work its musical motion, a "sense of propelling interconnection."[12] Thus musical form is at most a guide to the sequence of musical materials as they are heard; it is least of all an abstraction from that sequence.

Cadences offer a clear illustration of how a formal feature can function directly in auditory perception. Signifying formal divisions in a musical work, cadences are the notes or chords that conclude a musical phrase, a section of a piece, or an entire work, and they impose some kind of closure, momentary or complete. Some cadential patterns have been studied and classified according to their place in the modal or diatonic system in which they appear. Thus it is common to think of cadences as formulas to be brought out and employed at the appropriate divisions in a work to help define its structure. While this way of describing them reflects familiar and convenient usage, it says nothing about how cadences actually function, about the quality of completion, indecision, elusiveness, or evasion of the endings they articulate. More than with most words that designate formal features, the terminology used in classifying the harmonic formulas of cadences that were prevalent during the eighteenth and nineteenth centuries does, in fact, offer some descriptive suggestion of their auditory function, as in the case of perfect or full, imperfect, deceptive, and half-cadences. Other terms, such as authentic and plagal cadences, do not. Yet what really counts in a description of how cadences function are not the chord progressions or structures that distinguish one kind of cadence from another for taxonomic purposes, but how these are actually heard, the quality and strength of closure they convey. A composer's choice of a cadential pattern is guided, then, by the feel and force of the movement that is being shaped and by the perception of the demands of the musical materials. How much is the movement of the music to be slowed down or arrested? What sense of completion or incompleteness does the music require at that moment? What sort of cadential arrangement will hold just the right degree of closure for that point in a work? When is it right that a piece end, and what will give that ending the proper weight to balance what preceded it? These are the kinds of considerations that function here in forming a musical experience. Rather than choosing a cadence from a stock of formulas, the composer is sensitive to the demands of the music and is guided by its needs.

What is true of cadences applies equally to a common internal structural feature of tonal music—modulation or the transition from one tonal center to another. Modulation is typically analyzed according to harmonic formulas that clearly establish a new key, and yet nowhere is a composer's skill more apparent than in the ability to accomplish these transitions. When produced by formula, we get the clumsy announcement that such a change is now taking place, as in the embarrassingly awkward modulatory interludes that Schubert often resorts to. It is as if he were saying, in effect, "Wait a moment while I modulate. Then the music can continue on its melodic course." In contrast, the skillful modulations that occur in Mozart, Chopin, or Brahms seems the natural outgrowth of the musical movement as it seeks fresh tonal surroundings and eventually returns to its original place. Instead of a formula used mechanically to fulfill a requirement of the musical structure, modulation here becomes the aural discovery of new regions of tonality.

The larger divisions of musical form can be understood in much the same way as cadences and modulations. The standard forms of the classical and romantic periods may be treated either as structures or as experiential patterns. The ternary, or three-part song form, for example, embodies the basic idea of contrast in which a middle section offers a change in character from the similar sections that flank it. This is usually represented structurally as an A-B-A form, but it is heard as the experience of difference and familiarity. The same opposing accounts can be given the sonata–allegro form, a different, more complex and elaborate three-part order and the typical identifying structure of the first movement of the sonata, symphony, and concerto during the late eighteenth and nineteenth centuries. Yet in a similar fashion, the thematic contrast that is presented in the exposition, the working out of those ideas that takes place in the development, and the return of the original ideas that signifies the recapitulation can be understood either as a complex framework for the ordering of thematic materials or it can be heard as the pattern of their unfolding. What occurs as a characteristic way of hearing the natural elaboration of musical materials may be misconstrued in retrospect as a structure for the presentation of auditory information.

Other standard forms of the period lend themselves to the same contrasting interpretations: the rondo, with its constant alternation of new thematic ideas with the original one; the variation, with its succession of modified restatements of the initial theme; the scherzo, with its transfiguration into ephemerality of the decorous character and ceremonial order of the minuet. These, too, may stand either as formal structures or as successions of qualitative experience. Perhaps the fugue, a Baroque form that continues to attract composers, illustrates best the insufficiency of a formula. Even though fugues commonly begin with an expository introduction of the fugal subject in the various voices in an established order of pitch relationships, there is a good deal of flexibility in what follows, and the composer's sensitivity to the musical implications of the subject is mainly what determines the remainder of the piece. There are techniques and devices that lie at one's disposal, to be sure, but here, as in other musical forms, the sounds guide the choices, not the choices the sounds.

What lies at the heart of a phenomenological interpretation of musical form, however, is the operation of memory. For while sounds occupy a transitory and elusive moment, music is far more than the relentless passage of auditory instants. There is a relatedness and cohesion to musical sounds. Indeed, this entire discussion rests on the recognition of this but, more important, so does the very possibility of music itself, certainly in the Western classical tradition and probably beyond it as well. It is the capacity for aural memory that permits musical continuity and shape to appear and that allows the very possibility of repetition. Moreover, we can grasp the experience of form only by means of memory, whether form be analyzed as an abstract structure or construed as an integral experience. Memory is the experiential dimension of musical form.

The subject of memory is a major topic in philosophy and can hardly be developed here. What we should observe, however, is that the function of memory in musical experience is rather unlike its use in other places. Music does not require factual recollection or what has been called "durable memory." Memory here is rather a consciousness of the immediate auditory past, a consciousness that extends, moreover, as a projection from that reservoir into the future. Music functions within a mnemonic aura, so to speak, of past and prescience. Its sounds resonate for a while in imaginative perception and carry at the same time an anticipation of sounds to come.[13] There is, then, in this art, as in others, a phosphorescence of perception whose glow extends to enclose the musical work and become the shape of its experience.

This experiential rendering of musical form is a transformation that reflects the compositional process, not its methods. What is significant here are not the techniques of individual composers but rather the aesthetic significance of the process through which music comes into being. It is immaterial here whether a composer works laboriously at the development of his ideas, as Beethoven did, or whether the music issues easily, often fully formed, as the uniquely gifted Mozart wrote. Nor does it matter whether a composer uses the piano or another instrument for assistance or writes at a desk and relies solely on auditory imagination. These are biographical differences in techniques and working habits. But what is common to all composers, whatever their individual methods may be, is the process of fashioning an experience of the movement of sound in time and space.

Now it is this very process of shaping tonal experience that exemplifies the composer's engagement with musical materials. These materials, ephemeral though they be and wholly dependent on perception, possess an exquisite dependency on the composer's imagination. In no other art is that relationship quite so intimate as in the art of music. For here the means and materials are external to the sense to a degree more distant and foreign than in most other arts. The connection of painting with vision, of dance with the body, of literature with the word—all these media are consanguine with the perceptual qualities of their art. In music, however, they are not. As with film, the technology of the art is foreign to its material. The production of sound, with the possible exception of singing, uses means that are distant from the perception they stimulate—the complex mechanism of the piano, the chips and circuits of the synthesizer, the violin, which produces sound, as people have often remarked, by scraping horsehair across catgut. While the body is surely involved, ultimately identifying with the other means of tonal production, it is as the facilitator and not as the material of sound. In the composer's absorption in sound, however, lies the direct assimilation of creation and object. Here is full participation in the aesthetic object, a process originated by the composer and emulated by the listener. Musical generation requires the complete engagement of the composer in the auditory realm.

Musical improvisation offers an interesting test of this idea. At first glance it might seem as if improvisation were a spontaneous welling forth of music governed only by the impulse of the performer at the passing instant, as seems to be the case in the often subtle perambulations of jazz and the sometimes Dionysian frenzy of rock improvisation. However, some small knowledge of improvisational practice reveals the contrary: Most improvisation takes place within sharply defined boundaries of phrase and harmony, so that little is left to the performer's discretion but melodic turns and harmonic voicing, as in Baroque and rococo ornamentation, the realization of a figured bass, the cadenza in a classical concerto, or jamming a chorus in a jazz performance.

Stanley Cavell offers an idea that appears to reconcile both alternatives when he notes that, especially up to the time of Beethoven, much music sounds as if it were being improvised, yet this takes place in a context in which the conventions of music are understood so well that we always know where we are and where we are going. Thus the sense of spontaneity combines with the security of a familiar order. With the disappearance of conventions we have lost such meanings in arbitrariness or have resorted to the nihilism of total organization.[14] Francis Sparshott, however, refers to improvisation in pursuing the difference between a score and a performance by contrasting it with composition. A score is associated with a completed composition, while a performance conveys the quality of improvisation.[15] Both writers nonetheless identify improvisation with a sense of spontaneity and growth, with the quality of freshness that comes with direct creation.

While improvisation may have different degrees of freedom in different contexts of musical practice, it captures something of the dynamic character of the perception of music that we have been attempting to locate. In itself, actual improvisation is hardly the pure case of free creation in music. On one side, it is confined too much by conventions and formulas; on the other, improvisation is often too rapid to realize the nuances and to choose most truly from among the different dynamic forces that are present at any point in the unfolding of a work. Its freshness lies in the constant possibility of a chance arrival at an unpremeditated chordal structure or turn of phrase, where at times the hand leads the ear, not the ear the hand.[16] Improvisation, then, reflects the generative characteristics of musical material and offers a first approximation of where it might go. But there is something more. Improvisation conveys the impression of a freely unfolding progression of musical ideas, an impression that touches the life that lies at the heart of musical experience. Yet this is the face of freshness more than the fact of it, for while the sounds may actually not be newly contrived, they have the sense of spontaneity, of spontaneous generation, as it were. In this respect improvisation embodies the creative quality central to the experience of music, a quality that is the measure of every performance.[17]

Improvisation, in fact, combines both musical creation and performance in the same act. It is a dramatic instance of that generative process through which music originates out of an absorption in the musical materials, participating in their perceptual qualities and discovering their dynamic impulses. For the composer and the performer engage in the same reciprocal exchange with these materials, the composer in originating the score, the performer in revitalizing it. The score, of course, is never complete nor can it indicate every performance detail. The performer must therefore engage with the sounds and make them personal, so that performance at its best pursues the same process of fulfilling the dynamic forces of the music as did the composer originally.

Yet it is not only the composer and the performer who engage with the musical materials to realize their creative forces. As the trait central to the experience of music, the generative sense of musical development is found no less fully in the act of appreciation. All listening that is active and engaged shares this quality of live performance. An auditory event can no more be separated from the listener, whether as creator, performer, or audience, than dance can be regarded apart from the dancer. In musical experience there is no independent object—scores, records, and tapes being in themselves quite inconsequential things, devices to guide performance or to reproduce it. As Strawson points out, no distinction holds between the hearer and other things in pure auditory experience.[18] Moreover, even the illusion of separation is difficult to maintain, for there is no object visibly embodying the musical phenomenon, as the dancer does the dance or the book the novel. The sounds emanating from musical instruments are as intangible as those entering the ear. Spatial qualities are perceptually available in music, certainly, and a phenomenology of musical experience will surely discriminate distance, direction, and density. Yet these still are relative to the auditor and require the listener for them to occur at all, since they are perceptual, not physical features. Claudel's vivid description expresses the participation of the listener with a poet's eloquence: "We absorb him into the concert. He is no longer anything but expectation and attention."[19]

Certain musical occasions render this experience with extraordinary effect—such as hearing Gregorian chant sung in a Gothic or Norman cathedral. The long reverberation time, generally over six seconds, enables the sounds to persist, to rebound off the stone walls and lose their place of origin as they surround the listener in almost palpable fashion to produce an experience of immersion.[20] It is no surprise that Bachelard uses the auditory metaphor of reverberation to convey the meaning of sounds as the coalescence of time and space. Nor is it now strange to think of song as a unifier of singer and listener, for "the song sings itself in us; we are the song while the song lasts, identified at once with the singer and with the community."[21] Both Schopenhauer and Nietzsche, too, had good reason to believe that one can lose oneself in music.

Performance is not alone in emulating the participatory absorption of creation; appreciative listening is equally reconstitutive. Igor Stravinsky, never to be accused of pandering to romantic yearnings, acknowledges the participation of the listener in the creative process of musical generation, holding that

> the listener reacts and becomes a partner in the game initiated by the creator. . . . This exceptional participation gives the partner such lively pleasure that it unites him in a certain measure with the mind that conceived and realized the work to which he is listening, giving him the illusion of identifying himself with the creator. That is the meaning of Raphael's famous adage: "to understand is to equal."[22]

In appreciative engagement, no less than in creative activity, music is brought into being. As William James observed, every perceptual experience is, as such, original.

Participation in the dynamic character of musical experience is, then, equally the core of the creative act and the central trait of the regenerative acts of appreciation and performance. The same musical process is at work, whether original or reproduced, whether devised for the first time or renewed. The differences are more differences of agency than of perception, of history than of event. The engaged listener follows the direction that the composer originally shaped. We become a "composerly listener," to adapt Barthes's famous phrase,[23] regenerating the music by responding to the same internal forces that guided the composer originally and so pursuing the same process along the same path. "You are the music while the music lasts," wrote T. S. Eliot in *Four Quartets,* and when this happens there is no qualitative difference between the composer and the listener, only a chronological one.

In tracing out the notion of the generative character of musical creation, then, we are led to a metamorphosis of the conventional understanding of the features of music. Repetition now becomes regeneration, not duplication. Cadences are seen as pauses with different qualitative characteristics in the dynamic course of musical movement. Modulation is not a formula imposed to meet certain formal stipulations but is recast into the unstable movement of transition toward a fresh tonal region. Form and matter are transmuted into the shaping of tonal experiences out of the dynamic forces implicit in musical ideas. Memory becomes an aura of awareness persisting around the moving course of sounds, while improvisation evokes the unfolding life of musical ideas, the ideal of all performance and the vital force in musical creation. And the generative process that originated a musical work is emulated and paralleled by the perceptual experience of the performer and listener alike.

No art incorporates aesthetic engagement more thoroughly and more unassailably than music. It is, indeed, the art of engagement *primus inter pares,* and musical generation stands at the center of aesthetic participation. Shared by composer, performer, and audience, it is sound, in all its timbral, textural, dynamic, tonal, durational, and emphatic transformations that is the focal point of attentive listening. As a key to understanding how music is made, the concept of musical generation at the same time unlocks certain puzzles about its performance and appreciation. This becomes further evidence for the fecundity of the idea, for art has no separate parts, and recognizing the continuity among the different aspects of music assists in their mutual clarification. The original creation of musical objects and their re-creation in performance and in appreciation join together, then, as experiences of participation in generating and fulfilling musical ideas.

This discussion of musical creation began with a biological metaphor, one that rejected Baudelaire's love lyric of decay in favor of an image of growth. Mikel Dufrenne's equally Gallic sensibility also leads him to follow the same metaphor in an affirmative direction:

> Creation requires everything to stay in suspense, as if in gestation. In this sense the work also is open, as a wound that has not healed. . . . The rigor of perfection can become *rigor mortis*—to achieve it the work risks being killed. And is it not to elude such solemn petrification that the work calls for a participation which, in accompanying it, keeps the work alive? . . . The work of art does not conclude the matter of creation, as those philosophers who preach the death of man would describe it, but rather invites every individual to become a creator.[24]

While "generation" is an apt image for all the arts, it especially suits music. More than in the other arts, the sensory directness of musical experience requires no mediation of knowledge or recognition. And the immediacy of the musical event, an event in which the conscious body joins, reflects the directness of growth in which internal forces press forward to realize the potentialities that are inherent in the auditory materials. Growth can be guided, to be sure, but it is most successful when it develops, in art as in biology, by fulfilling the possibilities that lie in the materials themselves and not by imposing external demands. Musical generation expresses this intent, and the positive side of musical de-composition lies in freeing music from misleading models. While we need logic and rhetoric both, in philosophy as in art a true metaphor may be more eloquent than a valid argument.

CHAPTER SEVEN

Dance
as
performance

IT IS COMMONPLACE IN AESTHETICS TO DISTINGUISH BETWEEN those arts that center on a stable, relatively permanent object, such as a painting, a sculpture, or a building, and those that appear in the ephemeral form of a transient activity, such as music, theater and, most especially, dance. This division of the realm into performing and nonperforming arts has a certain common-sense plausibility that pleases our desire for order. Divide and organize has been the theme of Western intellectual life since classical times, reaching its zenith in the modern age of scientific analysis and technological mastery. Are there any alternatives to this powerful intellectual process? Need one *seek* any other mode of understanding?

As with many distinctions, that between the performing and nonperforming arts is suggestive more for what it does not explain than for what it does. How, for example, do we account for poetry, originating in song, as Valéry once noted, and still bound to the oral tradition of sound more than sight, even though our access is most often through the eye than the ear? Indeed, literature in general inheres in no physical form, the printed page being but an unintelligible series of hieroglyphs to those who have not learned its tongue, and the book an occasion for reading and not an artistic embodiment. Theater, moreover, is filled with scripts that read better than they play, like Byron's *Manfred*, Shelley's *Cenci*, and the dramas of Christopher Fry; or that play better than they read, such as Sam Shepard's *Curse of the Starving Class* and most farces; or that rely heavily on special production techniques of set, or lighting, or on nudity, such as *Oh, Calcutta!*; or that, like the *commedia dell'arte*, are improvisational theater in which there is no script at all. Less common is it for the same piece to work well both in and out of performance, as most of Shakespeare does or as sometimes happens when a fine novel is made into an equally good film, for the literary and theatrical arts are significantly different. In this last instance we have actually two different arts, of course, not just performing and nonperforming modes of the same work. Film is a curious case. Some, like Rudolf Arnheim, argue that it is primarily a visual art, while others, in the manner of Eric Rohmer, stress the dramatic portrayal of dialogue. In either case, film needs to be "performed" by being projected onto a screen for its traits to appear. Further, in nearly every case, film begins as the visual record of actual performances without which it could never exist. But film is an art as complex as it is provocative, and it deserves its own discussion.[1]

There is, then, this unsettled middle ground of arts that do not fit comfortably into either the performing or nonperforming camps. But other, more serious difficulties lie ahead. If we look closely at arts like painting and sculpture, we find, setting aside custom and tradition in aesthetics, that they actually function in appreciative practice more like performing arts than not. Whatever else performance requires, it is necessary for a person, alone or in company with others, to animate the art object, realizing the canvas, the script, the instructions of the creative artist in an active embodiment. Other common accompaniments of performance, such as a separate audience or a set, are not essential. One can perform a musical composition with no one else present, as is commonly done in a recording studio, or present a play without the usual embellishments of costume and set, as may occur in a minimalist production in street dress. In fact, one can even *rehearse* a performance, as in a dress rehearsal, allowing the work to proceed without interruption under its own momentum and with its own life. Although there is more to the subject than can be developed here, it is enough to recognize that performance is an integral, dynamic occasion that requires the contribution of what one can call the "activator" of the work.

Now such an activating agent is as essential in literature and the visual arts as in music, theater, and dance. Creative actualization carries the aesthetic event to realization in painting, sculpture, and literature as much as it does in any other art. The appreciation of painting requires a provoking eye—more than an eye, a searching sensibility that makes its own contribution to the movement of line, the interplay of hues, the shaping of space, the grasping of volumes, and the ordering of all its visual features into compositional integrity. These acts of apprehending art are activities of intelligent perception, for the viewer "performs" the painting in the process of perception, energizing the object and engaging with it in an active dialectic. Much the same happens, we have already seen, in the appreciation of literature, when the reader collaborates with the author and the text in a unified experience that carries a conviction of its own reality. There is activation here, too, as the reader performs the text by reading with an involved imagination that attends to its directions and its nuances and provides specific content to what is suggestively incomplete. Such a process of imagination complements and completes the text. In their own characteristic ways, then, painting and literature incorporate performance into their experiential process as much as does any other art. The performative factor is, thus, ubiquitous; active perceptual participation, not contemplative observation, is the order of aesthetic appreciation.[2]

Nowhere, however, is this activation more central and direct than in the art of dance. Of all the arts, dance embodies the energizing force of performance most completely. It has no separate object, like a canvas or a bronze. It has no readily accessible notational guide to its realization, like a printed text or even a musical score, Labanotation notwithstanding. As a consequence, object, artist, and audience join in a bond of extraordinary intimacy, directness, and force.[3] Because there are no overt intervening factors, dance may be regarded as an exemplar of the performative dimension in all the arts.

Dance, moreover, is an art bound more than any other to performance. It evolved through performance; it is composed through performance; it is learned through performance; it is appreciated in performance. Even though in recent times Rudolf von Laban and others have devised systems of notation that permit the recording of every movement—systems valuable for preserving choreography accurately—the best report of the character and quality of a dance remains the record of its performance on film or videotape.[4] Dance, then, embodies a remarkable coalescence of artistic creation, presentation, and active appreciation, all as part of the process of performance. What are the traits of this complex phenomenon so central to dance? What happens in dance performance? Can the grasp of this process be extended to other arts? These are the crucial questions here.

Whatever else is involved in performance, we must start by recognizing that performance is the creation of an occasion of experience. An innocuous statement, perhaps, but a necessary acknowledgment of several things. There is, to begin, an actual situation at hand, a situation in which a variety of features and forces comes into play. The form these take will vary with the art and the work, but there is always a circumstance, a setting, an occasion of some sort, perhaps ceremonial, perhaps social, perhaps simply personal. Central to this occasion is the fact that a direct actualization takes place. Something happens; an event occurs here and now. Von Laban identifies this in dance as gesture, conscious, goal-directed movement that passes from tension to release or from release to tension.[5] There is, therefore, an element of praxis that is inseparable from performance: For something is done, something is put into action, something is achieved. Perceptual activity here is, moreover, immediate and intrinsic. Performance is not primarily commentary, although it may indeed comment either directly or indirectly, the first by the direct appropriation of characteristic gestures, the second by irony. For a performance may incorporate recognizable material from other sources as part of its ongoing movement, or it may refer to such material. Yet even where there is external reference, a performance is an event. It stands present in itself as a primary fact. Merce Cunningham insists:

> When I dance, it means: this is what I am doing. . . . It is the connection with the immediacy of the action, the single instant, that gives the feeling of man's freedom. . . . This is not feeling about something, this is a whipping of the mind and body into an action that is so intense, that for the brief moment involved, the mind and body are one.[6]

Accounting for the kind of experience that is created in dance—a coherent situation that is directly actualized—requires a theory that reflects such practice.

As an active, integral situation, a performance implicates every factor in the occasion, including the audience. *Audience* is, in fact, a misleading term, for it suggests a false structuring of the situation, fragmenting its components into a field divided among the work being performed, its performer, and the recipients of an external event. That these functions can be distinguished is undeniable, but what is more important are the connections among them. Performers often comment on their sense of the audience and how the audience's responses affect and even transform their actions, just as the performers' actions affect and transform the audience. Such mutual interactions, moreover, determine not only the character of the occasion but the work itself, not just its embodiment but its being. These functions, then, are not separate parts of a performance but aspects of a continuity, and it is in this continuity that the art lies. Dance exemplifies the integrity of this situation in the directness, the force, and the primacy of performance. A vital performance generates a magnetic spirit that implicates everyone and everything present to experience, each of these making a distinctive contribution to the occasion. One might describe this as a halo effect: An effective dance performance creates an aura that encloses choreographer, dancers, audience, set, and music, each contributing to a common event. There is a synthesis here, not a summation.

The dance occasion, then, produces an immediate presence that binds all its constituent aspects into a continuous whole. But what happens in such a situation? Suzanne Langer offers a perceptive answer. An illusion, she holds, is created through gesture. Gesture differs from ordinary motion by possessing meaning; it is expressive movement that reflects vital force. When vital movement or gesticulation is a part of ordinary behavior, it is not art. Movement becomes art when it is removed from the sphere of telic behavior, from purposive action, and is placed in an imaginary, virtual realm. Here gesture is transformed into a symbolic form free from practical demands. As a symbol, gesture can express the forms of feeling, the nuances of sentient consciousness, without being constrained by the necessities of practical circumstance. In dance, as in theater and mime, such gestures are not "real" in the way ordinary movements are real actions and responses to actual conditions. They are, rather, illusory expressions of vital force. They are *virtual* gestures, Langer's term for things that have the semblance of actuality but occur instead in an illusory realm.

Here lies the difference between ordinary movement and dance movement. In dance the vital force of movement is transformed into a virtual realm of power, not actual, physical power but virtual power, "appearances of influence and agency" created by virtual gesture. This, then, is the primary illusion of dance, the creation of a virtual realm of power.[7] Bound as she was to an ontology of aesthetic illusion and to forms symbolic of feeling, Langer needed to locate a primary illusion in order that dance be an authentic art, and she had to place that illusion somewhere in a virtual domain. In identifying dance as virtual power, she was able to retain the coherence and distinctiveness of dance experience, but at the expense of its connections with other aspects of the human world. Safely symbolic, the virtual gestures of dance cavort in their own illusory realm.

It is at this point that Langer's perceptive characterization of dance goes awry. The notion of a region of powers is a rich one. Yet in her anxiety to dissociate its presence in dance from actual physical power, from the "field of forces" of physics, Langer locates it in its own separate region, "the subjective experience of volition and free agency" reminiscent of Kant's realm of the will. Elsewhere she points up the magical character of this "realm of 'Powers,' wherein purely imaginary beings from whom the vital force emanates shape a whole world of dynamic forms by their magnet-like, psycho-physical actions."[8]

Powers, unfortunately, do not separate safely into the traditional dualistic regions of illusion and reality. Power is both a primary percept and a unifying one, and the same force is experienced in imaginary as in physical circumstances, in dreams as waking, in thoughts, feelings, and states of awareness as in actions. We also recognize that the forces we sense in our own bodies are similar to those in other bodies, inanimate as well as living. One thinks here of Locke's easy transfer of the power we find in ourselves to begin or end an action to other kinds of objects like fire or a tennis ball.[9] Moreover, as we experience power, we encounter not just the forces that inhere in the physical actions of bodies on one another but the intangible influences that also affect us. For power includes invisible forces that work their influence at a distance, resembling those in a magnetic field, as well as the influence of psychic and psychophysical forces that are not yet adequately understood.

We can readily see the connections these powers have with a

primary source of dance—myth. Mythic and folkloric themes have inspired both classical ballet and modern dance, from Petipa to Ashton, from Duncan to Graham. We sense in myth the presence of powers, forces at work both in overt gesture and in the transparent vectors of influence among dancers and in their ambient space. In *Swan Lake* the insistent forces that emanate from von Rothbart's gestures are disarmed by the equally invisible power that flows from Siegfried's love for Odette. And in *Giselle,* with a love that transcends death as well as justice, Giselle, in an act intolerable to the liberated woman, enables Albrecht, who had so freely deceived her, to finally escape the deadly influence of the Wilis and their vindictive queen. Yet these powers are not just the "mystic forces" Langer locates as the central illusion of dance. They include not only attraction and repulsion, and they extend over the large and subtle range of perceived influences that pervade every human situation. Magnetic, electrical, physical, mystical—the "vibes" we sense in human interactions— the forces of dance differ from these mainly in their focus and their intensity. Such influences, ever present in fact and perception, are concentrated in dance experience. By joining into a single interacting field of forces the powers found in the interplay of bodily movement and the invisible lines of influence that implicate people, objects, and places, we begin to locate the realm of dance.

If so much centers on performance in a vital situation, how can we characterize dance? The answer to this question suggests a phenomenology of dance, a descriptive phenomenology of dance experience. We might perhaps think of it as exploring how dance feels from the inside. While suggestive, stating the goal of a phenomenological description in this way is actually misleading, for one cannot utilize a dualistic term like *inside* to describe dance experience but can only speak of an experiential whole. What, then, is dance like as an integral experience?

Dance, as we have just seen, creates a realm of powers, of forces at work. The appearance of dancers in a performance space charges that space. But this is no impersonal field of forces. More than in any other art, except perhaps architecture, dance involves intense physical activity. What music may call a theatrical factor, the deportment on stage that is an incidental accompaniment of its performance, dance takes as central: the active presence of the body. Dance makes explicit an essential constituent of the aesthetic field—the dynamic presence of the human body in its immediacy and in its possibilities. This refers not only to the bodies on the stage but also to the focus of forces on and in the human organism by which all that is present is drawn into this region of energy. Everything, moving or stationary, is affected—set, hall, onlookers, as well as dancers. Dance, indeed, exhibits an essential feature of all performance that is wrongly regarded as unique to this art: performance as a process of bodily engagement. What is obvious in dance may not be as clear in the other arts, for the long tradition in empiricism of psychologizing experience has obscured its somatic basis. What Merleau-Ponty calls "the flesh" is at the heart of all experience, but nowhere is its presence more insistent than in dance.

Movement is central to this field of forces that the body inhabits in the dance art. But movement occurs in all human activity. What distinguishes dance performance from other activity, from movement *simpliciter?* Is it being involved in an occasion? Is it the presence of an illusion? Is it the transformation of movement into gesture? It is none of these. Rather, movement in dance creates a presentational realm in which the body realizes itself in motion, a realm that fuses dancer and onlooker, body and consciousness, thought and perception in an intensely focused presence.[10]

For dance establishes a world through the moving presence of the body. By its extent, movement defines the boundaries of space, the region of experience; by its rhythm and rapidity it establishes the passage of time, the elastic medium of experience. Saying this does not prescribe the kind of movement that constitutes dance, since there are as many orders of movement, actual and implicit, as there are customs in traditional dance and styles in concert dance. Irish step dances, for example, are confined to the feet and legs. The dance tradition in India combines movements of the arms and fingers with those of the head and eyes. Much Balkan dancing joins arm and leg movement but keeps the torso largely vertical and stationary, while Turkish dancing often exploits bending at the waist. In different ways a supple, fluid torso generates a range of subtle body motions in African and Polynesian dancing. In some Pacific islands, movement is confined to the hands and fingers, while in parts of southern Tunisia it is the movement of the hair that constitutes the dance.[11] Nor does centering dance in the moving body overlook the fact that the dancer's body may be hidden by costume or set. Loïe Fuller's figure disappeared amid the voluminous silks she swirled about her. Martha

Graham's stretch jersey extended her volume and shape. Alwin Nikolais's use of body-concealing costumes, props, light and sound; the masks and heavy costumes of No dancers; body-enclosing bags and other fabrics and structures—all these have their source of motion in the human body and they enlarge the range of its form and volumes. However hidden or obscured, we nonetheless know the body is there and identify it as the vital source and center of such movement.[12] Each order of motion, then, every style that patterns the moving body, creates its own distinctive realm, its own peculiar presence, which is realized in the individual dance performance.

Much has been made of the rigorous training a classical ballet dancer must undergo to develop the distinctive carriage, to acquire the capacity for open movement through the painful artificiality of the turn out, and to achieve the ability to dance *en pointe*. But these difficult extensions of the body's capabilities are not so much sublimations of natural movement as they are the development and cultivation of certain physical potentialities in order to create impressions of weightlessness and ideal grace. The aerial, linear quality of classical ballet has often been contrasted with the sense of groundedness that characterized modern dance of the 1930s and 1940s. Movement here tended to reflect the pull of gravity, centering on the body as volume and on the proximity of the ground and of the ordinary objects and actions that stand and occur on its surface. Postmodern dance, yet another historical phase, began by attempting to purify dance of its dramatic, virtuoso, theatrical elements. It tried, in fact, to be deliberately anti-illusionistic, substituting undisguised effort for lightness and ease;[13] simplicity, often in the form of repetitive movement, for an intricate formal order; literal, non-referential actions for meaning and drama; the prosaic quality of task-like activity for brilliant or theatrical movement.[14] Douglas Dunn may have carried postmodernism's minimalist search for purity furthest in a work that had a dancer appear perfectly still for four hours a day for a month. Yet this produced strong emotional responses in the audience, and the dancer–choreographer, Senta Driver, claims that it is still an act of movement.[15] Postmodern dance has started to move away from the anti-theatricality of its original program, however, and the divisions between ballet, modern, and postmodern dance are increasingly vague, as dancers and choreographers cross the traditional boundaries with increasing frequency.

These are different developments that exhibit different sensibilities, not closer or more distant approximations of some single essential quality of the art. Such divergences in the kind and quality of movement may be the foundation of distinct genres or styles, as they are in the dance traditions of Spain, India, and Bali, but they do not decide questions of purity or superiority. Generic patterns of movement simply evoke different realms of spatial and temporal experience, and it is the effectiveness with which they develop those qualities that determines their success.

Sometimes gesture is distinguished from other kinds of movement and is identified as the form that movement assumes in dance. This ascribes a qualitative difference between dance and other movement that many now challenge, but it also points up the deliberate, studied form of dance motion, where movement may be taken for its own sake. Dance may employ pure gesture, movement shaped out of its own internal dynamic forces to stand sufficient in itself, as in Balanchine's formalist ballets *Symphony in C* and *Divertimento No. 15*. There may be descriptive gesture, where body movement emulates other things, as in Makarova's unforgettable winglike arms as the doomed Swan Queen in *Swan Lake*. Dramatic gesture is yet another form movement may take, and it is the basis of the many narrative dances that fill the repertoire, bringing dance close to mime.

As the art of the moving body, then, dance is embodied movement; it is the manifestation of the self in movement, *as* movement.[16] But movement is never isolated, nor is the self ever impervious to other forces. Movement always occurs in context, and this is the aspect of movement that forms the most distinctive feature of the dance art. For movement creates a realm of experience in which the forces that are present in every situation become the center of attention. Dance, in fact, literally embodies the basic powers of the human situation. It exhibits the primal conditions of the human realm in which space and time are generated out of movement. In a world without movement we would have no sense either of time or of space: The one could not be measured and would pass into eternity; the other could not be sensed, for the awareness of distance, which is the source of our perception of space, rests not only on movement of the eye but of the body as well. We are speaking here, of course, not of time and space as commonly understood physical concepts, but rather as they are experienced. In fact, with quantum mechanics these two orders approach identity.

Space and time, then, are always experienced through movement, and therefore we come to know them (in the physical sense of *know*) in personal, often intimate ways. Space has its source in the body. The body becomes the point from which space is measured and from which objects take their position. The perceiving body is "home," so to speak. Like the tortoise, we produce our accompanying place, no material shell here but a perceptual realm that we inhabit and with which we are continuous. The aware body is thus the center of our personal world, and as it moves it generates that world. This does not separate the body from the larger world, for we are not an interior that is opposed to its external surroundings. Rather, the perceptual organism is more like the nucleus of a cell, a concentration in its own fluid medium. So we can say that the body's presence determines what is present. Merleau-Ponty thinks of space in this sense as emanating from the body. We have seen how he takes the body as "the field of perception and action," incorporating familiar objects into its personal domain. Space becomes, then, not something exterior and objective but something I live inside. I reckon space, therefore, starting from myself "as the zero point or degree zero of spatiality."[17]

One might be inclined to characterize the body as the "here" from which other things are "there," as some have described it, but this mistakenly suggests that there is a separation between the body and its surroundings. Bollnow slips into such a division between self and world when he identifies the "natural place" to which someone belongs as different from the space where one may be at a given time, taking the house as the reference point from which one establishes his spatial world.[18] Dance *exhibits* the mistakenness of this notion. We are always "here," even though some conditions may be more welcoming and expansive than others, and dance gives presence to this immediacy of human being. Like all people, but with greater consciousness and deliberateness, the dancer engages in a complex choreography of centrifugal and centripetal movements. Responsive to every nuance of gesture from herself or others, the dancer reaches and withdraws, advances, turns, extends, and bends, employing a vocabulary of movement chosen by tradition, style, or choreographer from every imaginable kind of body motion. The dancer occupies "the cross-roads of in-working and out-going streams of power," as von Laban thought of it.[19]

It is possible to identify different spatial modalities, among them physical space, perceptual space, and spatial consciousness. Some or all of these may be used in various stages of the dance process. Certainly the choreographer must be conscious of the physical size of the performance space in shaping the dimensions and patterns of a dance. There is also a sense in which this actual space cannot be forgotten by the dancer in executing his or her movements. Yet space can be grasped kinesthetically through the movements of the body, apprehended in an almost tactual way by the skin, sensed by the moving eye, felt somatically as it envelopes and connects with the body and offers places for passage. Spatial consciousness occurs when space is grasped in this way. Space, in this sense, is alive, like the body, as Mary Wigman used to emphasize, pulling, pushing, lifting, lowering as we move in it and as part of it.[20]

At the same time, however, perceptual space supervenes and dominates the aesthetic occasion, embracing the body's spatial consciousness. This is space as it is perceived, not only somatically but in the full awareness of thought, memory, sentience, and imagination as well. In the directness of immediate experience, in fact, these are all continuous and inseparable.[21] Perceptual space is, in fact, one of the principal constituents of the dance medium. In film and television dance, for example, physical boundaries may be quite forgotten as the camera and the film editor collaborate in shaping the dimensions of perceptual space. Although they employ cutting as a means of accomplishing the choreographer's end, this technology is assimilated into the choreographic process.[22] Moreover, through our conscious awareness of the domain of perceptual space, we become active participants in the choreography of our world. In dance the vital human form exists in the realm of forces that define its space, and in this dynamic field of powers everything within its boundaries is charged. If there is any perceptual reference at all beyond the immediacy of this human space, it is small and weak.

When dance turns to plot and becomes dramatic, it might seem to belie the immediate presence of dance space. Doesn't plot take preeminence, imposing its own order on the spatial dynamics of the dance and replacing the abstractness of space with the definiteness of dramatic action? The development of narrative would appear to supplant the elaboration of movement in dynamic space, the growth of dramatic action replacing the energy of abstract forces.

Plot and space, however, are not opposed concepts. Indeed, an aesthetics of dance cannot hang on the opposition of the abstract and the dramatic, just as the same false polarities must fail between figurative and abstract painting, between absolute and program music, and between narrative and plotless novels. The aesthetics of any art should reconcile such different modalities, absorbing both into a more inclusive perceptual realm. In dance, these modalities are not pitted against one another; they are rather different patterns of spatial order, different paradigms for developing the interplay of forces in human space. Thus drama does not supersede energized space; it provides a frame for elaborating its vectors. Dance theater is but a concretization of the spatial interplay of dynamic forces, an order where they become dramatic rather than wholly abstract.

The greatest confusion to follow the introduction of dramatic elements comes from ascribing expressive properties to gestures. How convenient it is to speak of dance movements as expressing joy, anguish, love, grief—that entire, simple, and limited vocabulary of emotional qualities, which words alone but crudely identify. To think that dance, or any art, expresses feelings or ideas implies an act of translation from subject to object, from feeling to the work of art, from emotional state to dance performance, and it sets the art in a cognitive, symbolic frame as a vehicle for communicating emotions. Dance, however, belies the aesthetic concept of expression: Dance does not express; it is. It *embodies* characteristic experiences: the basic kinds of human interaction with their individual, subtle nuances; and the fundamental traits of experience—its dynamic quality, its speed, force, action, and response, and its shaping of time and space.[23] This incarnation of feeling, combined with the perceptual unity of perceiver and performer, is what gives dance its emotional force. Such embodiment is true, *mutatis mutandis,* of all the arts.

One of the most curious juxtapositions of the two modalities of the abstract and the dramatic suggests not only their compatibility but their reconciliation. There are instances, for example, in which reference is made to an absent person, as when Giselle dances her poignant hallucinatory solo as if she were still paired by the loving presence of Albrecht, before stabbing herself fatally. Here space that is empty but charged actually functions as part of the plot; negative space assumes dramatic form. This curious feature is not unique to dance; it occurs in theater and is central to mime. Such an issue could easily involve us in the fascinating question of the ontology of negation. It is enough here merely to mention that philosophers of our day, following Heidegger and Sartre, have helped us understand how absence supplies its own kind of presence. Nowhere is this revealed more poignantly than in the case of a loved one who has died and whose absence we experience as a kind of shadowy presence. The conventional license of theatrical dance sometimes renders this experience of absence explicit, as when Albrecht sees the ghost of Giselle emerge from its tomb to dance with him, or when the reunited lovers dance in the Kingdom of the Shades in the dream act of *La Bayadère*. Lisette's pantomime of her daydreams about marriage and children in Ashton's *La Fille mal gardée* is a more usual form of experiencing the presence of absence.

However, absence is more than an abstract dramatic presence. It has a place in dance analogous to the role that negative space assumes as an integral part of a sculpture with cavities or openings, and that the volume of a building acquires as an essential aspect of its structure. "Empty" space has its own distinctive charge, and it is as directly present in the plenum of the dance as any other spatial modality. Such space becomes dramatic not just in *Giselle*'s deranged dancing but more commonly in the lines of force that emanate from the extended arms of a dancer, as from a lover who is being drawn away from the beloved, one of the most frequent of dramatic gestures. Bending the torso, extending the arms or legs, even tilting the head or pointing a finger fill space with vectors of energy, creating a continuum not unlike the physical space of modern physics.

Dance space, then, is never empty. With different degrees of intensity and magnetism, energy fills the space that appears to separate the dancers. A dance performance is not a display of objects moving in empty space but an array of conscious human bodies moving in a field of forces, forces which they create and to which they respond. Through their movement, dancers generate the perceptual space of their dance. In this respect, the realm of dance epitomizes the human world we all inhabit.

Yet not just space originates in movement; so, too, does time. Writing with as much sensitivity about dance as he did about poetry, Valéry observed that the dancer encloses herself in a time that she creates. "This is a time consisting entirely of immediate energy, of nothing that can last," time that has its source in the dancer's instability.[24] Like space, time arises out of motion. A *tableau vivant* stands largely out of time, at the edge of eternity, as it were, the body consciousness of the viewer supplying the only awareness of temporal passage. For as *Sleeping Beauty* shows us, time stops with the cessation of motion. With movement at the heart of dance, however, time is necessarily present.

Arising out of the movement of the dancers, time becomes an essential part of the dance experience. Distinctions have often been drawn between various temporal modalities—clock time, subjective time, astronomical time, absolute and relative time. Does time proceed differently in dance from the larger world? Is temporality in dance distinctive, another modality still?

To answer in the affirmative is too convenient. For temporality in dance is more than an alternative form in which we cast an order of change. Rather, time here makes its primal, originary appearance, not as a surface occurrence but at the very center of experience. Dance exemplifies the *origin* of time as it does of space, not only as temporal consciousness but in relation to the activity of the human body as well. This is lived time, time generated and brought to awareness through the vital movement of the body. From its source in such movement derive all the special forms of temporal understanding devised for such specific purposes as comparison, measurement, abstraction, calculation, and even imagination. As the body moves, so too does time. The dancer embodies temporality, then, not just producing it but *being* it. So we, too, give rise to time as we execute the dance of life. What we do half-consciously, half-fortuitously, the dancer accomplishes with eloquence through deliberate and controlled movement.

Time, then, however it may be refined and abstracted, postulated in metaphysics and objectified in science, originates in perceptual experience. In some sense time, like space, is transcendental, as Kant held. It lies at the basis of experience, a condition without which perceptual experience could not occur.[25] Yet contrary to Kant, time is not a transcendental basis of apperception, an *a priori* intuition that is a *pre*condition of all experience; rather time is inherent *in* the very condition of experience. And experience must be extended to include the transition of thoughts, of perceptions, and of bodily actions and sensations: The awareness of their movement engenders our consciousness of temporality.

Time, then, originates in movement and is exemplified in the motion of the dancer's body. But what sort of time is this? It is a peculiar phenomenon, this temporality of dance. Dance goes on with us and before us; it is immediately present. Yet the temporal dimension also defines our dance experience. For dance always takes place now, in the present. As the source of time, the body originates time as it moves, and the body moves always in the present. That is why there are no tenses in dance, no past and no future. We stand, instead, at the very origin of temporality in the human body, at its center point. Time is neither an external condition, as Newton saw it, nor an internal consciousness, as Augustine would have it. Rather, time has its experiential origin in the vital movement of the aware body.

Motion is, of course, pervasive in the natural world. It occurs apart from humans and independently of human action. But both the impulse to move and our awareness of the power inherent in motion have their sources in our body consciousness. In originating action and response, the body enters into movement. And as the source of movement, the body originates time. It makes time present; it generates the present. Motion occurs in nature, but time does not yet exist. It is we who give order and focus to motion by gracing it with direction, shape, and meaning. Kant was right in considering temporality foundational in experience, but being a condition of experience does not make it a condition of nature. Time, in being human, becomes a dimension of conscious action, and dance embodies its origination.

Performance in dance, then, contributes in a special way to our understanding of the human world. It possesses the germinal features of that world, and it recreates their process of origination. Starting with the body moving in awareness, dance epitomizes how we generate our spatiotemporal realm, the condition underlying our experience of all the arts. That is why "the difference between the so-called space arts and time arts is merely one of emphasis," as Arnheim observes.[26] With their common origin in movement and energized by its inherent power, space and time form an inseparable continuity in experience.[27] As in modern physics, they join into a unified field. Moreover, the shaping of space–time through movement lies as much at the core of ritualistic, ethnic, and social dancing as it does of theatrical dancing. The embroidery may vary but the underlying fabric is the same. Performance as originary action, then, is strikingly apparent in dance. Examining how time and space emerge in dance movement illuminates the character of performance here and, *pari passu*, in all the arts. As the active, generative force in experience, performance epitomizes the process that catalyzes the human world into existence.[28]

The aesthetics of dance, more intensely than other philosophy, confronts the question of what it means to be human, Sparshott tells us, for dance is the art of human presence, at least in its artistic forms. The obscurity of this condition, however, does not condemn it, like all philosophy, to irreducibly multiple possibilities in answering the existential question, and even more dispiritingly, to the impossibility of a stable starting point, as Sparshott seems to think. In establishing a human realm through movement, the dancer, together with the participating audience, engages in the basic act out of which arise both all experience and our human constructions of the world. That is both as stable a point of departure as one can hope to get and as much as one needs. For dance is an originary art in a more direct way than any other. It answers the metaphysical quest for the dimensions of the world by finding them in the domain of human movement.[29]

Dance, moreover, offers a series of rich unities on which rests the reconstruction of experience. It stands as the direct denial of that most pernicious of dualisms, the division of body and consciousness. In dance, thought is primed at the point of action. This is not the reflection of the contemplative mind but rather intellect poised in the body, not the deliberate consideration of alternative courses but thought in process, intimately responding to and guiding the actively engaged body. The conscious body and bodily consciousness combine, then, in the dynamic process of dance. By joining the physical and spiritual, dance embodies the person as a unity.[30]

This unity of the aware body in movement has other consequences. We have seen how the very activity that constitutes the dance art removes it from the traditional frame of contemplative object and rests its aesthetic distinction on process and practice. Here is an art, then, like certain others, such as architecture and design, whose special beauty comes from the success of its practice. In this respect dance bridges the conceptual gap between beauty and practice, between the aesthetic and the functional.[31] As with the crafts, skill in the making is embodied in the object, and the admiration of the one becomes part of the beauty in the other. Performance in the arts, in general, shares this unity, but in much of dance the range of accompanying materials is distilled into the exquisitely functioning body. Nowhere is the functioning of the conscious human body revealed more directly.

The emergence of an integrated self is another striking feature of dance experience, a return to less inhibited and fragmented conditions of living, conditions not yet organized and divided into cognitive and somatic structures of order and control. Sparshott writes eloquently of the primary importance of self-transformation in dance, a condition brought about mainly by a focus on the activity for itself, by a concern for its quality, by its distinctiveness, by the special character of the places, the occasions, the costumes, and most important, the movements of the dancer's own body. But he unaccountably concludes that, unlike theater, in which actors use speech that binds us to the social world, dance is, in its immediacy, a nonsocial world.[32] Individualism dies hard. It is difficult to conceive how so social an animal as the human one can shed that body of consciousness and movement, that environment of space and time, all so inherently social in origin and significance, as if it were an external garment, and dance, as it were, in the nude. In fact even the nude, *especially* the nude, has a meaning that is thoroughly cultural, as does its quasi-synonym, the naked.

The transformed self is, though, only one aspect of the unity of the whole situation. We have already recognized the extraordinary bond that can develop between performer and audience, and this is a fact of much theoretical significance. Thinking of appreciation in any art as a psychological state, an aesthetic attitude, as it is commonly termed in aesthetics, both restricts the scope of appreciation and misdirects the experience. Dance betrays the inadequacy of this kind of account. In dance appreciation there is somatic involvement, what the critic John Martin called "kinesthetic sympathy," vicarious muscular experience from which we receive aesthetic satisfaction. He recognized the correlation of physical movement with psychological qualities, coining the term *metakinesis* to denote the common reality of which these are both aspects.[33] The use of the Greek word for motion, *kínēsis*, is not incidental here. It directs us again to the central factor in dance experience, movement, which is inherent in the vibrant presence of the human body, and locates the idea of dance as the art of the moving body.[34]

The energizing effects of dance, the sense of heightened vitality that the moving body brings, are felt as keenly by the audience as by the dancers. This is not surprising, given the integrity of the experience that unites them. Martin writes of "the inherent contagion of bodily movement, which makes the onlooker feel sympathetically in his own musculature the exertions he sees in somebody else's musculature."[35] Jamake Highwater finds, in addition, that this contagion leads the dancer to share with the audience in a nonverbal, nonsymbolic way even intangible ideas, feelings, and experiences. Visual and imaginative activity combine with somatic perception to become an integral part of the appreciative process.[36] When a dance performance *works*, this experiential unity is total. There is not only muscular sympathy and emotional empathy but a kind of unity of being that can happen as much with the formal group patterns in Balanchine's *Chaconne* as with the tragic drama of Graham's *Clytemnestra*.

Certainly the quality and character of the continuity between performer and audience vary with the dance tradition, style, artists, and situation. The connection, however, is never absent. On one end of the spectrum is classical ballet, characterized so often as creating an illusion for the beholder. Yet there is an illusion only when dance is judged against the prosaic world, and such a judgment is a cognitive act irrelevant in the immediacy of the dance experience. Illusion describes the enchanted quality of the experiential realm rather than the relation of audience to dancers, a realm that engages both of these in its own order of space, time, and movement. On the other end of the spectrum lies postmodern dance, which may deliberately seize on the continuity and commonality of experience of performer and onlooker.[37] African dance is one ethnic tradition that rests on the unity of performer and audience. Amadou Sissoko of Guinea's African Ballet identifies the gifted performer as one who is able to create the effective participation of the *bara* around him, the traditional circle that encompasses song, dance, instrumentalists, and audience. There is a single word in Swahili that expresses this—*ngoma*, incorporating drum, music, dance, dancer, audience. Primal people, furthermore, make full use of the contagious power of dance, focusing the energy that pervades the world to influence animals, nature, even spirits and gods. One can detect this in what is sometimes called homeopathic ritual; in fact, such sympathetic magic lies at the heart of most ceremonial dance. This same quality is a powerful force in the work of choreographers such as Erick Hawkins, whose dances are filled with the pulse that lives in the flow of natural events.[38]

The dynamic force in the kinesthetic experience of dance is common, then, to both the dancer and the audience.[39] The viewer may, in fact, regard the dancers with such intensity that a direct physical involvement in the movements develops. Some of the more spectacular leaps, such as the male dancer's series of *grands jetés en manège* around the circumference of the stage or the ballerina's running leap into a fish dive, often cause an involuntary flexing of the viewer's body. And if a dancer's foot should slip or appear to slip, the audience, almost as a body, as it were, will gasp as the dancer might and make an involuntary reflex, as if to regain its own footing. There is a sense in which the perceiver lives in the dancer's body, participating empathetically in the movements he or she undertakes. A large part of the exhilaration of a dance performance comes from this active somatic involvement.[40]

Sondra Horton Fraleigh notes how the qualities of flight, light, ease, and fluidity in Trisha Brown's dances act to open the viewer to the lived aesthetic of his own somatic perception. As lived bodies, both performer and perceiver share these qualities. She cites Mary Wigman's wonderfully evocative description of the relationship between the dancer and the audience: "the fire which dances between the two poles." The engagement of the audience becomes necessary to complete the dance art, for we enact the dance perceptually, making it a part of our own vital body.[41] Here in this art of human movement lies a direct physical experience of fusion, and performance embodies this trait of dance perception boldly and directly.

Perceivers, then, participate in the dance; they do not simply observe it. Within the continuous domain of the aesthetic field, an insuppressible bond connects the overt action of the dancer and the seemingly immobile observation of the audience. The originary actions of the dancer combine with the active response of the onlooker as both participate in the interplay of forces that constitutes the dance. The engagement of the viewer means, further, that dance cannot be objectified, for the region of powers encloses the whole experiential field. By joining in the field of forces that constitutes the realm of dance experience, the audience also performs the dance.

This participation in the dance, moreover, is not a private one. While it can be argued that even the most reclusive artist engages in a social act, dance is social for more reasons than the fact that it usually takes place before an audience, a characteristic it shares with theater and music. Some genres and traditions in dance depend on a communicative process to complete the dance experience. In Sanskrit dance and drama, for example, the principle of *rasa* formulates how the spectator must recognize and respond to symbol and suggestion, thus contributing to the development of mood and awareness. Such an exchange must occur between the performer and the spectator for the dramatic experience to be fulfilled.

Sociality, however, goes still deeper, for dance joins with singing in being the earliest and most common participatory art, deeply embedded in every human culture. In popular and folk culture the impulse to join in the dance is often irresistible. Havelock Ellis is but one of many to remark on how dance accomplishes social unification: "The participants in a dance . . . exhibit a wonderful unison; they are, as it were, fused into a single being stirred by a single impulse." We can see this occur in African dance, where the division between performers and audience is replaced by the practice of "call and response." There is a reciprocal interplay between the dancers and the drummers, each group at times challenging the other and leading it on to an ever more intense pitch of energy and excitement. The onlookers may join in by clapping, stamping, and shouting, they may move in and out of the dance, or they may contribute ongoing comments of approval or criticism. African dance extends at times to incorporate features from the physical and social environment, such as the position of the sun or the moon, the dust and heat of the day, the layout of the village, the reactions of the children surrounding the dancers, and even the intrusion of straying fowl. Although in the West conventional decorum intervenes in more formal performance settings, one may still discern the feeling of social unity as an implicit force.[42]

The sense of fusion in dance radiates outward in ever broader concentric circles. By generating the spatiotemporal medium of perceptual experience through movement, the activity of the body forms connections throughout human life–space. We begin to experience continuities with the larger environment and indeed with the cosmos. "To dance is to take part in the cosmic control of the world."[43] At this point the mythic nature of dance reveals itself. Dance becomes the medium, sometimes overtly ritualistic, in which the dancer participates in a realm of potent beings, bonding with the cosmos as an embodied symbol in the unity of meaning and being. This fusion of symbol and world is what Cassirer meant by "mythical consciousness."[44]

Although there is a performative factor in all the arts, dance is the exemplary art of performance. It fuses the creative and responsive activities of aesthetic perception in a work that exists only in and for that process. Performance and appreciation in dance join, then, not in reflecting the origination of a human world, not in reenacting the original act of creation, but in the very process of generating such a world. In accomplishing this, dance extends the human from its most fundamental to its most inclusive, from body to cosmos. Dance embodies this communal act of origination in a process in which everyone may participate and with an ardor that can become almost religious. At this point art approaches the divine.

Illustrations

It is quite impossible to illustrate aesthetic engagement, for no object can ever successfully represent experience. The following examples, therefore, are necessarily incomplete, since they unavoidably lack an essential factor: the participation of the viewer. The viewer contributes to the aesthetic occasion by catalyzing the painting or photograph into an active event or, as with the Bierstadt and Durand paintings, distancing and objectifying it. Of course, this contribution is not whimsical: visual features encourage and guide the response. And indeed the influence of such features suggests what aesthetic appreciation requires: a sensitivity to the qualities and features of the art object so that the response is appropriate and fulfilled, creating in this way what is literally the work of art, its active consummation.

These, then, are intended as illustrations, not of what an original painting or a scene looks like, but of how it may function in appreciative experience. As such, it represents only part of the event; the viewer represents another part.

Mark Di Suvero, *Atman*, 1978–1979. Courtesy of Richard Bellamy/Oil and Steel Gallery. Photograph, Arnold Berleant

This sculpture is not only directly accessible to the viewer, but also has a platform that invites people to sit and swing.

Albert Bierstadt, *Scene in the Tyrol,* 1854. Hirshhorn Museum and Sculpture Garden, Smithsonian Institution, Gift of Joseph H. Hirshhorn, 1966

This is a typical example of a panoramic landscape, which offers no visual connections between the observer and the scene but rather turns the environment into a contemplative object.

Asher B. Durand, *Kindred Spirits,* 1849. Oil on Canvas, Collection of The New York Public Library, Astor, Lenox and Tilden Foundations

Several levels of interpretation mark this painting as a contemplative object, both to the viewers within the painting and the viewer of the painting. Visual cues work to divide the figures from the landscape they inhabit and to separate the beholder of the painting from the pictorial space.

Francesco de Guardi, *Piazza San Marco*, 1740–1760. Venetian, The Metropolitan Museum of Art, Bequest of Mary Stillman Harkness, 1950

This painting, which appears as a distant, self-contained scene when viewed from the usual distance (above), opens its space to the viewer who steps inside the triangle of perspective. By moving close to the pictorial surface, the boundary demarcated by the frame disappears from view and one can join the public scene, moving from group to group as a participant in the pictorial space (see details opposite).

Salomon van Ruysdael, *Country Road*, 1648. The Metropolitan Museum of Art, Rogers Fund, 1906. (06.1201)

The transformation of a painting from a visual object (above) into a participatory landscape occurs when the viewer moves close to the pictorial surface and enters its space (detail opposite).

Vredeman de Vries, Perspective drawing, 1604/1605. From Jan Vredeman de Vries, *Perspective*. Courtesy of Dover Publications, Inc.

This classic rendition does not display the lines of perspective originating at the eye of the viewer. By moving inside that triangle, we, like the figure in the foreground, can enter the pictorial space and be transformed from an observer into a participant.

Stairway to church, Šibenik, Yugoslavia. Photograph, Arnold Berleant

The gentle curve of this stairway invites the pedestrian to ascend to the church, which does not stand as an opposed, monumental object but rather as the goal of the viewer's movement.

Path, Plitvice Lakes National Park, Yugoslavia. Photograph, Arnold Berleant

Curving paths and roads often have a compelling effect, urging the viewer to move along them into the landscape, a phenomenon well known to landscape painters and architects.

Art
and reality

PART THREE

CHAPTER EIGHT

Cinematic reality

FILM IS THE MASS ART OF OUR DAY. IT APPEARS TO PURVEY FANTASY to a huge market of people hungry for distraction from dull routine and for deliverance from a sense of anonymity and powerlessness. But cinema is not so much an art of escape as an art of entry. In this modern equivalent of crystal gazing everyone becomes his or her own clairvoyant, able to see beyond the ordinary limits of time and place to the farthest distances of artistic imagination. For film is a composite of magic carpet and time machine, capable of transporting us instantly to any place in the world and any moment in history. Yet cinema represents more than the ability of modern optical and chemical technology to produce waking dreams, dreams that realize the intent of both Middle Eastern romance and modern science fiction. What makes film so remarkable an artistic means is its capacity to completely shape the perceptual materials that constitute human reality in ways that go far beyond the usual physical and chronological constraints of ordinary life.

More than any other art, film can order the pure dimensions of experience directly and without any apparent physical intermediary to create a convincing and absorbing reality of its own. Unlike most other arts, there is a clear separation in film between the physical materials of the art and their perceptual forms. Film does not distract us with physical objects, living bodies, acts of producing sound, or usually, with linguistic symbols that stand as surrogates for experience. There is no paint, no stone, no dancers, and ordinarily, no printed words. Like recorded music, the substance of film is exclusively perceptual, while its technical origins remain hidden. The cinematic world, then, is purely phenomenal. Here is perhaps the quintessential art form of mid twentieth-century technology, joining electricity, optics, and chemistry with mechanics in the motion picture camera, the darkroom, and the cutting room to fashion a total perceptual experience.

Cinematic art may also be unique in the complete control it grants the artist in shaping the dimensions of experience. For the perceptual environment that cinema creates is fashioned out of the fundamental constituents of the human world, using space, time, and movement to combine visual images, ambient sounds, spoken language, a social and physical setting, and the mental images of memory and imagination into a continuous whole. Through the skillful use of camera and movement, processes of developing and printing film, sound recording, and especially through the distinctive and powerful technique of editing, the director can create a seamless and all-enclosing sequence of experience that embodies all the perceptual qualities of the human world. Because of its comprehensiveness and the fact that perception is synaesthetic, joining together all the sensory modalities, cinema is able to draw the audience into a degree of engagement to which access is easier, more direct, more complete and compelling than in any other art. How, precisely, does film accomplish this?

Most obviously through its use of time. Filmmakers manipulate time the way composers order sound. Time in film is not the chronological time it takes for the film to run; it is more than plot time in which the action unrolls. It is experiential time, the time of perceptual awareness. The director not only creates in time out of temporal segments but creates time itself, bringing temporality into conscious experience and imparting to it a distinct quality and character. Time here is not a linear, one-dimensional, and unidirectional phenomenon. It becomes almost like a solid. Our ordinary perception of temporality is as a fluid medium, but the filmmaker handles it as if it were a tangible material that can be manipulated at will. And indeed it seems as if it can. Slowing down and speeding up the camera's shutter speed alters the course of the action and displays the elasticity of time, which is closer to our actual experience than the regular movement of the clock. Stopping the camera freezes time. Tracking or panning shots may halt the progress of time, for when the camera moves forward or to one side to present a scene or a character's life at different periods it effectively displaces the passage of time and evokes a sense of timelessness.[1]

But it is especially through the technique of montage that the filmmaker has the power to freely create a temporal order. The unidirectional movement of time disappears and temporality becomes multi-dimensional, multi-layered, so to speak, as we move among different chronologies without regard for their historical sequence. Through montage the filmmaker can also transcend the linearity of time, moving horizontally, at right angles, as it were, to achieve simultaneity, doubling back to repeat or reenact events, standing still to stop the action, and in other ingenious ways changing the course and direction of time. The techniques are familiar: Cross-cutting divides and interchanges film sequences, so that the camera moves back and forth between two or more actions taking place concurrently to give the impression of simultaneity.[2] The flashback allows sequences depicting past and present to be exchanged and rearranged in any order, producing an effect more true to psychic experience than the irreversible order of the clock, since we engage in this process of temporal reordering not only in waking and sleeping dreams but also in the deliberative activities of remembering and planning. There are still other effects that can be achieved through editing, such as repetitions of the same shot, which arrest temporal progress entirely.

This remarkable capacity to shape temporality led Panofsky to compare the treatment of time in film to the manipulation of space, describing it as a spatialization of time through the rearrangement of celluloid strips.[3] By means of the editing process the film artist fashions a temporal mosaic, ordering time sequences as if they were a collection of multi-colored stones to be placed in any pattern that pleases the creative purpose. Any need to conform to standards of regularity, uniformity, and objectivity is disregarded. The time of the film is the time of the mind, still more, the time of experience.

More vividly than theater or the novel, Arnold Hauser has argued, film exemplifies the temporal experience of our age, experience that focuses on an awareness of the present. He associates the beginning of this mentality with Bergson's philosophy of time, as Deleuze has more recently, and finds that the cinematic ability to spatialize time exemplifies the modern experience of simultaneity more forcefully than does any other art.[4] This is an illuminating claim, for the complete freedom of film to manipulate temporal segments and sequences leads, in fact, to the loss of forward momentum, the disappearance of a sense of the irreversibility and inevitability of time, and thus to a focus on the present moment. If time is infinitely malleable, continuity and directional order vanish. Since temporal sequences can now be arranged at will in any order whatsoever, they all become "timeless" segments of an extended present.

Does this signify the effective abandonment of temporality? Not at all. Film represents rather the constantly shifting qualitative experience of temporality around its focal point in an extended present. Such a time consciousness was actually prefigured by St. Augustine, for whom the past and the future are grasped as forms of the present, "a present of things past, a present of things present, and a present of things future."[5] The objectivity of time has been transmuted into temporal experience, and film, one of the youngest of the arts, has come to embody the temporal mentality of advanced age, in which time contracts to the present and the present expands to embrace the fullness of past and future.

Yet time, so to speak, cannot stand alone; it requires a spatial coordinate in order to transpire. Time in film is inseparable from the space in which the action moves pursued by the camera's eye, and in which the two dimensions of the cinematic image are transformed into a three-dimensional experience. The passage of time in film, however it be manipulated, must occur in a spatial context, for spatiality is the condition for its very perception. And since temporal perception must occur in a spatial medium, pure temporality is unattainable here. Yet the converse is equally true. Cinematic space demands time in which to expand and develop. It is transformed, in fact, into a temporal mode. For cinematic space is not the space of physical action but of perceptual experience. There can be no physical space in film, only perceptual space, and the fixed dimensions of the so-called objective world dissolve into the changing horizon of human action.[6] Like the space of dreams, cinema space is fluid and its periphery mobile, and it can be manipulated and ordered in whatever way the director decides. Yet by being presented sequentially, space is apprehended through a temporal mode. The dynamization of space thus becomes the mirror image of the spatialization of time.[7]

Cinematic space, then, cannot be grasped apart from time. Nor is it abstract. Space in film becomes place, the place of human habitation, action, and meaning, for in some sense a human presence is pervasive. Unlike so-called physical space, the absolute space of Newtonian physics, cinema space is not homogeneous. It is associated with human personality, human feeling, human endeavor. Space is the place in which life is lived, thus becoming particularized and individual, and assuming the qualities of the characters who inhabit it. A multitude of vivid places fills the landscape of film history, from the expressionistic set of *Dr. Caligari* and the great steps of the Odessa massacre in *Potemkin,* to the highway landscapes of *Easy Rider* and the convalescing hero's room in *Rear Window.*

Except for giant, curved screens that extend beyond our peripheral vision, the perceived dimensions of the screen, like those of the frame of a painting, appear fixed and limiting. Yet the space within the screen is endlessly plastic. Proximity and remoteness lose their usual meanings entirely. Distances are under the director's control and can be bent in a multitude of ways, short distances becoming endless and great ones being gained instantly. The cutting room is thus the modern technological equivalent of the magic carpet. The camera creates the perceptual space of action, and by cutting and splicing we leap instantly from one location to any other. There is, in addition, the inherent virtuosity of the camera. Like the space of a map, cinema space is elastic and can be made to expand or contract. By dollying back or by panning, the camera can cause space to grow, opening wide to assume the impersonality of a public place, while through a close-up space can become more intense, contracting and taking on greater intimacy. Space can flatten by taking advantage of the distorting effect of the telescopic lens and can deepen by using a wide-angle lens or increasing the depth of field. Through cross-cutting, the viewer can inhabit several places at the same time. Characters, too, may appear and disappear instantly or be transformed before our eyes, while physical barriers prove no impediment to the eye of the camera. We can even enter those places that lurk in the recesses of memory or imagination. Space, moreover, can change its density by controlled lighting and through multiple exposures that allow images not only to be superimposed on one another or become translucent but also to be visible simultaneously. These are well-known techniques, and this catalog only details the devices whose cumulative force shapes our spatial perception in film.[8]

Cinema space has a powerful attraction for the viewer. It invites one to enter, persuading us "to abandon our ordinary lives and live wholly within the world of the film."[9] This is the essential realism of film, a subject debated endlessly but often conceived mistakenly as an attack on or defense of the recording function of the photographic process. The genesis of the image is a different matter from how it is perceived in the movie theater. Realistic images and modified images that result from techniques that alter what has been recorded may both be equally real in filmic experience. Such experience, and not an *a priori* principle, becomes the touchstone of artistic effectiveness.

Spatial perception is, in fact, historically and culturally variable. It is convenient but misleading to associate changes in the depiction of space in painting, for example, with the development of techniques for representation, linear perspective being the usual example. A history of perception, however, would show that spatial awareness is different under different geographical and cultural conditions. It would be revealing to explore the tendency of preliterate cultures to find a continuity between the space of imaginative action and that of physical action, instead of regarding them, as we do, as being dissimilar spatial orders. Primitive rituals draw no clear distinction between image and reality. Totems, for example, are tokens of the animal itself. This connection helps explain the remarkable fascination of preliterate peoples with photographs, since with these they hold reality in their hands. Even in modern society people will sometimes tear up photographs to remove a person from their lives. Panofsky has shown how the medieval cathedral presents spiritual space, the reality of the interior world. In entering the cathedral one penetrates the celestial realm, noble, lofty, sacred. The nave, the aisles, the choir offer spatial regions of the spiritual world, together the virtual embodiment of a dualism with the earthly space outside. The skyscraper is often taken, following Gropius, as the cathedral of modern industrial society, a lofty monument to the power and aspirations of scientific technology. But the skyscraper is in some respects more a survival of Newtonian space, a collection of impersonal, objective, neutral, standardized cubical units. Cinematic space is a more convincing paradigm of the modern world, because it projects the experience of a relativistic and malleable quantum universe, the space of satellite communication and instantaneous electronic transmission and transformation.

Furthermore, spatial perception, like temporal, is never self-contained. Space and time are, in fact, correlative perceptions, each requiring the other in order to occur at all. In this respect, as well, the spatiotemporal domain of modern physics is embodied in film. Through its continuity of space and time, film offers encounters that may be even more convincing than those in ordinary life, where we are hampered by habitual disjunctions that bifurcate our world into separate spatial and temporal realms. Film transcends such divisions, providing experience that is closer to what contemporary physics has given us, where space and time are inseparable and continuous, much like our lived world.

There is still another basic component in this process of constructing a cinematic universe (or of cinema constructing a human universe). Space and time demand a third dimension, for spatiotemporal perception is not an exclusively visual act. A multi-sensory, kinesthetic engagement occurs in film, since spatial perception involves the apprehension of distance, of distance traversed, and the awareness of temporal progression occurs as a process of passage through space. To be experienced as three-dimensional, space must be fused with movement, as it is in the everyday world. And for time to transpire, the actions of characters, the movement of events, the eye of consciousness itself are necessary. We require movement, overt or implicit, to apprehend depth and passage.

Film has the remarkable capacity to accomplish this. It offers us spatiotemporal experience through the movement of the camera, proceeding as the body's eye around a room, through a building, down a street, and into the landscape, not bound by the constraints of size or of gravity, of obstacles or of distance, to give us an awareness of space as it is grasped through our bodily apprehension. The means of producing movement combine both camera motion and screen action. The camera can produce the perception of motion by speeding up or slowing down the number of frames per second, by zooming in for a close-up or back for medium and long shots, by tracking and panning, by tilting and rolling. Here the camera acts as the viewer's eye, but more freely and with greater versatility than the human organ. As the camera moves the eye moves, becoming an active participant in the perceptual process. At the same time, the events in the screenplay contribute another kinetic layer through bodily action and changes of place.

Slavko Vorkapich uses motion to characterize film in general, not only including the shapes that movement creates but enlarging the notion to incorporate montage, since, through cutting, the shapes of movement are arranged into a dynamic visual organization that gives a film its total structure.[10] Other more recent writers have also developed theories of film that take motion as basic and not reducible to a collection or sequence of instants. Pierre Rouve elaborates the outlines of a systematic film grammar whose syntactic root unit is the *filmeme*, the dynamic temporal relation between two frames out of which other, larger structures are generated.[11] Gilles Deleuze finds his focal idea in the *movement-image,* an element or unit that is the "mobile section of a duration." This is the matter of film, an identity of image and movement that he derives from Bergson's *Matter and Memory.* "The plane of immanence or the plane of matter is a set of movement-images; a collection of lines or figures of light; a series of blocks of space–time." The film is generated out of movement-images by the process of montage, which combines three varieties of images: perception-images (long shots), affection-images (close shots), and action-images (medium shots).[12] None of these manifestations of movement can occur apart from temporal and spatial parameters, and the dependency is reciprocal. Time, space, and movement thus unite into an integral perception of the world, and every film exemplifies more or less successfully this fusion of spatiotemporal kinesis into a perceptual realm.

Filmic experience, then, is not in itself illusory. Cinematic art works with the actual materials of perception and meaning to bring a human reality into being. This is where the debate over realism in film is misplaced. The issue is not whether film, because of its capacity to record the surfaces of things, is committed to representing such appearances essentially unaltered. The claims of theorists such as Kracauer and Arnheim that "the film is mimetic by its very nature" mistake the medium for the message.[13] By being formed out of the constituents of perception, cinema cannot help but offer the real, whether that be in a representational mode or one of fantasy. Even animated films create their own worlds. As in the magical realism of many recent South American novels, the significance of the distinction between the real and the unreal disappears. They are continuous, and they combine in art as they do in life. It is only by adopting an external stance, that is, the position of still another order of being, that we are able to distinguish the modality of the experience.

This situation resembles dreams. Dreams, like magic, present us with the inexplicable. The dream is, in fact, a mode of magic, a socially acceptable form of magical vision. Yet while asleep we recognize its authenticity for, as Dewey once noted, all experience is real as it is experienced.[14] Which, then, is truly real, the knowledge that we are asleep or the dream that we have and remember even after it is over? But perhaps this is a false question, since from the standpoint of living experience, no reality has precedence over any other. Moreover, at its most successful, film quite surpasses the division between dream and reality, as Marcel claims.[15] The only significant question in any particular case is how effectively it achieves its reality.

The claim for the reality of the cinematic domain is not as outrageous as it may seem at first. Some film theorists have approached the idea, although usually they remain bound by the preconception that regards film primarily as image, and they do not pursue the notion consistently. Siegfried Kracauer, for example, recognizes the ability of film to weaken the spectator's consciousness but speaks disapprovingly of the desire of some viewers to submerge themselves in the film to such a degree that they lose their sense of separate identity.[16] Others find the process of reality beginning at the point where movement is incorporated into the visual medium. Rouve, for example, locates it in the filmeme which, he holds, exists within a different reality, one that is "co-real" with the ordinary world.[17] Vorkapich finds reality appearing in the process of montage, which combines visual-dynamic-meaningful elements into "living entities."[18]

Michael Roemer presses the idea further still. Film portrays the ordinary surfaces of things, yet it remains an object fashioned of images, not the things themselves. Paradoxically, however, the film image acquires an intrinsic reality that results not so much from being the image of actual surfaces as from what is cinema's greatest power—the ability to *render* experience rather than merely to *cite* it. This is the power of film to present events directly and with a vividness that may be more intense and real than even life itself. Roemer decries the common tendency of filmmakers to manipulate the response of their audience by using cinematic clichés, sequences of incidents whose effects are predictable. References to war in films of the 1940s or to atomic catastrophe in the 1960s often merely cite events and play upon the viewers' feelings about them. A truly cinematic image, however, is "derived from life and rendered in concrete, physical terms." When an event is not just referred to but is experienced directly and vividly in a particular instance, its power is realistic and convincing. There must be a feeling of "spontaneity, the sense that what is happening on the screen is happening for the first time and without plan or direction," for reality to be established in a film. We can actually acquire the illusion of a "primary experience," Roemer holds, so intense that we will participate in subjective, fantastic, dreamlike sequences, entering eagerly into images we know to be "unreal."[19]

Roemer's argument is a strong one, and he offers many examples of films that achieve a level of audience participation in a cinematic reality. But because he retains the convention of regarding film as image and illusion, he avoids passing through the image, through the surface of reality, into its very substance. Indeed, the technology of the film medium is easily misleading here, for there is actually no difference between surface and substance. Although the film product is composed of surfaces, so to speak, of images of surfaces, to be more accurate, that is a fact of the technological process by which it is fabricated, not of the experiential one in which the viewer participates with the film. The distinction between surface and substance is, in fact, entirely misleading. The medium of cinematic experience is actually a spatiotemporal kinetic activity, as we have seen, and it is only here in such active experience that we can find the true locus of the filmic world. Roemer is right in recognizing the central impulse of cinema to be the rendering of reality in a way that requires the audience to take an active part in the filmic process. But because it shapes the conditions of experience, film does more still than render reality: It *constitutes* it. By its capacity to determine and control completely the conditions and contents of experience, film achieves reality.

Jean Cocteau's *Blood of a Poet* exemplifies how we can pass through the image into the real. This early surrealist film is something of a cinematic analogue of Alice's journey into the looking-glass world. The poet is told by an armless statue to enter the mirror, which leads into the Hôtel des Folies. Here he views different bizarre scenes through the keyholes of various rooms, and eventually finds his way out. In *Blood of a Poet* the space of imagination is indistinguishable from the space of action. Ordinary barriers become insubstantial and, in the spatiotemporal kinetic creation of a perceptual realm, are easily transgressed. The viewer goes beyond the surface of the film, like going through the surface of the mirror, into the space of a cinematic world to grapple with the strange mysteries of human actions. With the poet's eye we enter the space of this world to discover that it has its own independence and its own plausibility. Gazing through the crystal eye of the camera, we move through filmic space and time to inhabit a realm different from our ordinary one but no less convincing. Images and surfaces vanish and in their place is the spatiotemporal kinetic world of all human experience, the only reality we know and have.

Rouve has carried the argument for cinematic reality thoroughly and consistently through to its conclusion. "Films," he argues, "do not mirror empirical reality but structure a *sui generis* technological reality." Analyzing the semiological status of the film object, Rouve elaborates the syntax of a cinematic language derived entirely from the technological process out of which the cinematographer is able to construct a genuine experiential reality that acquires its own legitimacy. "In the cinema, technosyntactic structures and their semantic transformations are *not restitutive, but constitutive.*"[20]

Mizoguchi's masterwork *Ugetsu* (1953) achieves this constitution of reality not only for the viewer but within itself as well. Genjuro, an ambitious rural potter in sixteenth-century Japan, risks the dangers of traveling across a war-torn countryside to the principal city of the region, where he can sell his wares at great profit. Delivering some bowls to the Lady Wakasa, who lives in a nearby palace, Genjuro spends some idyllic days in which he is first enticed into remaining with the beautiful young noblewoman and eventually urged by her nurse to marry her. While Genjuro is on a trip into the city, a priest observes the sign of death on his face and warns him that Lady Wakasa was killed along with her family years before and the castle burned, and that he is consorting with ghosts. It is only with extraordinary difficulty that Genjuro is able to wrench himself out of his eerie predicament. His return to his village, weary and without money, nonetheless gives him deep relief and joy. He is welcomed by his faithful wife, is fed, and falls asleep, exhausted, next to his infant son. The next morning he is awakened by the village leader who is searching for the boy, whom he has been caring for ever since Genjuro's wife was killed by foraging soldiers. This ghostly relationship, however, is redeeming rather than treacherous. Even after the potter returns to his craft, chastened and diligent, the voice of his wife accompanies him in his work. There is no clear difference in *Ugetsu* between what is real in the film and what is magical. Everything inhabits the same terrain, and we share Genjuro's credulity as he lives in both worlds, or rather in his world, accepting, as he does, the plausibility of experience.

Film thus possesses a metaphysical capacity, an ability to arrange the conditions and constituents of perceptual experience so as to construct a human world. Kant's transcendental aesthetic can be extended to the cinematic order, where the deliberate selection and manipulation of the conditions of experience—time, space, and motion—provide the perceptual foundation of experiential reality. And as these display different patterns and regularities, so does the world that they underlie. Like Genjuro, we live easily in a realm that combines orders of reality that are conventionally separated, finding nothing odd or implausible in the transition between entering the movie theater and being conscious at times of the seat, the audience, and extraneous noises, and the more insistent and compelling perceptual region of the film into which we are so readily enticed.

This metaphysical capacity of the cinematic art becomes at times a subject for its own virtuosity. In film we often find ourselves shifting from one world to another or inhabiting two or more different realms concurrently, much like the multiple realities of modern consciousness, so that instead of a single filmic world, we may enter several. In *The French Lieutenant's Woman*, two plot levels develop concurrently: one, the nineteenth-century story of Sarah Woodruff; the other, the somewhat parallel but underdeveloped tale of the actors making the film of that story. The film cuts easily from one plot line to the other with little confusion. What is of special interest is how easily we are able to adjust from one place and time to the other which, though acted in by the same individuals, does not jar or confuse us. The use of overlapping sound tracks makes the transition smoother, and it is easy for us to adapt to whatever world is before us. We are accustomed to such frequent transitions in ordinary waking life, shifting from the immediate present to a projected future and returning in the next instant to the various strands of the past that jostle for attention in our memory. Like the film, human reality is often multiple.

Woody Allen's *The Purple Rose of Cairo* turns the juxtaposition of worlds into a maze. Here cinematic reality becomes both the subject and the substance of the film. During the Great Depression, Cecelia, a plain, small-town housewife, seeks relief from the impoverished and vulgar conditions of her marriage by going to the movies obsessively. This innocent escapism takes an unusual turn when Tom Baxter, a character in a film she has seen repeatedly, decides to break out of the dull routine of the drama he is playing and leave the film. He literally steps out of the screen and into Cecelia's life, courting her across the small New Jersey town with a charming innocence of the "real" world she inhabits. Meanwhile, the film cannot go on without Baxter, much to the chagrin of the other actors whom he has left behind on the screen. The situation precipitates a crisis in the movie industry, and the film is about to be withdrawn. None of this concerns Tom, who is intent on Cecelia, while for Cecelia his attentions, although disquieting, are the fulfillment of her fantasy life. Even though Baxter carries with him the beliefs and expectations of the way things happen in the movies, which is the only world he knows, his courtship of Cecelia has the dramatic tensions, elations, and disillusionments that accompany all love affairs, when two people attempt to reconcile the separate domains of their lives.

This confusion of worlds becomes even more involved when Gil Shepherd arrives on the scene. Shepherd is the "real-life" actor who plays Baxter in the film (but whose "real" name, as he confides to Cecelia, is Herman Barnibinian). Gil flatters Cecelia and attempts to engage her affections in a desperate effort to save the film and his career. Meanwhile, Tom persuades Cecelia to accompany him back into the film, for that is the world in which he knows how to function. He takes her out on the (movie) town which, of course, has disastrous effects on the plot of the film. Shepherd finally confronts Baxter in the theater. Forced to decide between them, Cecelia chooses the actor, Shepherd, over the personage, Baxter, since he represents the "real" and not the film world. The greatest disappointment of all, however, comes when Cecelia packs her bag, abandons her crude and insensitive husband, and goes to the station to meet Shepherd, only to learn that he has already left. Here is a bittersweet commentary on the interplay between the film world and the ordinary world, or rather between the film world in the film and the ordinary world in the film or, even closer, between a plurality of film worlds and the ordinary world of the film's viewers. One is left wondering which, if any, is the most authentic. In its constant interpenetration of ambiguous realities, *The Purple Rose of Cairo* resembles Calvino's novel, *If on a Winter's Night a Traveler,* which also juxtaposes a variety of interconnected but distinct plot lines. In cases like these, the legacy of postmodernism joins with the irreconcilable alternatives of deconstruction.

The classic example of multiple filmic co-realities is arguably Kurosawa's *Rashomon.* Like *The Alexandria Quartet,* Lawrence Durrell's tetralogy in which each of the four interrelated novels portrays the same period and events from the standpoint of a different principal character, *Rashomon* prefigures the metaphysical indeterminacies that deconstruction now reveals to us. At the inquest into the slaying of a warrior who, with his lady, had been waylaid by a bandit while passing through a forest, each of the witnesses gives a different account. According to the lady, she was raped by the bandit in front of her husband, whom the bandit had tied up. Afterwards, when the warrior refused to forgive her for her unwilling complicity, she stabbed him in a fit of insanity. The bandit claims that he had subdued the warrior fairly in honorable combat. Even the warrior contributes his version through the assistance of a medium, maintaining that he committed suicide after his wife went willingly with the bandit. Finally, a wood gatherer states that he witnessed the entire affair and that all three participants had acted in a cowardly and hysterical way, the bandit killing the warrior in a parody of a sword fight. Yet this account does not settle the matter, for the wood gatherer's credibility is itself placed in question when he is shown to have had a meddling interest in the events, tacitly acquiescing in the implication that he had removed a valuable dagger from the slain warrior. Each account is rendered equally vivid by the skillful use of flashbacks, and each can claim equal reality. Can we ask what actually happened? Is one account the true one? Are all true? None? These questions are never answered, and the ambiguity of realities is never resolved. As in the rest of life, no reality is more real than any other.

These examples of the cinematic manipulation of reality point up what occurs, perhaps sometimes less strikingly, in every film. Cinema does not create the image of reality. It does not produce its illusion. Because film exercises virtually complete control over the very conditions of experience, it is able to create full perceptual reality. This encourages a degree of participation so complete and profound that the viewer may easily come to accept the world of the film and enter fully into its domain. The boundaries of the ordinary, everyday world fade away as the cinematic realm encloses each member of the audience with a force at times so compelling that there is no escape short of wrenching oneself bodily from the seat and leaving the theater.

More, too, than any other art, cinema embodies the antinomy of artistic self-sufficiency and aesthetic continuity with the entire range of human events with which this discussion began. The cinematic realm can become so complete as to exclude all other orders of experience. Yet, at the same time, its resemblances and structural similarities with the other worlds we inhabit are so powerful that these resonate within filmic experience. Our engagement with film thus exemplifies many of the interconnections and confusions between the worlds of art and the so-called real world. And as with film, we begin to discover that the differences fade away.

Film is not the grand synthesis of the arts that Wagner intended the music drama to be. It does not achieve the ideal of the artists of the Vienna Secession, the *Gesamtkunstwerk*, a work that combines architecture, design, painting, sculpture, and even music. The cinematic art is rather a complex union of features and elements, some garnered from other, older arts, others generated out of film's own needs, the inventiveness of its creators, and the technology of our age. These form an artistic synthesis that, through the extraordinary ability of film to shape the conditions and contents of perceptual actuality, is able to constitute worlds in all their rich ambiguity of location, scope, and meaning. The cinematic sphere is so comprehensive, so persuasive, and so powerful that it easily displaces the apparent reality of everyday life and seduces us into entering its own domain as silent yet active participants. When it succeeds in drawing us fully into its perceptual universe, film becomes an art of total engagement.

CHAPTER NINE

*The
realities
of
art*

IN AN EXHIBITION IN THE MID-1980s AT THE POMPIDOU CENTER IN Paris, the philosopher J.-F. Lyotard attempted to show how our postmodern sensibility cannot allow us to accept the world simply as it is perceived. Reality, he holds, has become transformed into a complex and infinite network of meanings and codes, so that the appearances of our modern world offer only uncertain and unstable messages. These infinitely complex "immaterials" underlie and subvert the realities of our time, and the only recourse for perception and imagination, overwhelmed by the transformation of reality into elusive and indeterminable meanings, is to the concept of the sublime. This contrasts sharply with Kant, for whom the sublime lay in our response to the inability of our imagination to accommodate the size or might of nature. For Kant this led imagination from admiration for nature's power and grandeur back to confidence in reason and to the superiority of human moral dignity.[1] The rational indeterminacy of deconstruction, however, ends by diminishing both nature and human reason. We have come a long distance from Kant to this intimidation of meanings.

There is something distinctly anaesthetic in this displacement of perception by intellect, a sign, perhaps, of their unhappy inversion. Is it a symptom of our own inability to grasp the bizarre, self-created magnitudes of our mass world that the sublime has itself been trans-formed from an affirmation of natural grandeur and human worth into an involuted consciousness overwhelmed by its own inade-quacy? Does not such an approach exhibit its own failure? Perhaps the cycle must now return from rationalism to empiricism, from intellect to experience. Perhaps we must return to the things them-selves, as Husserl advised, to the directness of perception that ante-dates every presupposition, including the existence of objects.

This is no easy advice to follow, for perception itself harbors a history of meanings, as Husserl's own reduction of descriptive con-sciousness to a transcendental ego reveals.[2] Yet accepting the fact that there is no pure perception from which to begin, no Archime-dean starting point for inquiry or knowledge, we must be content at least to explore the regions of direct perception before we have deliberately filtered our experience through the formative influence of the conscious intellect. To this effort art can make a contribution, for in art direct perception achieves its most complete fulfillment.

Yet we cannot entirely escape the burden of thought by turning to aesthetic experience, since meanings are reflected as much in the course of the arts as in our theories of them. Implicit in every phase of artistic change is a mode of perception, and implicit in every mode of perception are presumptions about what experience is, what it means, and what it entails. Moreover, a theory of perception is implicit in every conception of art. So it may be, as I have already suggested, that the history of the arts is more than anything else a history of changes in the way we experience and comprehend our world. The word *experience* is used in this broad sense, because at bottom the meanings of the two terms *perception* and *experience* co-alesce. This diverges from the empiricist tradition in philosophy, which has continually narrowed the purview of experience until for some it has been reduced to pure, isolated elements of sensation. Such a straitening of the term distorts its bond to actual perception by excluding the complexity and range that provide most of its content.[3]

Aesthetics can serve as a corrective to this abridgement of expe-rience. Although its foundation lies in sense perception, the scope of aesthetic experience leads us to extend the domain of perception to include the rich regions of imagination, fantasy, memory, and dream. Perception lives in these provinces, too, and while it assumes differ-ent modalities there, it becomes at times more vivid and full than under more ordinary conditions. Experience must also be broadened to encompass the implicit realms of memory, imagination, and meaning, for the attempts to circumscribe its scope have had the same effects as they have imposed on perception, replacing its vital presence by a pallid experimental object or importing ungrounded assumptions. In fact, all this tampering with the range of perception and experience leads one to wonder about the truth of the usual boundaries between the real and the unreal.

Perceptual experience in its inclusive sense is, of course, central to the arts. In tracing how such experience is fashioned in painting, architecture and environmental design, music, literature, dance, and film, we have found a common structure in an aesthetic field that exhibits similar artistic, objective, appreciative, and performative aspects in all the arts. While some of the structural factors may be more pronounced in certain arts than in others, the isomorphism among them suggests how a response may be framed to some of the troublesome questions regarding the unity and diversity of the arts. At the same time we have discovered that the arts, in shaping their characteristic experiences, employ the very features that constitute the foundation of the human world. All the arts are bound together in their common source in the universal conditions of sensible experience and in the power these extend over the broad expanse of awareness and meaning. Now after having pursued some of the typical and distinctive ways the arts work with their perceptual materials, we can explore their ground more directly. For the study of aesthetic perception not only reveals a continuity among the many arts but lays bare the very foundations of the human world itself. We begin to realize that aesthetic theory is bound to metaphysics. But this is a query that may best be pursued indirectly.

Is it any longer possible for us to approach an art with simplicity, to engage it innocently and purely? I do not refer to the untutored eye or the blank mind, impediments, these, and not the liberators they are sometimes thought to be. In fact, such guises of pure perception resemble intellectual myths designed, like the state of nature of seventeenth- and eighteenth-century political theory, to promote a particular conclusion, for we now realize that perception and consciousness are never empty and unintentional. The allusion here is rather to the capacity to enter into the region that art opens to our awareness. What appears when an artist sketches a portrait? Lines?

An image? Something beyond this? What emerges when a flautist breathes a song? A succession of tones? A melody? Yet more? And when a dancer moves with controlled grace about a stage? Gesture? Depiction? Something further? When an architect shapes a structure? And when a poet's metaphor joins images to evoke a new and startling awareness? The aesthetic web is multidimensional.

For the arts reach out in the same act both to a perceptual substratum that underlies their individual processes and to a region that extends beyond them. Every art dwells in its own sphere of experience, and yet it transcends that domain with connections, tenuous or strong, to other regions—the world of practical action, of ordinary objects, of "real" people and places. Ingarden recalls this in describing the shift in perception that occurs when we move from seeing the Venus de Milo as a piece of marble to perceiving it aesthetically as the body of a woman, of the Venus herself.[4] We come to recognize that each art shapes a distinctive world, its own condition of being. Faces emerge from the canvases of Rembrandt, faces of persons who are present in our experience, as well as in the world of their own time and place, and with whom we must come to terms. The tonal realm of Mozart differs from the worlds of Bach, Chopin, and Bartók, as each composer constructs his own distinctive sphere of auditory shapes, of dynamic patterns of tension and release, from the sounds and silences that emerge from human breath and action. Dance takes the movements of the body but transforms them into the music of the body, originating and energizing space–time through gesture and creating a human realm of energies and lines of influence. And the aesthetic transfiguration of environment turns the masses, volumes, and empty spaces of physical structures into complex configurations of bulks, surfaces, and open space whose interacting forces join with their inhabitants in processes of movement and change.

An uneasy dialectic is at work between the realm of art and the world before and beyond art. This provokes an ambiguity of status, which is an experiential counterpart to the interpretive dilemma of deconstruction. Not only may we be unable to determine the true interpretation of a text; we may even be unable to decide on the actual locus of reality. Art can evoke what Ingarden called a "moment of conviction," "a belief that what is represented in the aesthetic object (when it does represent something outside) has a real existence in the world."[5] One can identify different orders of experience, such as religious, erotic, social, playful, and humorous, each of which can claim its own authenticity and yet may at the same time enter into reciprocity with the aesthetic. But it is the capacity of the aesthetic to encourage the shift in awareness, the conviction that comes from full and sustained engagement that is our entry into the realm of art.

Several strata combine, then, in aesthetic engagement: There is our involvement with the individual object or event. There is the perceptual realm of that art from which the particular occasion draws and to whose store of meanings and awareness it contributes. And there are the various regions of experience that lie beyond the aesthetic occasion but that contribute to it in ways that may be subtle or direct, and that introduce the insuppressible issues associated with representation.

These matters return us once again to theory. They require a rephrasing of our understanding of the arts, which we now can no longer grasp naively. Many of the explanations of artistic significance that populate the history of aesthetics try, in one way or another, to connect art with the larger world on the one side, and with the directness and immediacy of foundational experience on the other. This is sometimes expressed as the objective and subjective referents of art, its reference to the art object or to whatever that object may depict, and its effects on sensible or conscious experience. Theories, in fact, have been classified according to such a difference. The distinction, however, is greatly misleading, since it rests on a dualistic division of experience which renders separate what is always continuous. Object, perception, and meaning coalesce in aesthetic engagement.

A similar difference in emphasis between perceptual directness and extended referentiality may also be found among the arts themselves, some stressing the former, others the latter. Arts that tend to reach toward what lies outside are exemplified by portraits, optical art (including the visually magnetic graphic art of Escher), icons (in which, for the believer, the power of the saint portrayed in the icon extends into the room), posters, sculpture, and *trompe l'oeil* painting. Arts that tend to lead one into their own sphere include literature, landscape painting, environmental sculpture, design, architecture, environmental design, music (especially antiphonal and other environmental music), and theater-in-the-round. However, the stress on perception or on reference is a matter of emphasis only, illuminated by the unique qualities that occur in our engagement with different individual arts, and varying still more in the individual case. All the arts lead in both directions.

While it is often said that art offers us entrance to new regions of sensibility and awareness, questions arise when we attempt to determine the kinds of sensory and conscious experience that are germane to the arts and how and what they signify. The history of aesthetics exhibits in large part a continuous effort to answer these questions. The oldest and most persistent theories are those that claim that art should give us a true account of how things are. Imitation, though, is often dismissed as ingenuous: Surely there is more to art than providing a realistic representation of the world. And so other theories have appeared that explain in different ways what art is and does and that thereby determine its peculiar identity. We have had proposals that account for art as the representation of ideal beauty or form, as the expression or communication of emotion, as the symbol or language of feeling, as a distinctive kind of pleasure, as lyrical intuition, or as an ambiguous object dependent on interpretation, to mention some of the best-known theories. In one way or another, a connection is drawn between the art object and our response to it. Even those explanations that find beauty inherent in the forms of visual or auditory qualities value them for their effects on feeling and awareness. Yet whatever their direction or ploy, these are all surrogate theories. Each takes a phase or aspect of the aesthetic situation and its connection with the larger sphere of experience as the basis for a full explanation, yet none provides an inclusive account of the scope of art. Is aesthetics another case of synecdoche masquerading as truth?[6]

Most striking, however, is the fact that, whatever their explanation, these views share the common presupposition that art has some kind of tie with the larger world. It is easiest, of course, to see this in the imitation theories, whose leading idea is that art is not an utterly separate domain but that it reflects the world beyond its borders. This notion persists even when art takes abstract form, for connections are still discovered with the structures and qualities of the larger world. Abstract art "does not thereby cease to be representational," Leo Steinberg writes. "Only the matter that now calls for representation is drawn from a new order of reality. . . . Representation is a central aesthetic function in all art."[7] Even formalist theories acknowledge a bond with the world in the qualities inherent in the artistic medium, which evoke powerful associations with the very sensory material of human life.[8] Subjectivistic theories may also draw connections that extend beyond the art object, but they do so less directly. By operating through the agencies of human feeling, intuition, and psychological perception or communication, or by employing the cognitive media of language or symbol, these theories search regions beyond the object that are suffused with human presence and significance. All these accounts acknowledge the interpenetration art has with different objects, events, and experiences, both personal and cultural.

Art connects in some way, then, with other domains of experience. Yet there is also a sense in which art retains a certain independence of other things. It is not only formalist theories that insist on this: Any acknowledgment of the inherent value of art or of the irreducibility of art and the aesthetic to other kinds of objects and experiences does so as well. The question for this Kantian kind of antinomy is what kind of truth both autonomy and heteronomy retain. How can we reconcile the self-possession of art, its intrinsic significance, with its connections and associations across its borders?

Of the many answers to this question, Suzanne Langer's is especially sensitive to the inherent qualities of the individual arts, while maintaining their link with the world beyond. Art, she holds, possesses the form of living things. It does not *represent* things but embodies the *form* of experience, what life *feels* like. Art does this by constructing forms symbolic of human feeling, forms that inhabit a virtual realm, not the real one.[9] As instances of the first truth, that art is self-contained, the formalism of Eduard Hanslick and Roger Fry is paradigmatic. Hanslick maintained that musical beauty consists solely in the artistic relationships of sounds in melody, harmony, rhythm, and timbre, and that it does not have as its content the representation of specific feelings. "The content of music is tonally moving forms."[10] Similarly, in writing of the visual arts, Fry set aside the likeness of a painting to nature and urged us to consider only the emotional elements of design, such as line, mass, space, light and shadow, and color, and their relationships.[11] For both writers art possesses an intimacy and directness that carry their own authenticity, and the force of this immediacy is the paramount reality. In art the sensibility of the world is irreducible; at the same time, art makes the irreducibility of the world sensible. Artists are, in Marianne Moore's words, "literalists of the imagination."

Yet the problem remains of the relation that both kinds of theories acknowledge holds between art and the so-called real world. To the imitation and symbolic views of art one may respond that art does not mirror or represent actual things and experiences but rather elaborates and enlarges them. And to the formalist position, we may join Fry in admitting that art is never entirely self-contained but causes emotional responses based on our physical and physiological traits.[12] We do not enter the world of art through a special doorway and leave it behind later by simply closing the door after us.

Even when a connection is drawn between art and the world, it is nearly always to the detriment of art. There seems to be a suspicion of aesthetic power, for the vocabulary common in discussions of art recognizes its larger scope and at the same time finds art defective in the face of that range. To speak of art as an illusion ascribes to it a deceptive character, just as when we refer, perhaps even admiringly, to distortions in an artist's representation. Langer's notion of semblance, her realms of virtual time, space, powers, and memory, all harbor the idea of illusion in contrast with what is real. The concept of representation, itself, bespeaks a derivative status in presenting an object again, as do words like *appearance, imitation,* and *reflection,* based as each of them is on a contrast with what is actual. The recognition of deficiency is no less the case when art's difference is described eulogistically as a work of fantasy or imagination, or as possessing the character of dream. These suggest something delightful, evocative, or intriguing, yet all carry the connotation of having little substance and even less credibility when held against the real world of concrete objects and objective events. Even Coleridge's "willing suspension of disbelief" implies the underlying falsity of art. Such cases as these may explain the frustration in Matisse's retort to the viewer who remarked to him disapprovingly that she had never seen a woman who looked like the one in a painting of his: "Madame, that is not a woman; that is a picture."[13]

The tendency to confine art to the realm of the unreal is so deep rooted and well established as to seem unchallengeable. Surely no convention more clearly reflects the obvious than this. Yet a puzzle remains to which this view has no ready answer: If art is only a reflection of reality, if it is dependent on the world beyond its boundaries, if its purview is the imaginative, the fantastic, and the false, where does its power come from? If art is but an illusion, why should we be so troubled by it as to want to control it? And why, moreover, should we be so vulnerable to its touch? The ability of art to push aside the insistence of ordinary things and demand our attention is more than the strength of a dream or the force of imagination. For the history of the arts is also a history of disturbance and suspicion, disturbance from comfortable presuppositions and suspicion of unsettling tendencies. What is the connection of art with our world and our lives that gives it such force?

Perhaps the problem of the inferior status of the artistic order comes from the tendency to hold up the realm of art against the common world outside, to think of this world as the real and objective order of things and to judge art against it. This is surely a misleading comparison, for the modes of being and meaning in art are different. At the same time, however, there are strong ties that bind art to other domains in the larger human sphere. The arts have a bearing on the modes, qualities, and dimensions of the human world, and this underlies its power, however abstract or irrational artistic forms may become.

The differences between what is artistic and what is literal, between imagination and truth, between the aesthetic mode and the ontological order are logical, and they can be elucidated by Spinoza's distinction between substance and attribute. Like substance, human experience has an ontological unity. It is not divided into radically different kinds, as so much of the philosophical tradition seems to maintain by isolating and separating reason, will, feeling, sensation, and purely vegetative or vital awareness; by labeling humans as religious beings or political beings; and by all the divisive dualisms that impose oppositions on the continuity of experience. This unity, however, assumes distinctive patterns, aspects, and perspectives on different occasions and through different activities. Such patterns result from the kind of emphases given to the features of experience that dominate those occasions. They are not, however, inherent in the order of things.[14] As a scholar, for example, one exercises abstractive rational skills, verbal and social skills, and perhaps experimental skills. Yet at the same time one continues to sense, feel, eat, breathe, desire, love, and engage in all the other activities that make up a human life. The structure of a particular mode of experience determines what is germane to the situation and what is not. That order is not fixed in advance but emerges from the activities, conditions, and requirements of the situation, and it can always be redefined. Many recent debates revolve, in fact, around what the proper components of a mode of experience are: whether a scientist has moral responsibility for the kind of uses to which his or her work can be put; what and who may decide the legitimate scope of an individual's self-determination in various contexts—social, sexual, political, economic, biological, moral; and in aesthetic theory, whether art occupies a domain separate from telic activities.

To see art as a mode of activity and experience of its own, then, is not to deny its wider connections with other regions of the human universe. Rather it recognizes the claim for the equal legitimacy of the artistic–aesthetic mode with every other. Only in this way can we begin to understand the extended relationships and continuities of aesthetic with other regional experiences. But these cannot be decided in the abstract. By considering how some of the arts grasp the human world, we may be able to draw certain conclusions about the legitimacy of the aesthetic mode.

WHEN ALICE stepped through the mirror into the looking-glass world, she found things quite different from the world she was accustomed to. For a century readers have entertained themselves by accompanying Alice on her fantastic adventures, and scholars have amused themselves exploring the peculiar logic of the creatures and events she encounters. Alice's experiences did not seem at all logical to her, however, and she found things most confusing and unreasonable, even though everyone she met on her travels regarded them as quite ordinary. Yet Alice couldn't fathom the looking-glass world precisely because she insisted that it conform to her usual expectations of how things are, whereas that world could only be understood according to its own ways.

Perhaps, like Alice, we must learn to see what is *in* literature and not look for what literature is *about*. In the world Alice comes from, her encounters in the looking-glass world would be quite absurd, yet when she goes through the mirror they are not at all odd. There is nothing internally inconsistent about an order of things in which time goes backwards, reversing the sequence of cause and effect so that the White Queen's finger bleeds before it is pricked. Nor is there anything inherently unreasonable about a shop in which you have to find things for yourself (now commonplace), and where the egg Alice buys gets farther away from her the closer she comes to it, while other things turn into trees as she approaches them. Like reversing glasses, we quickly adjust to a world opposite from what we are accustomed to, as long as it exhibits regularity. And of course we now readily accept the idea that words are conventional symbols and so are not at all distressed when Humpty Dumpty wants to reverse the usual practice of assigning general meanings to common nouns and giving names particular referents. It is perfectly plausible (and not that unusual) to let ordinary words mean whatever one wants them to mean, or to follow the practice of taking metaphorical expressions literally, instead of as they are commonly understood or, again, to deny the principle of noncontradiction and allow a hill to be really a valley. Moreover, what is more reasonable in a mirrored world than that all paths should lead back to where you started from or, in a world in constant motion, that you should have to run at breathtaking speed to stay in the same place, so that "if you want to get someplace else, you must run at least twice as fast as that?" Finally, our idea of the regularity of time is clearly illogical to the Red Queen, since in her country days and nights mostly come two or three at a time, and sometimes in the winter they take as many as five nights together "for warmth, you know."[15]

We are very much in Alice's place when we enter the world of literature, for we tend to take ordinary experience as our standard of reality and regard everything that diverges from that standard as less than real. This common-sense attitude is both puzzling and presumptive for, as we have seen, clear divisions are difficult to discern, and the realms of art, like those of dream and fantasy, merge with and sometimes displace the apparent stability and regularity of the ordinary world. Perhaps, like Alice, we must learn to think in unaccustomed ways so that we may discover the unusual logic of the domains of art.

Many writers have recognized, as Kafka did, the ability of art to reveal "a reality which surpasses our conceptual ability."[16] Gaston Bachelard grasps this in a poetic comment on poetic images:

These images [such as of the roundness of being] blot out the world, and they have no past. They do not stem from any earlier experience. We can be quite sure that they are metapsychological. They give us a lesson in solitude. For a brief instant we must take them for ourselves alone. If we take them in their suddenness, we realize that we think of nothing else, that we are entirely in the being of this expression. If we submit to the hypnotic power of such expressions, suddenly we find ourselves entirely in the roundness of this being, we live in the roundness of life, like a walnut that becomes round in its shell.[17]

J. R. R. Tolkien, the master fabulist of our time, recognized the metaphysical capacity of literature in theory as he embodied it in practice.

Any great fantasy must take place in time and space, i.e., a world, and that world must have an internal consistency—the ability to draw a person in and make him one with that world. The writer is a "sub-creator" who must create a world that can be real, because when a world can become real or believable on all levels of consciousness, the reader can experience that world fully as a human being with all the emotions and feeling with which he can experience this world.[18]

Such recourse to imagination may suggest, however, that we have left the ordered logical world of everyday life far behind and have entered a realm of pure fantasy. But these worlds are not so removed from our own more ordinary one: They interpenetrate each other. There is, Bachelard observed, "the immanence of the imaginary in the real."[19] Wallace Stevens meditates on the interplay of reality and imagination, maintaining that they are not opposed but possess a "universal interdependence," which renders them "equal and inseparable." Imagination erupts from the pressure of a new reality, Stevens insists, as the poet abstracts reality by placing it in his imagination. Indeed, he recognizes that imagination and reality are not opposite poles but are so entirely interdependent that they become equal and inseparable. The subject matter of poetry becomes, then, not the objects that exist out in the external world "but the life that is lived in the scene that it composes."

There is, in fact, a world of poetry indistinguishable from the world in which we live or, I ought to say, no doubt, from the world in which we shall come to live, since what makes the poet the potent figure that he is, or was, or ought to be, is that he creates the world to which we turn incessantly and without knowing it and that he gives to life the supreme fictions without which we are unable to conceive of it.[20]

What Ben Jonson observed about literature, "Speak, that I may see thee," a novelist of my acquaintance expressed more directly when he remarked, "Once it is written down, it has already happened."[21]

Apollinaire tells the story of the unusual behavior at an art exhibition of that irrepressible prose speaker, M. Jourdain. "M. Jourdain then turned on a landscape. He charged, running like a madman, but that painting of Cézanne's was not a canvas, it *was* a landscape. [He] dived into it and disappeared over the horizon, because of the fact that the earth is round."[22] The lore of art history, as well as of literature and dance, contains a surprising variety of accounts of the converse of this, of art that comes to life or that oversteps the limits of illusion. Moreover, we find these attempts to evoke the reality in art in many traditions and not just those of the West. In Japanese art, for example, before realistic painting became clearly demarcated from the actual world, a sensibility prevailed that found the continuity between them significant. During the Heian period, however, painting took on a reality of its own, a reality easily considered magical. A typical story concerns the painter Kose no Kanaoka, who had depicted on a palace screen a horse that was said to wander off each night to graze on the flowers Kanaoka had painted on another door. Only after the artist painted a halter on his neck did the horse cease to stray.[23] Many other cultures preserve accounts of works of art that had to be tied down to keep them from moving of their own accord and of artists whose work was so realistic that they had to stop before the final touch to prevent their forms from coming to life, as in the Pygmalion myth in the West.[24] Byzantine and Ethiopian artists, moreover, never portray evil figures like Judas as looking out of the picture for fear that their evil eye may harm the beholder.[25] It is easy to dismiss the belief in the magical power of art as a fanciful exaggeration, but this is a condescending response to a more serious intent.[26]

Representational art is often experienced as more than representation when the distance between image and referent disappears and the two merge into a single identity. Unlike the experience of foolish M. Jourdain, this need not result in a loss of the aesthetic, as Bullough feared it would, but may become a necessity for the aesthetic and indeed, perhaps, its fulfillment. In a recent discussion Arthur Danto seems to acknowledge the insight in this prescientific, perhaps animistic state of things by his distinction between "mere real things" and the "is" of artistic identity. The second of these involves embodiment. Breughel's painting, *The Fall of Icarus*, does not portray Icarus by an image; the image *is* Icarus. Danto cites Barnett Newman's *Stations of the Cross*, a series of fourteen panels that switch in the twelfth panel from a black "zip" (to use Newman's word) on a white ground to a white "zip" on a black ground. This reversal, Danto maintains, does not simply "represent" a change in Christ's character. By understanding that these panels are more than an ordered collection of related abstract canvases but correspond in a general way to the stages of Christ's dreadful ascent up Golgotha, the paintings are transfigured. The interpretive grasp of what the twelfth panel means (it is called *The Death of Christ*) transforms the work in the eyes of the observer. This subtle point about the artistic embodiment of reality is rendered still more elusive when applied to abstract art, yet it becomes there perhaps even more profound. For here we are not speaking of identity achieved through physical resemblance nor even of an identity grasped isomorphically but of an identity apprehended in the most inclusive sense of all, ontologically. "Interpretation," Danto holds, "is the agency of . . . transfiguration."[27]

It is a curious border, this line between image and reality, epistemologically troublesome and aesthetically unstable. Imitation theories of art struggle with the difference, recognizing the connection but striving to maintain the separation, while theories that liken art to a form of play rest on the ambiguity of the boundary. The fact is that art represents a continuing challenge to this division between the real and the illusory because it is unwilling to accept an importance that is merely reflected. Not only does art claim its own reality; it refuses to remain apart from the "real" (read "ordinary") world and stay in its own place. Relinquishing the purity and safety of isolation, the aesthetic mode of experience insists on overstepping the limits imposed from without and intruding into every province of experience and activity.

Painting and sculpture press these claims in visible forms. They render living experiences, creating occasions for us to enter different worlds and encouraging us to engage in them. Toward the end of his life van Gogh did several groups of paintings, each of the same scene but in subtly different tonalities. Unlike Monet's repaintings of the same view, which caught the evanescent quality of light changing the solidity, the very substance of haystacks, the cathedral at Rouen, the town of Vétheuil, and his garden at Giverny, van Gogh's last works are more profound still. They create veritably different realms. The two versions of *Daubigny's Garden* (1890), *Wheatfields* (July 1890), and *The Road Menders* (December 1889) display even more forcefully the peculiar strength found in so much of his work by the striking contrast between the versions. Here is not the insubstantiality, the ephemerality of objects dissolved into sunlight that the Impressionists caught so successfully, but the complete transformation of the character, the very being of those places through the elusive agency of the prevailing tonality. The slight variation in the cast of the coloration between the paintings, visible but indescribable, produces not duplicate scenes or even different interpretations of the same scene: It creates totally different worlds. Perhaps these are the pictorial analogue of the constant transmutation of van Gogh's own disordered reality.[28] They remind one of Klee's comment, "Art does not oppose the visible; rather it makes visible."[29]

Other artists have given powerful example to this trait implicit in all art. Rothko's last works, in which he pared his palette down mostly to a narrow but subtle range of grays, make still more compelling the profound, powerful presence found in his previous work. The evocations of these late works cover a range as wide as did the choice and juxtaposition of the modulated hues of the vague horizontal rectangles in his earlier mature ones. In these final paintings, chromatic warmth and scope are discarded along with bounded forms. The horizontal areas now extend to the edge of the canvas and the elusive distances of the gray fields resolve into the receding spatiality of landscapes. These are not ordinary places, however. One enters metaphysical landscapes of terrifying loneliness, moving through barren realms to approach a horizon line that seems to mark the edge of an abyss.

Instances multiply easily. The magic nets of Eva Hesse's hanging fiberglass cord sculptures generate a field of forces that radiate outward to entangle the viewer. These are strange works that act to magnetize and entrap us in their eerie world. George Segal's sculptures produce an aura of timelessness and anonymity. Because they are not set on a pedestal above us but inhabit the same space as we do, they draw us into their world. We consort with the motionless white plaster figures and can easily sense ourselves joining with them in an introspective, frozen reverie. Even when his works depict a temporal environment, as in *Times Square at Night, The Subway,* and *The Red Light,* the unmoving figures seem transported beyond the urgency of the place. They (and we) almost become sleepwalkers, paled as an urban population is by its frenetic, gaudy setting.

As the traditional territories within the visual arts merge with the larger human environment, these arts change from distinct objects into worlds that assimilate both beholder and image. "This precession of what is upon what one sees and makes seen, of what one sees and makes seen upon what is—this," wrote Merleau-Ponty, "is vision itself." Such a coalescence led him to recognize that "vision encounters, as at a crossroads, all the aspects of Being."[30] If one looks at a painting as a picture of something, it becomes an object. If one experiences it as a presence, it is transmuted into a reality. In his "Reminiscences" Kandinsky gave forceful expression to this idea: "Painting is a thundering collision of different worlds intended to create a new world in and from the struggle with each other, a new world which is the work of art. . . . The creation of works of art is the creation of the world."[31]

We have already discovered the cinematic constitution of reality in the process of shaping time, space, and movement in writing, shooting, and editing a film.[32] But what happens when we go from the film world to the world beyond the movie theater? Can we find the same artistic and perceptual process at work in the environment of daily life? Although the circumstances here may not appear to be as fully under our explicit control, identical factors are at work. For space, time, and movement are the fundamental conditions of all experience, beyond the film as much as within it. In the domain of the everyday world occur the shapes and forms of masses and volumes, the dynamic forces that join and repel them, the sensuous features of surface and texture, the auditory and olfactory qualities that surround and penetrate the conscious body. The same magnetic influences operate in the ordinary world as operate in the worlds of film and the other arts, and an editing process comparable to the cinematic one occurs in the ways we shape and experience the daily environment. What Piaget points out in the child's construction of space—that space results from the organism's interacting with the environment—is true more generally.[33] One cannot speak of the organization of the world we are perceiving apart from our active perception of it.

Thus the ways we organize and act in our spatiotemporal motile world utilize the same processes that we see in film. As the director and technicians select a site and build a set, we construct the physical circumstances of daily life through urban planning, landscape architecture, building and domestic architecture, and interior design. As the script guides the actions and speech of the characters in a film, social roles and conventions, traditional linguistic forms, and the culturally established patterns of practical activity direct our own behavior. As the film editor cuts and chooses his or her materials, we pursue our conscious lives through our choice of activities, selective attention, and fantasizing, dreaming, and other imaginative constructions. And as the viewer cannot remain aloof and removed, so we cannot avoid participating in some fashion in daily life.

This process of physical action and perceptual involvement in constructing the human domain finds remarkable expression in the traditional Japanese concept of *ma*. This richly complex notion brings together space, time, and movement with the individual conditions under which people live and perceive their world, joining these with a sense of the sacredness of place. Unlike the absolute, objectified idea of space and time that the West still retains as the basis of a common "objective" culture, *ma* reflects their continuity. In its most literal meaning, *ma* is the interval between two phenomena. Thus it can be applied equally to what Westerners call spatial and temporal phenomena. As in film, space here is inseparable from the events occurring in it, and so it is conjoined with a temporal process. Similarly, time can be sensed only in connection with movements and spaces. Not only are space and time indivisible; they cannot be abstracted from human perception and participation. In traditional Japanese music, for example, there is no common metronomic beat that guides all the players. The individual musicians each contribute intuitively sensed time patterns, which render the movement of the music subtly differentiated. In another case, living spaces are not concretions of abstract units but rather are inseparable from the traits and taste of their inhabitants as affected by their social class, taste, understanding, and the climate in which they live. *Ma* represents the cultural unity of space, time, and human activity.[34]

Ma, then, articulates the basic process of constituting a human environment. This process lies hidden beneath a surface of objective structures and established divisions, which disguises their origins in the engaged activities of people constructing their world. As with film and the other arts, the environment is the result of the same actions by which we fabricate every reality. What is central to them all is human involvement in a perceptual matrix. Here, through our activities of sensing, moving, acting, and making, we contribute to the formation of a world in which the physical and perceptual are but aspects of the same constructive process. Perhaps understanding this as an artistic/aesthetic activity gives credence to Mondrian's prediction of "the end of art as a thing separated from our surrounding environment, which is the actual plastic reality," and leads us toward his goal of "a surrounding not merely utilitarian or rational but also pure and complete in its beauty."[35]

Thus at the moment when art transcends the opposition between the instrumental and the intrinsic, the aesthetic and the ordinary come together in the larger human sphere. As in the realm of art, everything is both its own particular self and its ties and ramifications with others. Yet this is not an aestheticization of the world but the converse: It is an acknowledgment of the central place of the aesthetic process in the formation of the human domain. In the broadest view, the worlds of art are the arts of the world.

This ambiguity of the real inhabits all the modes and forms of art, and it links in curious ways the worlds that lie both within and beyond art. In the arts we have probed, the same dimensions of our world manifest themselves: space, time, movement, mass, force, factors of interdependence and of continuity. Some of these dimensions assume an apparent preeminence in certain arts—space in painting, movement and mass in architecture and environment, temporality and force in music, the imaginative construction of place and historical time in literature, the generation and embodiment of the spatial and temporal conditions of the human world through the movements of dance, the shaping of a total perceptual realm in film. But these dimensions, we now know, are not peculiar to certain arts; all of them are active aspects of the creative synthesis that occurs in every artistic realm, indeed in every order of being.

These explorations of the ontological order of literature, painting, film, and environment only begin the process of discovering the realities of the aesthetic realm. They both exemplify and confirm from the standpoint of the arts Buchler's principle of ontological parity, by which no order can claim greater authenticity than any other.[36] All are equally real, and art, as an important domain of the human universe, possesses its own inherent legitimacy. Yet that universe does not come in layers or compartments. Distinguishable modalities of experience are nonetheless continuous with others, and this is surely true of the aesthetic. The constant interplay between the aesthetic and other modes of the human realm, such as the practical, the social, and the moral, threatens many common convictions and issues. The belief in the autonomy of art, the puzzles over representation in the arts, and the defense of the artist's freedom to engage in cultural and political criticism are only a few of the conventional ideas prevalent in modern aesthetics that begin to fall away or require radical restructuring. It does not illuminate the meaning of art or enhance the significance of the aesthetic to isolate them in an exclusive realm. Besides being false in fact, this isolation serves ultimately to weaken the aesthetic sphere and to question the equal standing of art with the other domains of human culture.

Yet the ontological parity of art has still another implication. It recognizes that the contribution the appreciator makes to the completion, indeed to the very actuality of the aesthetic field, does not diminish the meaning or importance of art. Although art can no longer be identified with objects like paintings, sculptures, poems, and novels, it does not thereby become less genuine or important.[37] We have, in fact, not so much an ontology of the work of art as a metaphysics of aesthetic experience. Nor is the realm of art less real than any other by not being objective, absolute, or eternal. Such an impersonal and independent status we now recognize as both unnecessary and impossible in any human enterprise, scientific, practical, or moral, as well as aesthetic. But the personal contribution to art is constitutive to a degree greater than in most other domains of experience, and that is why perceptual participation is so crucial a factor here. Aesthetic engagement is the very condition of art and aesthetic reality its ultimate achievement.

CHAPTER TEN

Epilogue:
*art and
the end
of
aesthetics*

PURSUING THE COURSE AND SIGNIFICANCE OF ART IN EXPERIENCE, history, and theory has led us beyond aesthetics proper into regions of philosophical query that we have only begun to probe. Yet the connections of aesthetics with other domains of philosophy are not casual, and there are unusual insights to be found here. Strong bonds tie aesthetics with epistemological and metaphysical inquiry, since taking experience as foundational leads to common or related concepts and structures. There are ethical and social implications, as well, carefully excised though they were during the eighteenth century, for normative experience is pervasive and knows no disciplinary boundaries. These connections must come as no surprise, in spite of the tendency of modern aesthetics to build barriers against the incursions of political uses, social conventions, moral orthodoxies, and cognitive significance, and to protect the arts from the leveling threats of ignorance and insensibility.

The arts do not gain, however, by remaining aloof and unsullied. Nor, in fact, have they ever really stood apart from the commerce of culture, in spite of efforts to insulate them. To recognize the social context in the creation, appreciation, and use of the arts is to strengthen their importance and their powers, not weaken them. And grasping the wider scope of the aesthetic makes it all the more important that we understand its workings better. Part of this consists in realizing that aesthetic theory is not intellectually derivative or subsumed under philosophical disciplines mistakenly considered more basic. It also means repudiating the tendency to regard the arts as an inessential adjunct to practical studies. Education has not dealt kindly with the arts, nor has philosophy with aesthetics.

It may, in fact, be more enlightening to reverse the conventional order of influence and consider instead the implications of aesthetics for social and philosophic thought in general. For the phenomena of aesthetics reach to the very source of perception and meaning in direct experience, and thus they become in some sense foundational. While there is no truly primary experience, no "given," so to speak, the arts bring us closer than any other social form to the immediacy of the human world as we live it. It may then truly follow that "the philosophy of art is the *heart* of philosophy."[1]

Like the fundamental axioms of metaphysical systems, the basic concepts of aesthetics do not lend themselves to logical demonstration. At the start of a primary inquiry we can only establish methods of proof, not utilize them. What we have discovered here, then, is more the result of recognition than of logical demonstration. The capacity for aesthetic recognition reminds one of Plato's doctrine of *anamnesis*, which sees learning as a process of recollecting what we once before knew but which has since become obscured by subsequent experience and cultural overlay. These discussions of the aesthetic in theory, art, and experience, then, are not intended to decree how one must come to the domain of the arts nor to insist peremptorily that all appreciation be participatory. My purpose has rather been to demolish the conceptual barriers erected by a limiting tradition in the Western world of some two centuries duration and to disclose the condition of engagement that has always been present when our aesthetic encounters have been most effective and fulfilling.

All kinds of forces have obstructed this kind of experience, however, for by its directness and vitality it undermines the legitimacy of institutions that seek to substitute their "truths" for the immediacy of our own experience. Yet the fatal weakness of such authorities lies in the same place as their power, the fact that they are removed from direct experience and mediated instead by social institutions and prohibitions. Their claims to legitimacy are therefore structural, while the arts, in contrast, carry their claim to authenticity solely in themselves. For art is in some sense always Dionysian. It has an intoxicating power, a strength that turns its back on safe conventionality, bypassing the restraints of reflection and insisting on its own genuineness. In an age pervaded by irrationalisms, from drugs to deities, from terrorism of the gun to terrorism of the mind, the artist is the ultimate anarchist, offering to save us from all such solutions by returning us, with gratuitous benevolence, to our own essential and free place in the human world.

We come, then, not so much to the end of art as we have known it, as to the end of aesthetics as we have learned it.[2] What can replace the aesthetic tradition of the last two hundred years? A revision, it may be, of both the theory of the past and the theory of the future. We need to investigate the forms and contribution of the aesthetic dimension of experience in non-Western and pre-literate cultures. We need a renewed inquiry into earlier periods of our own tradition, pursuing the insights concealed in such ideas as *catharsis* and *mimēsis*, notions that suggest participation in the arts and their connection with other domains. We need a new guiding theory, an aesthetics that will expand its traditional vision and enlarge its goals. Fresh concepts are required that help explain art and the aesthetic without legislating what they must be and without co-opting them to serve other purposes. We must learn to look at the domain of the arts without preconceptions about what they must show, do, or mean. And we must develop an understanding of aesthetic activities that rests on the arts and their experiences and not on external standards such as official policies or epistemological and metaphysical presuppositions.

The rewriting of aesthetic theory is not a task for a lone scholar. It requires the distinctive insights, experiences, and imagination of everyone who seeks to understand the aesthetic field. Such a collaboration joins aesthetics with the other cultural studies by which we attempt to illumine the human world, this tiny point in cosmic space–time that we inhabit. Art history, the psychology of art, music history, the sociology of art, dance history, the criticism and theory of the various fine and popular arts, cultural anthropology, intellectual and cultural history, as well as philosophy—these are some of the disciplines that can contribute to aesthetic inquiry. Approaching aesthetics in this way leaves it open in all directions: open to relevant information from the sciences, physical as well as human, open theoretically to revision and reformulation, and above all, open to the data of our experiences in the arts, experiences that never duplicate each other and are never entirely predictable.[3]

This book has attempted to carry forward such an effort by developing and documenting a framework for aesthetic inquiry free from the restrictive ideas of the recent past. Its underlying principle is that aesthetic activity is a unified process that conjoins the distinguishable aspects of art and aesthetic appreciation into an inseparable experiential whole. This has led us to identify aesthetic engagement as both the common feature of aesthetic experience and as the factor whose theoretical significance is most fundamental. The four dimensions of the aesthetic situation or field that have emerged—creation, object, appreciation, and performance—occur not as things or as people but rather as functionally interdependent aspects of a unified occasion.[4] In the directness and eloquence of such experience lies the identity and the power of art.

The idea of aesthetic engagement, grounded on theory, on history, and on its preeminent place in the modern arts, supplied the basis for this journey of discovery through a number of individual arts. Each art exemplified at least one basic dimension of the aesthetic field, and we have seen how the idea of engagement enriches our understanding of that aspect and makes our awareness more vivid. Landscape painting exhibits some ways in which the art object demands our active perceptual participation in order to be realized. Architecture and environmental design document the role played by structures and places as fields of forces that engage the inhabitant in a reciprocal relation of activity and response. Literature exemplifies how the appreciative reader joins with the written word to complete a literary experience. Music reveals artistic creation as a generative process, which both performer and audience share with the composer. Dance offers a focus on performance so complete that it draws choreographer, dancer, and viewer equally into the process of originating a human present. While each of these arts was chosen to represent a particular feature of aesthetic experience, all these dimensions are present in every art. At the same time, the ways in which they occur vary with the characteristics of the art form and the distinctive traits of every aesthetic occasion. Finally, film fulfills most forcefully a metaphysical capacity inherent in all the arts. By utilizing a medium that shapes the total conditions of experience, film entices us into an all-encompassing realm, an order of reality that exists only through our active perceptual engagement. Together, the various discussions in this book offer both theoretical and empirical support for the idea of aesthetic engagement.

Art, then, is one answer to the skepticism of intellect that has bewildered our time. In the directness and immediacy of aesthetic experience, art precedes reflective judgment and so forestalls the difficulties and indeterminacies of philosophy and science. This is not a strategy of avoidance or a tactic of delay. While recognizing that the idol of certainty is a false god, the quest for understanding is a legitimate human need, which art neither replaces nor subverts. What we find in the particular arts and in aesthetic experience more generally is something that is different yet necessary, at the same time a truth of experience and a touchstone for the truths of knowledge. Recognizing this undermines the practice still common among philosophers to judge art by the standard of scientific knowledge and thereby to find it wanting. Intellectualizing art risks making sows' ears out of silk purses.[5]

We might, in fact, invert the usual order of subsumption. When the aesthetic becomes the criterion of authenticity, science finds a rightful place as a powerful force in its own sphere, a sphere that is, however, but a single sector of the larger universe of experience. Recognizing the inseparability of the knower from the known has culminated in an epistemological revolution in which, even in science, presumably the most objective of disciplines, the investigator not only cannot be excluded from the knowledge process but becomes a necessary factor in determining the very nature of its product.[6] Indeed, as a model of engaged experience, perhaps the most effective one, the aesthetic may well serve as a model for science.

Aesthetics can become, then, both a standard for the cognitive enterprise and the occasion for returning cognition to normative and consummatory experience in all its uniqueness and incommensurability. The study of aesthetics reaffirms human participation in the natural and cultural world. And it realizes the influence of engagement both on direct perceptual experience and on the creative interplay of the arts within the larger culture. While there are universes of understanding to discover here, we have no rigid frame, no universal criterion, no final answer. It is with proper humility, then, that aesthetics should end, as philosophy began, in wonder.

NOTES

CHAPTER ONE

1. See Frank Sibley, "Aesthetic Concepts," in Joseph Margolis, ed., *Philosophy Looks at the Arts* (New York: Scribner's, 1962), pp. 63–87.

2. In *The Book of the Courtier* (1528), for example, the Italian Renaissance nobleman Count Baldassare Castiglione grouped in undifferentiated order such activities as the appreciation of poetry, music, and painting with fencing, horseback riding, the collection of coins, medals, and natural curiosities, and classical learning. The classic account of the historical coalescence of the various arts into a stable group of fine arts composed of painting, sculpture, architecture, music, and poetry is Paul Oskar Kristeller's essay, "The Modern System of the Arts," in his *Renaissance Thought*, vol. 2 (New York: Harper & Row, 1965), pp. 207, 222–23, 225.

3. The brief account of the emergence of modern aesthetics that follows here summarizes part of my developed study in "The Historicity of Aesthetics, I," *British Journal of Aesthetics*, 26, no. 2: 101–11, and in "The Eighteenth Century Assumptions of Analytic Aesthetics," in V. Tejera and T. Lavine, eds., *History and Anti-History in Philosophy* (Dordrech, The Netherlands: Kulwer, 1989), pp. 256–74 (used by permission of Kluwer Academic Publishers). How the notion of disinterestedness arose to denote a special kind of attention, how it was disentangled from moral considerations of ends and consequences, and how it became established as the central trait of the aesthetic attitude are questions that have attracted continuing attention.

The seminal discussion of the historical emergence of aesthetic disinterestedness is Jerome Stolnitz's, "On the Origin of 'Aesthetic Disinterestedness,'" *Journal of Aesthetics and Art Criticism* 20, no. 2: 131–43. More recent scholarship has contested Stolnitz's claim that a clear sense of "aesthetic disinterestedness" can be found as far back as Shaftesbury. Saisselin detects the notion earlier in the French Enlightenment, while Townsend finds it entangled with the sense of 'experience,' showing no steady evolution but developing gropingly in the Earl of Shaftesbury, Francis Hutcheson, and the Scottish Enlightenment writers, and finally emerging in its modern sense at the end of the eighteenth century in Kant. See Remy Saisselin, "A Second Note on Eighteenth Century 'Aesthetic Disinterestedness,'" *Journal of Aesthetics and Art Criticism* 21, no. 2: 209; Dabney Townsend, "From Shaftesbury to Kant," *Journal of the History of Ideas*, 48: 2; and "Archibald Alison: Aesthetic Experience and Emotion," *British Journal of Aesthetics* 28, no. 2: 132–44. Attention to this important period in the history of modern aesthetics continues also in the work of George Dickie, Peter Kivy, Stephanie Ross, Noël Carroll, and Ted Cohen, among others.

4. Anthony, Earl of Shaftesbury, *Characteristics of Men, Manners, Opinions, Times* (1711) (New York, 1900), vol. 1, p. 94; vol. 2, pp. 136–37, 130–31. Shaftesbury, "A Notion of the Historical Draught or Tablature of the Judgment of Hercules" (1712), quoted in Michael Fried, *Absorption and Theatricality* (Berkeley: University of California Press, 1980), p. 89.

5. Francis Hutcheson, *An Inquiry into the Origin of Our Ideas of Beauty and Virtue* (1725) (3rd ed.; London, 1729), sect. 2, paras. 1, 3.

6. Thomas Reid, *On the Intellectual Powers of Man* (1785), "Of Beauty."

7. Immanuel Kant, *Critique of Judgment* (1790), sects. 43, 45.

8. Kant, *Critique of Judgment,* sect. 5. Further, when Kant describes taste as universal (sects. 6–9), he frames his view within the cognitivist tradition that has dominated Western thought since classical times.

9. Kant, *Critique of Judgment,* sects. 11, 16. Kant, of course, was himself not as exclusive as this account may suggest, for he distinguished between pure and impure judgments of taste and admitted a relationship between the arts and culture. However, Kant's enormous and continuing influence, like that of most seminal thinkers, derives from a selective and therefore unbalanced interpretation of his theory. The descendants of a theoretical giant are frequently more orthodox than the originator. It appears, furthermore, that this tendency toward enshrining disinterested perception as peculiarly aesthetic was not consistently or universally maintained at the time it was being formulated. See Fried, *Absorption and Theatricality,* pp. 103, 104, 131–32.

10. Hugo Münsterberg, *The Principles of Art Education* (1905), see Calogero's more recent description of the aesthetic attitude as "lyrical equi-

librium" in Max Rieser, "The Aesthetics of Guido Calogero," *Journal of Aesthetics and Art Criticism* 30, no. 1: 19–26.

11. Edward Bullough, " 'Psychical Distance' as a Factor in Art and an Esthetic Principle," *British Journal of Psychology* 5 (1913); reprinted in Melvin Rader, ed., *A Modern Book of Esthetics,* 3rd ed. (New York: Holt, Rinehart & Winston, 1960), pp. 394–411. José Ortega y Gasset, *The Dehumanization of Art* (Garden City, N.Y.: Doubleday, 1956).

12. Jerome Stolnitz, *Aesthetics and Philosophy of Art Criticism* (Boston: Houghton Mifflin, 1960), p. 35.

13. See Maurice de Wulf, *Philosophy and Civilization in the Middle Ages* (Princeton, 1922), p. 28.

14. It is obvious that any general statement (this one included) must be qualified in particular cases. The history of aesthetics, like the history of art, indeed like any history, includes such variety as to provide exceptions to any generalization. However, the task of historical review (and, in fact, the reason for its constant revision) is to identify from the ever-changing perspective of the present the dominant influences and trends that have shaped the course of things. That is part of the purpose of this chapter.

15. John Locke, *Essay Concerning Human Understanding,* bk. 2, chap. 1, sects. 2, 3. George Berkeley, *Principles of Human Knowledge,* pt. 1, sect. 1. David Hume, *An Inquiry Concerning Human Understanding,* sect. 2.

16. Henri Bergson, *An Introduction to Metaphysics* (Indianapolis: Bobbs-Merrill, 1955), pp. 21ff.

17. Theodor Lipps, *Asthetik,* 2 vols. (1903–1906); 2nd ed. (1914–1920). See "Empathy and Abstraction," in Rader, *A Modern Book of Esthetics,* pp. 376, 379.

18. John Dewey, *Art as Experience* (New York: Minton, Balch, 1934), pp. 15, 25.

19. Maurice Merleau-Ponty, "The Primacy of Perception," and "Eye and Mind," both in J. M. Edie, ed., *The Primacy of Perception* (Evanston, Ill.: Northwestern University Press, 1964), pp. 16, 164.

20. Mikel Dufrenne, *The Phenomenology of Aesthetic Experience,* trans. E. Casey et al. (Evanston, Ill.: Northwestern University Press, 1973), pp. 51, 205, 71, 218, 219, 56, 55.

21. Ibid., p. 232.

22. The history of appreciation stands independent of the history of the theory of appreciation, and it is likely that doctrines of disinterestedness have been more influential in academic circles than in artistic ones.

23. If the axioms are inadequate in any important instance, they are inadequate in general. Moreover, these developments cannot be dismissed merely as exceptions to the rule since, for universal claims, exceptions are contradictions.

24. Quoted in Annie Dillard, *Living by Fiction* (New York: Harper & Row, 1982), pp. 28–29.

25. Ibid., p. 176.

26. Collection of the Guggenheim Museum, New York, New York.

27. Danto regards the essential place of interpretation in such art as the final stage in the transformation of art into philosophy and thus the end of its history. This provocative thesis animates much of his work. See Arthur C. Danto, *The Transfiguration of the Commonplace* (Cambridge: Harvard University Press, 1981), and *The Philosophical Disenfranchisement of Art* (New York: Columbia University Press, 1986).

28. See André Breton, "Lighthouse of the Bride," in Robert Lebel, ed., *Marcel Duchamp* (New York, 1959), p. 92; and William S. Rubin, *Dada, Surrealism and Their Heritage*, exhibition catalog (New York: Museum of Modern Art, 1968), pp. 19–21. See also Katherine S. Dreier and Matta Echaurren, *Duchamp's Glass: An Analytical Reflection* (New York, 1944); and Arturo Schwarz, *The Large Glass and Related Works* (Milan, 1967).

29. Collection of the Philadelphia Museum of Art, Philadelphia, Pa.

30. Ursula Meyer, ed., *Conceptual Art* (New York: E.P. Dutton, 1972), pp. 2–7, 174–79.

31. See Allan Kaprow, *Assemblage, Environments and Happenings* (New York: Abrams, 1966), pp. 195–98.

32. Samuel Beckett, *Waiting for Godot* (New York: Grove Press, 1954), p. 10. Quoted by permission.

33. Quoted in Walter Kerr, "What If Cain Did Not Know *How* to Kill Abel?," *New York Times,* 9 February 1969, sec. 2, p. 1.

34. Alain Robbe-Grillet, "New Novel, New Man," in *For a New Novel* (New York: Grove Press, 1965), p. 137.

35. Alain Robbe-Grillet, *The Voyeur* (New York: Grove Press, 1958).

36. Ralph Manheim, in "Preface" to Louis-Ferdinand Céline, *Death on the Installment Plan* (New York: New American Library Signet, 1966), p. vii.

37. Dillard's *Living by Fiction* traces such features as I have been treating here through the landscape of contemporary fiction.

CHAPTER TWO

1. This discussion derives in part from the suggestive observations of Lewis Mumford. See his *Technics and Civilization* (New York, 1934).

2. A good example of the provocative flights in this direction is Edward Rothstein's "Making-Believe Crazy," *New Republic,* 25 August 1986, pp. 28–29.

3. See J. P. Hodin, "The Aesthetics of Modern Art," *Journal of Aesthetics and Art Criticism* 2, no. 2: 184–85.

4. See my essay, "The Sensuous and the Sensual in Aesthetics," *Journal of Aesthetics and Art Criticism* 23, no. 2: 185–92.

5. One notable example is Gerald Arpino's ballet *Astarte* as performed by the Joffrey Ballet, which blasted rock music and directed flashing lights at the audience to help create an ecstatic occasion. Another is Pierre Boulez's work, *Répons*, in which the conductor is surrounded first by six soloists, behind each of whom is an amplifier, which produces an electronically modified echo of his playing, then by more distant performers, and finally by the audience, behind which speakers are positioned. The recent interest in environmental music has its origins at least as far back as the Venetian Renaissance in the antiphonal brass choirs of Andrea and Giovanni Gabrieli.

6. John Cage has noted that pop art takes its style and subject matter from the world of commerce and advertising, a setting devoted to making one go out and buy, and disengages such material from this context. The practical claim persists here, and pop art derives its satirical relevance from this.

7. "The obligation—the morality, if you wish—of all the arts today," Cage has observed, "is to intensify, alter perceptual awareness and, hence, consciousness. Awareness and consciousness of what? Of the real material world. Of the things we see and hear and taste and touch." "We Don't Any Longer Know Who I Was," an interview with Cage, *New York Times*, 16 March 1968, p. D9. See "An Interview with John Cage," *Tulane Drama Review* 10 (Winter 1965): 66.

8. See Walter Kerr, "The Theater of Say It! Show It! What Is It!" *New York Times Magazine*, 1 September 1968, p. 10f.

9. Jerome Stolnitz characterizes these innovations as a kind of childish self-indulgence in the "The Artistic and the Aesthetics 'In Interesting Times,'" *Journal of Aesthetics and Art Criticism* 35, no. 4: 411, 412.

10. Morris Berman resurrects the history of this tradition in science and discerns its current force and meaning in *The Reenchantment of the World* (Ithaca: Cornell University Press, 1981).

11. The actress Mercedes McCambridge expressed the same idea speaking of radio drama: "I am a member of a team, and the other person of the team is the person listening," in an interview on "All Things Considered," National Public Radio, 14 December 1983.

12. In *Overlay* (New York: Pantheon, 1983), Lucy R. Lippard describes in detail many ancient sites of earth and stone work and discusses their social and cosmic significance, as well as the recent work of artists inspired by them.

13. The continuities of art and the aesthetic are a major theme of John Dewey's *Art as Experience* (New York: Minton, Balch, 1934), pp. 230–32.

14. See D. W. Gotschalk, *Art and the Social Order* (New York: Dover, 1962). See also Arnold Berleant, *The Aesthetic Field: A Phenomenology of Aesthetic Experience* (Springfield, Ill.: Charles C Thomas, 1970), which is a systematic attempt to develop a contextualist aesthetic along the lines sketched out here.

15. From "Theory," in *The Collected Poems of Wallace Stevens* (New York: Vintage, 1982), p. 86.

CHAPTER THREE

1. See Chapter One.

2. Max J. Friedländer, *Landscape, Portrait, Still-Life* (New York: Schocken, 1963), p. 12.

3. The contribution of the viewer to painting is a major thesis of E. H. Gombrich's influential book, *Art and Illusion,* 2d ed. (New York: Pantheon/ Bollingen Foundation, 1961). See "Part Three: The Beholder's Share," and *passim.*

4. See page 13.

5. However, landscape painting was well established by the fourth century in the Far East.

6. Friedländer, *Landscape, Portrait, Still-Life,* p. 16.

7. Leon Battista Alberti, *Della pittura* (1436).

8. In *The Perception of the Visual World,* James J. Gibson identifies no fewer than thirteen types of perspective (Boston: Houghton Mifflin, 1950).

9. Milič Čapek, *Philosophical Impact of Contemporary Physics* (Princeton: Van Nostrand, 1961), pp. 176, 161.

10. This account of the relativistic position in physics goes beyond what Einstein himself proposed. Einstein continued to subscribe to the conventional belief in the impersonal character of the world and the insignificance of the observer, considering his theory to be about the covariance of content and the space–time frame. If we regard the observer, however, as a body possessing gravitational mass and not as a disembodied mind, then there is a change in the curvature of space–time that is brought about by the presence of the observer. This is Čapek's "fused dynamical reality," and it is the beginning, not the extent, of the reciprocity between perceiver and perceived.

11. Necker cubes are optical illusions in the form of two-dimensional outline drawings of transparent three-dimensional cubes. The cubes are angled so that they may be seen as occupying different positions, depending on how the perceiver identifies their planes. Examples may be found in Don Ihde, *Experimental Phenomenology* (New York: Putnam, 1977). The Ames room is a classic experimental room in transactional psychological research. It is built with converging side walls, floor, and ceiling. A person inside, who

is viewed through a window opening, appears to increase or decrease sharply in size while walking from one end of the room to the other. See Hilde Hein, *The Explorations* (Washington, D.C.: Smithsonian Institution Press, 1990), pp. 76–77 and illus.

12. See note 22.

13. See Patrick A. Heelan, *Space-Perception and the Philosophy of Science* (Berkeley: University of California Press, 1983), pp. 28–35, 44, 72.

14. In his persuasive arguments for the hermeneutical nature of scientific knowledge, Patrick Heelan employs the "anthropic principle," which holds that human beings are the determining and interpreting factor concerning the cosmos. Although Heelan recognizes that a certain family of Riemannian geometries can characterize the spatial structures we perceive in our visual environment, visual space reflects Aristotelian geometrical models. These acknowledge that real space is perceived as finite and that there is a qualitative perceptual difference between close and distant space, although the observer is central in both. Patrick Heelan, "Science, Art, and Hermeneutics," Paper delivered at the conference, For Interpretation—Hermeneutics Across Disciplines, at Adelphi University, 4 April 1986. See Heelan's *Space-Perception and the Philosophy of Science;* see also John D. Barrow and Frank J. Tipler, *The Anthropic Cosmological Principle* (New York: Oxford University Press, 1986).

15. Edmund Husserl, *Cartesian Meditations* (1931) (The Hague: Nijhoff, 1960), pp. 21, 33.

16. Maurice Merleau-Ponty, "Eye and Mind," in J. M. Edie, ed., *The Primacy of Perception and Other Essays* (Evanston, Ill.: Northwestern University Press, 1964), p. 176.

17. Maurice Merleau-Ponty, *The Phenomenology of Perception* (London: Routledge and Kegan Paul, 1962), pp. 267, 265, 266, 329.

18. Merleau-Ponty, "Eye and Mind," pp. 176, 178, 180.

19. Friedländer, *Landscape, Portrait, Still-Life,* pp. 19, 26.

20. Alberti, *Della pittura.*

21. *Webster's New World Dictionary,* 1959, College Ed., S.V. "Landscape."

22. In "Perception of Perspective Pictorial Space from Different Viewing Points" *Leonardo* 10, no. 4: 283–88, Rudolf Arnheim illustrates the tendencies (1) to allow the geometry of perception to dominate the phenomena of perception (pp. 286/1, 287/1) and (2) to objectify the spatial object so that it is disparate from the viewer's space.

23. Collection of the Hirshhorn Museum and Sculpture Garden, Smithsonian Institution, Washington, D.C.

24. Collection of The New York Public Library, New York, New York.

25. Collection of the New-York Historical Society, New York, New York.

26. Jean-Paul Sartre, *Essays in Aesthetics* (New York: Philosophical Library, 1963), pp. 66–67 (my italics).

27. Collection of the Metropolitan Museum of Art, New York, New York.

28. Henry James, *The Ambassadors* (Boston: Houghton Mifflin, 1960), bk. 11, chap. 3, pp. 318–23.

29. Wassily Kandinsky, "Reminiscences," in R. L. Herbert, ed., *Modern Artists on Art* (Englewood Cliffs, N.J.: Prentice-Hall, 1964), p. 31.

30. Vredeman de Vries, *Perspective* (1604/1605) (New York: Dover, 1968), pt. 1, plate 30.

31. James J. Gibson, *The Perception of the Visual World* (Boston: Houghton Mifflin, 1950).

32. As Michael Kubovy describes it, "perspective is robust in the face of changing vantage points." *The Psychology of Perspective and Renaissance Art* (Cambridge: Cambridge University Press, 1986), p. 103.

33. Merleau-Ponty, *Phenomenology of Perception,* 325.

34. Both van Ruisdael's *A Forest Marsh* and Guardi's *Landscape* are in the collection of The Hermitage, Leningrad.

35. E. C. Goosan, "The Big Canvas," in G. Battcock, ed., *The New Art* (New York: Dutton, 1973), pp. 63, 65.

36. The Frick Collection, New York, New York.

37. Collection of the Metropolitan Museum of Art, New York, New York.

38. Kuo Hsi, "An Essay on Landscape Painting," in Lionel Giles, ed., *The Spirit of the Brush* (London: John Murray, 1906).

39. Sherman E. Lee, *Chinese Landscape Painting,* rev. ed. (New York: Harper & Row, 1971), p. 18. See also "Roman Art," in Harold Osborne, ed., *Oxford Companion to Art* (Oxford: Clarendon, 1970), p. 999.

40. Michael Fried regards both conceptions as overcoming the estrangement of the beholder from the scene being regarded. See Fried, *Absorption and Theatricality,* pp. 103, 104, 131–32. In an ongoing series of studies of Courbet, Fried carries forward the theme of the presence of the beholder in certain of his paintings by means of the space the artist has provided. See Fried, "The Beholder in Courbet: His Early Self-Portraits and Their Place in His Art," *Glyph* 4 (1978); and "The Structure of Beholding in Courbet's *Burial at Ornans*," *Critical Inquiry* 9 (1983).

In *Painting as an Art* (Princeton: Princeton University Press, 1987), Richard Wollheim develops an elaborate case for the claim that the spectator's experience of a painting, while a single experience, has two aspects. On the one hand, the beholder is aware of the surface of the painting. On the other, one can engage in what Wollheim calls "seeing-in," which precedes representation. This is a kind of direct access to the picture's content, at times through the presence of an internal spectator, at other times by centrally imagining oneself as such a spectator and even becoming an agent in the painting (pp. 44, 46, 47, 129, 160–64).

41. E. H. Gombrich emphasizes "the beholder's share" in viewing a portrait. See "The Mask and the Face: The Perception of Physiognomic Likeness in Life and in Art," in M. Mandelbaum, ed., *Art, Perception, and Reality* (Baltimore: Johns Hopkins University Press, 1972), p. 17. See also David Carrier, "Art and Its Spectators," *Journal of Aesthetics and Art Criticism* 45, no. 1: 5–17; and my reply, "Does Art Have a Spectator?" *Journal of Aesthetics and Art Criticism* 45, no. 4: 411–12.

42. I am indebted to the late painter and art historian Palko Lukács for this example.

43. Donald Posner, "Caravaggio's Homo Erotic Early Works," *Art Quarterly* (1971):11, 24, 26.

44. See the discussion of active perception in both portrait and landscape in Edward Hall, *The Hidden Dimension* (Garden City, N.Y.: Doubleday, 1966), chap. 7.

45. Friedländer, *Landscape, Portrait, Still-Life*, pp. 14, 149.

46. Erwin Straus, *The Primary World of the Senses* (1935) (Glencoe, Ill.: Free Press, 1963), p. 322.

47. Georges Braque, in an interview with Jacques Lassaigne, 1961. Braque continues, "Instead of starting with the foreground I always began with the center of the picture. Before long I even turned perspective inside out and turned the pyramid of forms upside down *so that it came forward to meet the observer*" (my italics). Quoted in the catalogue for the exhibition, *Les Cubistes*, Galerie des Beaux-Arts, Bordeaux, 1973. See Suzi Gabelik, *Progress in Art* (New York: Rizzoli, 1977), pp. 81–82. The unnamed final quotation is from William Butler Yeats, *Essays and Introductions* (New York: Macmillan, 1961), p. 159.

CHAPTER FOUR

1. J. B. Jackson, "Landscape as Theater," *Landscape* 23, no. 1 (1979): 3–7.

2. Heidegger enlarges on this phrase from Hölderlin in Martin Heidegger, *Poetry, Language, Thought*, trans. Albert Hofstadter (New York: Harper & Row, 1971), "Poetically Man Dwells," pp. 213–29.

3. Eckhard Schulze-Fielitz, "The Space City," in U. Conrads, ed., *Programs and Manifestos on 20th Century Architecture* (Cambridge: MIT Press, 1970), pp. 175–76; and Paolo Soleri, *Arcology: The City in the Image of Man* (Cambridge: MIT Press, 1969).

4. To my knowledge, Jusuck Koh was the first to use the terms

ecological architecture and *ecological aesthetics* in this sense. See Jusuck Koh, "Ecological Design: A Post-Modern Design Paradigm of Holistic Philosophy and Evolutionary Ethic," *Landscape Journal* 1, no. 2 (1982): 76–84. Allen Carlson proposes the notion of functional fit to describe the integrated relation of a building to its physical and cultural environment, in "Reconsidering the Aesthetics of Architecture," *Journal of Aesthetic Education* 20, no. 4 (Winter 1986): 21–27.

5. One environmental design researcher locates environment in the physical correlate of the social situation, providing nonverbal communication through its fixed and nonfixed features. See, for example, I. R. Manners and M. W. Mikesell, eds., *Perspectives on Environment,* Publication no. 13 (Washington, D.C.: Association of American Geographers, 1974); see also Amos Rapoport, *The Meaning of the Built Environment* (Sage, 1983). Philosophers, not surprisingly, come closest to making this most basic term explicit, and it occurs appropriately in discussions of environmental aesthetics. For Hilde Hein, environment "entails a distinction between object and surround, a figure and a ground. . . . Our environment is the context—spiritual, physical, living and non-living—which defines us." Hilde Hein, "Conceiving Environmental Quality, Toward an Aesthetic of the Environment" (unpublished paper, 1972–73). After reviewing six possible relations between a person and other things and people, Francis Sparshott identifies the most likely ones in talk about the environment as the relation of self to setting and, secondarily, of traveler to scene. Francis E. Sparshott, "Figuring the Ground: Notes on Some Theoretical Problems of the Aesthetic Environment," *Journal of Aesthetic Education* 6, no. 1 (1972): 13. One of the few books concerned with environmental aesthetics approaches the definition metaphorically, describing the environment as "a continuing theatre for sensing and acting," and suggests that environmental perception concerns the quality of our surroundings, a usage closer to the one argued for here. See B. Sadler and A. Carlson, eds., *Environmental Aesthetics,* Western Geographical Series, vol. 20 (Victoria, Can.: University of Victoria, 1982), p. 1. See also *Oxford English Dictionary,* 1933 ed., s.v. "environment," def. 2. The citations in the *OED* begin with Carlyle in 1830. Of course the etymology may be followed back to the French *en* (in) + *viron* (circuit) < *virer* (to turn, to sweep round), which less substantiates the usual meaning of environment than suggests human activity in a place.

6. A fuller development of the following typology of environment and of the instances of participatory environments appears in my paper, "Towards a Phenomenological Aesthetics of Environment," in H. Silverman and D. Idhe, eds., *Descriptions* (Albany: State University of New York Press, 1985), pp. 112–28.

7. See, for example, Kevin Lynch, *The Image of the City* (Cambridge: MIT Press, 1960), pp. 43–44.

8. See Robert J. Yudell, "Body Movement," in K. C. Bloomer and C. W. Moore, eds., *Body, Memory and Architecture* (New Haven: Yale University Press, 1977).

9. "Perception of *scenery* is only open to those who have no real part to play in the landscape." David Lowenthal, "The American Scene," *Geographical Review* 58, no. 1 (1968): 72.

10. In *The Collected Poems of Wallace Stevens* (New York: Knopf, 1954), p. 75.

11. Mikel Dufrenne, in a lecture on Merleau-Ponty's "Eye and Mind" at the State University of New York at Stony Brook, 13 October 1979.

12. Christopher Tunnard puts the point eloquently: "Is man a part of all he sees or a spectator only, studying landscapes as Burckhardt advised his readers to study history, as one would contemplate a storm at sea, safe on the shore? Should we not be terrified that the storm may touch *us*? Are we not involved, emotionally and physically, in nature, and is not our role one far more deeply committed than that of mere guardianship or good behavior toward the wild?" *A World with a View* (New Haven: Yale University Press, 1978), p. 29.

13. John Dewey, *Art as Experience* (New York: Minton, Balch, 1934), pp. 43–44, 48, 3, 13, 25, 29, 58, 60, 65, 75, 162.

14. Maurice Merleau-Ponty, *Phénoménologie de la perception* (Paris: Gallimard, 1945), pp. 119, 158; *Phenomenology of Perception*, trans. Colin Smith (London: Routledge and Kegan Paul, 1962), pp. 150–51, 234; Eugene F. Kaelin, *An Existentialist Aesthetic* (Madison: University of Wisconsin Press, 1966), pp. 239, 240; M. Merleau-Ponty, "The Primacy of Perception," in J. M. Edie, ed., *The Primacy of Perception* (Evanston, Ill.: Northwestern University Press, 1964), pp. 14, 16, 42; and "Eye and Mind," in *Primacy of Perception*, p. 178.

15. O. F. Bollnow, "Lived-Space," *Philosophy Today* 5 (1961): 31–39. Reprinted in N. Lawrence and D. O'Connor, ed., *Readings in Existential Phenomenology* (Englewood Cliffs, N.J.: Prentice-Hall, 1967), pp. 178–86.

16. Calvin O. Schrag, *Experience and Being* (Evanston, Ill.: Northwestern University Press, 1969), pp. 136, 137, 170, 192.

17. Bloomer and Moore, *Body, Memory and Architecture* p. 105.

18. Lawrence Halprin, *Cities*, rev. ed. (Cambridge: MIT Press, 1972), p. 194.

19. The ideas described here as the active model of environment bear a strong resemblance to Lakoff's theory of cognitive science, which he calls experiential realism. See George Lakoff, *Women, Fire and Dangerous Things* (Chicago: University of Chicago Press, 1987); and also George Lakoff and Mark Johnson, *Metaphors We Live By* (Chicago: University of Chicago Press, 1980). The participatory model of environmental experience, however, goes still further in the direction of experiential integration and continuity.

20. Magoroh Maruyama has identified four metaprinciples of environmental design that are reflected in different cultures and historical periods and that represent alternative ways of ordering the human world. See his "Mindscapes: The Limits to Thought," *World Future Society Bulletin* (September–October, 1979): 13–23; "Mindscapes and Science Theories," *Current Anthropology* 21, no. 5 (October 1980): 589–600; "Heterogenistics and Morphogenistics: Toward a New Concept of the Scientific," *Theory and Society* 5, no. 1 (1978): 75–95.

21. See Kurt Lewin, *Principles of Topological Psychology* (New York: McGraw-Hill, 1936), p. 205; Robert W. Leeper, *Lewin's Topological and Vector Psychology* (Eugene, Oreg.: 1943), pp. 14, 35–36, 37, 63, 65, 66; Kurt Lewin, "Defining the 'field at a given time,'" in Melvin H. Marx, ed., *Psychological Theory* (New York: Macmillan, 1951), p. 311; James J. Gibson, *The Senses Considered as Perceptual Systems* (Boston: Houghton Mifflin, 1966), p. 319); *The Perception of the Visual World* (Boston: Houghton Mifflin, 1950); and *The Ecological Approach to Visual Perception* (Boston: Houghton Mifflin, 1979), pp. 127, 129, 137, 138–39, 255.

22. Barbara Sandrisser explores this perceptual integration in "Climate Responsive Design: Accepting Seasonal Change," in Richard Austin et al., eds., *The Yearbook of Landscape Architecture* (New York: Van Nostrand Reinhold, 1985), pp. 26ff.

23. This idea is developed further in my essay, "The Environment as an Aesthetic Paradigm," *Dialectics and Humanism* 15, nos. 1–2 (1988): 95–106.

24. Yi-Fu Tuan deals with some of these issues in "Surface Phenomena and Aesthetic Experience," *Annals of the Association of American Geographers* 79, no. 2 (June 1989): 233–41.

25. Bernard Berenson, "The Aesthetic Movement," in *Aesthetics and History* (New York: Pantheon, 1948).

26. Geographers continue to follow Sauer in regarding the landscape as visual and distant, or at least as a separate background. "The geographic landscape is a generalization derived from the observation of individual scenes." Carl O. Sauer, "The Morphology of Landscape," in J. Leighly, ed., *Land and Life* (Berkeley: University of California Press, 1967), p. 322. When a phenomenological analysis is applied, this may change: "Landscape is not, in its essence, made to be looked upon, but, rather, is an insertion of man into the world, a site for life's struggle, the manifestation of his being and that of others." Eric Dardel, *L'Homme et la terre: Nature de la réalité géographique* (Paris: Presses Universitaires de France, 1952), p. 44. Both quotations and the translation of the second are from Edward Relph, "Geographical Experiences and Being-in-the-World: The Phenomenological Origins of Geography," in D. Seamon and R. Mugerauer, eds., *Dwelling, Place and Environment* (Dordrecht: Nijhoff, 1985), pp. 15–31.

27. Maurice Merleau-Ponty, "Eye and Mind," p. 173.

28. Jean Piaget, quoted in E. H. Hall, *The Hidden Dimension* (Garden City, N.Y.: Doubleday, 1966), p. 63.

29. Edmund Carpenter, *Eskimo* (University of Toronto, 1959), cited in Hall, *Hidden Dimension*, p. 73.

30. Paraphrased from Gelb by Merleau-Ponty, in *Phenomenology of Perception*, p. 119n.

31. The work of transactional psychologists demonstrates this brilliantly. The Ames room is the best known of many instances that exemplify the perceiver's contribution to what is perceived. When the perceiver takes visual cues in customary ways to infer the proportions of the room and the size of a person within it, the ingenious manipulation of those cues produces incongruities that dismay our expectations. For example, a person seen walking from one end of the room to the other quickly changes from a pygmy to a giant. See Chapter Three, note 11; also Hall, *Hidden Dimension*, p. 74.

32. Arata Isozaki, in *Ma: Space-Time in Japan* (New York: Cooper–Hewitt Museum, 1979), p. 13. Chapter Eight discusses the concept of *ma* more fully.

33. Martin Heidegger, "Building Dwelling Thinking," in *Poetry, Language, Thought*, pp. 155–57.

34. See K. Tange and N. Kawazoe, *Ise* (Cambridge: MIT Press, 1965). See also Maruyama, "Mindscapes."

35. See Halprin, *Cities*, pp. 208, 214–15.

36. Techniques are being developed to simulate environmental perception to guide design decisions. The environmental simulation laboratory at the University of California at Berkeley has pioneered in these efforts.

37. In a sense, the perceptual environment is preeminently, indeed unavoidably, aesthetic, both etymologically speaking and theoretically. The environment is always sensed, and the richness and inclusiveness of perception, its roundness, one might say, makes that fact undeniable. This has extraordinary implications for environmental theory and for the applications of theory to environmental design and policy.

38. In Japan an arrangement of several buildings can be appreciated only by moving through the space, allowing each building gradually to come into view. It cannot be grasped from a single stationary viewpoint. See Isozaki, *Ma*, p. 36. Arnheim, however, does not quite agree with de-emphasizing the visual. See Rudolf Arnheim, *The Dynamics of Architectural Form* (Berkeley: University of California Press, 1977), pp. 101, 108–9, 115. Writers from different disciplines have placed architecture within an ecological framework. Jusuck Koh argues for "a holistic view of the human–environment system and . . . an evolutionary and open-ended view of culture and of design and building," in "Ecological Design," and Allen

Carlson applies the ecological model to architecture, in "Reconsidering the Aesthetics of Architecture."

39. The philosophy and design of museum exhibitions are developed in my essay, "The Museum of Art as a Participatory Environment,"*Curator* 33, no. 1 (March 1990): 31–39.

40. Malcolm Lowry, *Hear Us O Lord from Heaven Thy Dwelling Place* (London: 1969), p. 272.

41. Bollnow, "Lived-Space," p. 38.

42. See Ian L. McHarg, *Design with Nature* (Garden City, N.Y.: Natural History Press, 1969); and Christopher Alexander, *The Timeless Way of Building* (New York: Oxford University Press, 1979); and *A Pattern Language* (New York: Oxford University Press, 1977).

43. See Fritz Steel, *The Sense of Place* (Boston: CBI Publications, 1981), p. 187.

44. Tuan describes how the deliberate design of certain ancient Chinese cities embodies cosmological relations. Yi-Fu Tuan, *Topophilia, A Study of Environmental Perception, Attitudes, and Values* (Englewood Cliffs, N.J.: Prentice-Hall, 1974), chap. 11. I have developed some of the ideas and examples in this chapter in a number of essays on environmental aesthetics, which will appear in my book, *Aesthetics and Environment: Ideas for a New Synthesis* (Philadelphia: Temple University Press, forthcoming).

45. Gabriel Marcel, *Metaphysical Journal* (Chicago: Henry Regnery, 1952), entries for November 6, 8, and 9, 1920.

46. Hall notes this force clearly: "The relation between man and the cultural dimension is one in which both *man and his environment participate in molding each other.* Man is now in the position of actually creating the total world in which he lives, what the ethologists refer to as his biotope. In creating this world, he is actually determining *what kind of an organism* he will be." Hall, *The Hidden Dimension,* p. 4. Tuan recognizes the possibility of changing cultural beliefs by changing environment. See Tuan, *Topophilia,* chap. 7. See also my "Aesthetic Paradigms for an Urban Ecology," *Diogenes* 103 (Fall 1978): 1–28.

47. Heidegger, "Building Dwelling Thinking," pp. 152, 153, 156–57.

CHAPTER FIVE

1. Italo Calvino, *If on a Winter's Night a Traveler,* trans. William Weaver (New York: Harcourt Brace Jovanovich, 1981), p. 92.

2. See Roman Jakobson, "Closing Statement: Linguistics and Poetics," in T. A. Seboek, ed., *Style in Language* (Cambridge: MIT Press, 1960), p. 356. Although Jakobson recognizes the role of the reader in the scheme of communication, he assigns it functions other than the poetic. See also

Michael Riffaterre, "Describing Poetic Structures: Two Approaches to Baudelaire's 'Les Chats,' " in Jacques Ehrmann, ed., *Structuralism* (New Haven: Yale French Studies, 1966); reprinted in Jane P. Tompkins, ed., *Reader-Response Criticism: From Formalism to Post-Structuralism* (Baltimore: Johns Hopkins University Press, 1980), pp. 26–40; also Terry Eagleton, *Literary Theory* (Minneapolis: University of Minnesota Press, 1983), chap. 3.

3. Jakobson, "Closing Statement," 358ff.; Riffaterre, "Describing Poetic Structures," especially p. 36.

4. Saussure, quoted in Jonathan Culler, *Saussure* (Glasgow: Fontana/Collins, 1976), p. 5; see pp. 9, 21–24, 29; and Ferdinand de Saussure, *Cours de linguistic générale* (1916), ed. Tullio de Mauro (Paris: Payot, 1973); and *Course in General Linguistics* (London: Peter Owen, 1960), pp. 117.

5. Quoted in Eagleton, *Literary Theory*, pp. 96–97.

6. Riffaterre, in Tompkins, *Reader-Response Criticism*, p. 36.

7. Walter Benjamin suggests that Proust, who suffered from asthma, developed a syntax through which we experience fear of suffocating. See Benjamin, *Illuminations* (New York: Schocken, 1969), p. 214. See also R. Murray Schafer, *The Tuning of the World* (New York: Knopf, 1977), p. 228.

8. Calvino, *If on a Winter's Night*, p. 185.

9. Roland Barthes, in *S/Z* (New York: Hill and Wang, 1974), quoted in Eagleton, *Literary Theory*, p. 138. The reader, the writer, and the speaker occupy different roles, certainly, but by their activation of signs in use their diverse functions coalesce. While this discussion centers on the reader, similar observations could be made about the other relations to the literary process.

10. William Empson, *Seven Types of Ambiguity* (Harmondsworth, England: 1965), p. 1. See Eagleton, *Literary Theory*, p. 52.

11. "Tragedy, then, is an imitation of an action that is serious, complete, and of a certain magnitude; in language embellished with each kind of artistic ornament, the several kinds being found in separate parts of the play; in the form of action, not of narrative; *through pity and fear effecting the proper purgation of these emotions.*" Aristotle, *The Poetics*, 1449B, chap. 6, in S. H. Butcher, *Aristotle's Theory of Poetry and Fine Art*, trans. S. H. Butcher, 4th ed. (New York: Dover, 1951), p. 23; my emphasis.

12. Laurence Sterne, *Tristram Shandy*, II (London: Everyman's Library, 1956), p. 79. Quoted in Wolfgang Iser, *The Act of Reading* (Baltimore: Johns Hopkins University Press, 1978), p. 108.

13. Henry David Thoreau, *Walden* (New York: Heritage Press, 1939), "Reading," p. 108.

14. Joseph Conrad, "Preface," *The Nigger of the Narcissus* (Garden City, N.Y.: Doubleday, Page, 1926), p. xiii.

15. Jean-Paul Sartre, "What Is Writing?," in *What Is Literature?* (New York: Philosophical Library, 1949). Quoted in Iser, *Act of Reading*, p. 108.

16. For one of many surveys of this movement, see Tompkins, *Reader-Response Criticism*, pp. ix ff. See also "Introduction," in Susan R. Suleiman, *Reader in the Text*, pp. 3–45.

17. Stanley Fish, *Is There a Text in This Class?* (Cambridge: Harvard University Press, 1980), pp. 7, 13, 14, 15, 17, 67, 307, 317, 321, 322, 338, 355.

18. Roman Ingarden, *The Literary Work of Art* (Evanston, Ill.: North-western University Press, 1973). See Eagleton, *Literary Theory*, pp. 80–81.

19. Mikel Dufrenne, "The Philosophy of Poetry" (lecture delivered at the University of Buffalo, September 1960). In *The Phenomenology of Aesthetic Experience* (Evanston, Ill.: Northwestern University Press, 1973), Dufrenne elaborates on the multifaceted intimacy of this relationship.

20. See Iser, *The Implied Reader: Patterns of Communication in Prose Fiction from Bunyan to Beckett* (Baltimore: Johns Hopkins University Press, 1975); and *Act of Reading*.

21. Starobinski draws the proper conclusion from this process, which Iser never quite articulates for himself: "Strictly speaking, what we see arising here is a complex reality, in which the difference between subject and object disappears." This is a synthesis which, in Edmund Husserl's terms, is passive because it is prepredicative and prejudgmental. We shall pursue this idea later in the chapter. See Jean Starobinski, *Psychoanalysis and Literature* (German trans., 1973), quoted by Iser, *Implied Reader*, p. 135. See also Iser, *Act of Reading*, pp. ix, x, 21, 36, 53, 54, 67, 68, 69, 85, 96, 131, 132, 135, 169–70, 182, 203, and elsewhere.

22. "We have only to understand the mirror stage *as an identification*, in the full sense that analysis gives to the term: namely, the transformation that takes place in the subject when he assumes an image." Jacques Lacan, "The Mirror Stage as Formative of the Function of the I as Revealed in the Psychoanalytic Experience," in *Ecrits*, trans. Alan Sheridan (New York: Norton, 1977), pp. 2, 4.

23. Norman N. Holland, "Unity Identity Text Self," in Tompkins, *Reader-Response Criticism*, p. 130.

24. Bachelard's position is somewhat elusive. At times, as here, he is clearly a subjectivist; at others, he acknowledges a more equal reciprocity of reader and text. Gaston Bachelard, *The Poetics of Reverie* (Boston: Beacon Press, 1969), p. 53; also pp. 1–2, 3, 4, 15; see also his *On Poetic Imagination and Reverie*, trans. Colette Gaudin (Indianapolis: Bobbs-Merrill, 1971), p. 22; and *The Poetics of Space* (New York: Orion Press, 1964), p. 233.

25. It appears that the formalist mode of studying language and literature (at least as Culler interprets Saussure) and the subjectivist focus on response and inner state enter into a grand dialectical relationship whereby this opposition of contraries shares a common center in the indi-

vidual subject. Yet what seems to be opposite poles of explanation become here manifestations of a more basic idea, the ultimate grounding of theory in the individual subject. The subject in the one case contributes his intuitions and judgments to form what are taken as linguistic facts (Culler, *Saussure*, p. 77), becoming the central point in the analysis of language. The subject in the other is the seat of inner experiences that combine memories, associations, perceptions, and conceptual frames in personal ways. Deconstruction dismantles the subject, turning meanings into interpersonal systems of convention, and the subject itself into a construct, the product of systems of conventions (p. 78). Yet even Saussure concludes from his study of characters in German legends "that what one speaks of as the character himself is nothing other than the creation of the reader" in bringing together "the disparate elements which one encounters as one reads through the text" (p. 106). Quoted by Culler in *Saussure*, from D'Arco Silvio Avalle, "La sémiologie de la narrativité chez Saussure," in C. Bouazis, ed., *Essais de la théorie du texte* (Paris: 1973), p. 33.

26. Georges Poulet, "Criticism and the Experience of Interiority," in Tompkins, *Reader-Response Criticism*, pp. 41–49; see p. xiv; see also Poulet's "Phenomenology of Reading," *New Literary History: A Journal of Theory and Interpretation* 1, no. 1 (October 1969):

27. Plato, *Ion*, 535.

28. See Steven Mailloux, *Interpretive Conventions* (Ithaca, N.Y.: Cornell University Press, 1982), p. 23.

29. Tompkins, "The Reader in History," in *Reader-Response Criticism*, pp. 225–27.

30. Joyce Cary, *Art and Reality* (Cambridge, England: Harper University Press, 1958), p. 165.

31. See Justus Buchler, *The Metaphysics of Natural Complexes* (New York: Columbia University Press, 1966); see also *The Main of Light* (New York: Oxford University Press, 1974).

32. Eagleton, *Literary Theory*, p. 80.

33. Rosenblatt's views on the experience and teaching of literature derive from the epistemology and aesthetics of John Dewey and the perceptual psychology of Adelbert Ames and Hadley Cantril. See Louise M. Rosenblatt, *The Reader, the Text, the Poem: The Transactional Theory of the Literary Work* (Carbondale: Southern Illinois University Press, 1978), esp. preface, p. 12, and chap. 4. This is a valuable study, closer, perhaps, than any other to the direction taken here.

34. Calvino, *If on a Winter's Night*, p. 68.

35. For example, when they begin with the exordium, "*Aixo era y no era*" ("It was and it was not"), Majorcan storytellers not only recognize the ambiguous status of literature but acknowledge also its different claim to

truth. Quoted by Jakobson in *Style in Language,* 371, from W. Giese, "Sind Märchen Lügen?" *Cahiers S. Puşcariu,* 1 (1952), pp. 137ff.

36. Calvino, *If on a Winter's Night,* p. 255.

37. See Colette Gaudin, "Introduction," in Bachelard, *On Poetic Imagination and Reverie,* pp. xix, xxxiv–xxxv.

38. V. S. Naipaul, *The Enigma of Arrival* (New York: Knopf, 1987), p. 133.

39. A discussion of Sartre's comparison of Guardi with Canaletto occurs in Chapter Three. Italo Calvino, *Invisible Cities* (New York: Harcourt Brace Jovanovich, 1978); Hans-Georg Gadamer, *Truth and Method* (New York: Crossroad, 1975), p. 145.

40. James T. Farrell, "On the Function of the Novel," in F. Puma, ed., *7 Arts,* no. 3 (Indian Hills, Colo.: Falcon's Wing Press), pp. 25–40.

41. Alain Robbe-Grillet, "Time and Description in Fiction Today," in *For a New Novel,* trans. Richard Howard (New York: Grove Press, 1965), pp. 143–56.

42. See John Barth, "A Few Words about Minimalism," in *New York Times Book Review,* 28 December 1986, p. 2.

43. Friedrich Nietzsche, *The Birth of Tragedy,* sect. 8, trans. C. Fadiman, in *The Philosophy of Nietzsche* (New York: Random House, 1954), p. 988.

44. Takeshi Kaiko, *Darkness in Summer,* trans. Cecilia Segawa Sieger (Tokyo: C.E. Tuttle, 1974), pp. 110–11.

45. Conrad, "Preface," *Nigger of the Narcissus.*

46. George Lakoff and Mark Johnson develop a similar approach in *Metaphors We Live By* (Chicago: University of Chicago Press, 1980).

47. Bachelard, *Poetics of Space,* p. 47.

48. Saigyō, in the *Shinkokinshū* (ca. 1205).

49. Dylan Thomas, *Collected Poems* (New York: New Directions, 1957), p. 112.

50. Paul Valéry, *The Art of Poetry* (New York: Vintage, 1962), p. 211. In *The Body in the Mind: The Bodily Basis of Meaning, Imagination, and Reason* (Chicago: University of Chicago Press, 1987), Mark Johnson views meaning as embodied. Bodily experience, including its emotional conditions, is part of meaning, and communication is an activity that is creative and problem solving.

51. Calvino, *If on a Winter's Night a Traveler,* p. 72. Again, "I expect readers to read in my books something I didn't know, but I can expect it only from those who expect to read something they didn't know" (p. 185).

CHAPTER SIX

1. Charles Baudelaire, "La Charogne," in *The Flowers of Evil* (Norfolk, Conn: New Directions, 1946).

2. Arthur Schopenhauer, *The World as Will and Representation*, vol. 2, trans. E. F. J. Payne (Indian Hills, Colo.: Falcon's Wing Press, 1958), pp. 453–54.

3. Arnold Schönberg, *Fundamentals of Music Composition* (London: Faber and Faber, 1967), p. 93.

4. "Sound and motion" is Gustav Cohen's translation (Eduard Hanslick, *The Beautiful in Music* [Indianapolis: Bobbs-Merrill, 1957], p. 48); "forms moving in terms of a tonal system" is Francis Sparshott's ("Aesthetics of Music—Limits and Grounds," in P. Alperson, ed., *What Is Music?* [New York: Haven, 1987], p. 45); "tonally moving forms" comes from Geoffrey Payzant's important new translation of Hanslick (see his "Essay: Towards a Revised Reading of Hanslick," in Eduard Hanslick, *On the Musically Beautiful* [Indianapolis: Hackett, 1986], p. 101); and "forms of moving tones" is my own preference.

5. Igor Stravinsky, *Poetics of Music* (New York: Vintage, 1956), p. 28.

6. Suzanne Langer, *Feeling and Form* (New York: Charles Scribner's Sons, 1953), p. 125.

7. Sam Morgenstern, ed., *Composers on Music* (New York: Pantheon, 1956), p. 48. Marcello was specifically denying the composer's need to master mathematical relations in order to write music.

8. Allen Edwards, *Flawed Words and Stubborn Sounds: A Conversation with Elliott Carter* (New York: Norton, 1972), p. 101.

9. Zuckerkandl and Schenker have explored certain aspects of these traits of musical tones and motives in important ways. See Victor Zuckerkandl, *Sound and Symbol* (Princeton: Princeton University Press, 1956); and Heinrich Schenker, *Free Composition*, trans. Ernst Oster (New York: Longman, 1979).

10. Bach's famous "Chaconne" actually has thirty variations, the final repetition being a reprise of the opening eight bars. The variations in the Brahms finale are followed by a brief coda. See Willi Apel, *Harvard Dictionary of Music* (Cambridge: Harvard University Press, 1953), pp. 126–29, for a discussion of the distinctions between a chaconne and a passacaglia.

11. From *The Principles of Psychology*, reprinted in B. Wilshire, ed., *William James: The Essential Writings* (New York: Harper Torchbooks, 1971), p. 47.

12. Edwards, *Flawed Words and Stubborn Sounds*, pp. 89–90, 95, 101. "The constant and overall phenomenon of music is one in which every 'moment' is in the process of coming from some previous moment and leading to some future moment—only *thus* contributing to what is happening in the present" (pp. 99–100).

13. Bachelard uses the auditory metaphor "reverberation" to convey the meaning of sound as the unity of time and space, because in this word both space and time are present and indistinguishable. This may be taken as

an empirical argument, so to speak, for the inseparability of musical form from its dynamic materials. See Gaston Bachelard, *The Poetics of Space* (New York: Orion, 1964), p. xii.

14. Stanley Cavell, "Music Discomposed," in William H. Capitan and D. D. Merrill, eds., *Art, Mind, and Religion* (Pittsburgh: University of Pittsburgh Press, 1967), pp. 86–88.

15. Sparshott, "Aesthetics of Music," p. 56.

16. David Sudnow develops this in connection with jazz improvisation in *Ways of the Hand* (Cambridge: Harvard University Press, 1978).

17. Elliott Carter grasps this point precisely: "From a purely musical point of view, I've always had the impression of improvisation of the most rewarding kind when good performers take the trouble to play music that is carefully written out as if they were thinking it up themselves while they played it—that is, when with much thought and practice they come to feel the carefully written-out piece as part of themselves and of their own experience, which they are communicating to others directly from themselves in the moment of the performance, in an alive way." Edwards, *Flawed Words and Stubborn Sounds,* p. 78.

18. P. F. Strawson, *Individuals* (Garden City, N.Y.: Anchor Books, 1963), p. 61. See A. J. Ayer, *The Foundations of Empirical Knowledge* (New York: Macmillan, 1955), pp. 253–55.

19. Quoted by Aaron Copland in *Music and Imagination* (New York: New American Library, 1959), p. 10.

20. See R. Murray Schafer, *The Tuning of the World* (New York: Knopf, 1977), p. 118.

21. Mark W. Booth, *The Experience of Song* (New Haven: Yale University Press, 1981), pp. 15–16.

22. Stravinsky, *Poetics of Music,* p. 81. Stravinsky was not the only composer to acknowledge a partnership with the listener. Hindemith did so as well, although without Stravinsky's verbal gifts: "While listening to the musical structure, as it unfolds before his ears, [the listener] is mentally constructing parallel to it and simultaneously with it a mirrored image." Paul Hindemith, *A Composer's World* (Cambridge: Harvard University Press, 1953), p. 16.

23. Used by David Schiff in a lecture on Carter's music at Vassar College, Poughkeepsie, N.Y., 2 April 1989.

24. Mikel Dufrenne, "Aujourd'hui encore, la création," in *Esthétique et Philosophie,* vol. 3 (Paris: Klincksieck, 1981), pp. 67–73. My translation.

CHAPTER SEVEN

1. Film is considered at length in Chapter Eight in a manner similar to the aesthetics of dance.

2. In *The Concept of Criticism* (Oxford: Clarendon Press, 1967), for example, Francis Sparshott argues that every art involves performance.

3. Katharine Everett Gilbert recognizes this, in contrast to Aristotle and Bullough. See her "Mind and Medium in the Modern Dance," *Journal of Aesthetics and Art Criticism* 1 (Spring 1941): 106–29. Reprinted in R. Copeland and M. Cohen, eds., *What Is Dance?* (New York: Oxford, 1983), pp. 289–302, esp. p. 299.

4. Notational systems and film or videotapes obviously perform different functions. One does not displace the other. A visual record is particular: a recording of an individual dance performance. Choreography, however, provides a formal identity which allows alternative interpretations, and this is what a notational system attempts to specify. Notation is general. It indicates the arrangement of the movements that constitute the dance, much as a musical score specifies an arrangement of sounds and silences. A performance embodies these, making them particular and specific, and it is infused, furthermore, with the nuances that escape notation but give vitality and personality to the individual performance.

5. Von Laban defines dance as "a sequence of gestures rounded into an artistic whole." Rudolf von Laban, *Die Welt der Tänzers* (Stuttgart: 1920), p. 20. See Gilbert's account in Copeland and Cohen, *What Is Dance?*, pp. 292–93.

6. Merce Cunningham, "The Impermanent Art," in Richard Kostelanetz, ed., *Esthetics Contemporary* (Buffalo: Prometheus, 1978), pp. 310, 311.

7. "The dance creates an image of nameless and even bodiless Powers filling a complete autonomous realm, a 'world.' It is the first presentation of the world as a realm of mystic forces." Susanne K. Langer, *Feeling and Form* (New York: Scribner's, 1953), p. 190.

8. Ibid., pp. 176, 184.

9. John Locke, *An Essay Concerning Human Understanding* (1690), vol. 1 (New York: Dover, 1959), pp. 308–16.

10. Of course the quality of the intensity will vary with period, tradition, and choreographer. Sondra Horton Fraleigh has rightly noted, in a personal communication, the varying character of dance: contemplative, as in Japanese No and Eric Hawkins; acrobatically vital, as in much new Canadian dance; mesmerizingly repetitious, as in the work of Laura Dean; tough, as in the dance of Senta Driver; delicately feminine, as in romantic ballet; starkly formal, as in certain works of Balanchine. In all these cases there is, as she puts it, "an attentiveness to bodily lived values," to the body aesthetic. This is the sense of the claim that dance is intensely present.

11. "In some districts of Southern Tunisia dancing . . . is dancing of the hair, and all night long, till they perhaps fall exhausted, the marriageable girls will move their heads to the rhythm of a song, maintaining their hair, in

perpetual balance and sway." Havelock Ellis, "The Art of Dancing," in Copeland and Cohen, *What Is Dance?*, p. 485.

12. See Sondra Horton Fraleigh, *Dance and the Lived Body* (Pittsburgh: University of Pittsburgh Press, 1987), p. 54.

13. Tom Johnson's "Running Out of Breath," is one example. See "Running Out of Breath," in Copeland and Cohen, *What Is Dance?*, pp. 332–35, for his descriptive account of this dance.

14. Yvonne Rainer, "A Quasi Survey of some 'Minimalist' Tendencies in the Quantitatively Minimal Dance Activity Midst the Plethora, or an Analysis of Trio A," in Copeland and Cohen, *What Is Dance?*, p. 325.

15. Gordon Fancher and Gerald Myers, eds., *Philosophical Essays on Dance* (Brooklyn: Dance Horizons, 1981), p. 109.

16. Fraleigh expresses the dancer's standpoint well: "My movement is not an object to me—the dance is not my object, because I am living its moving. The being of the dance is there in its moving. My being is in my moving." *Dance and the Lived Body*, p. 41.

17. Maurice Merleau-Ponty, "The Primacy of Perception" and "Eye and Mind" in J. M. Edie, ed., *The Primacy of Perception* (Evanston, Ill.: Northwestern University Press, 1964), pp. 14 and 16, and p. 178 respectively. See the discussion of space in Chapter Four.

18. O. F. Bollnow, "Lived–Space," in *Philosophy Today* 5 (1961): 31–39. Reprinted in N. Lawrence and D. O'Connor, eds, *Readings in Existential Phenomenology* (Englewood Cliffs, N.J.: Prentice-Hall, 1967), pp. 178–86 (esp. pp. 178–80). This point was discussed somewhat differently in Chapter Four.

19. Gilbert's characterization in "Mind and Medium in the Modern Dance," p. 296.

20. Fraleigh, *Dance and the Lived Body*, p. xxvi.

21. This claim of the continuity of imaginative and actual perception differs from Sartre, who found them mutually exclusive. See Jean-Paul Sartre, *The Psychology of Imagination* (New York: Philosophical Library, 1948).

22. Sparshott refers to Jerome Robbins's emphasis on recognizing that dancing goes on in actual space. Actual space is hardly secondary in dance in the way that physical space of the canvas is to the perceptual space the painter creates. Francis Sparshott, *Off the Ground: First Steps to a Philosophical Consideration of the Dance* (Princeton: Princeton University Press, 1988), pp. 377–78.

23. The mere imitation of shapes and actions can convey *ideas* of emotion and allow us to say, for example, what a dancer is representing. However, as Selma Jeanne Cohen argues, more is needed for communication to take place, and she refers to Doris Humphrey's modes of stylization

that intensify "the dynamic qualities of strength or weakness, tension or release, that assure communication." See Selma Jeanne Cohen, *Next Week, Swan Lake: Reflections on Dance and Dances* (Middletown, Conn.: Wesleyan University Press, 1982), p. 96. Yet the common appeal to communication to explain aesthetic expression adds another difficulty to the first and embroils us in a continuing series of artificial problems that are part of a larger tradition of philosophical speculation concerning self, other, intersubjectivity, and the external world. Cohen cites Arnheim, who steps deftly outside these difficulties by characterizing what the choreographer achieves when successful as "the kind of stirring participation that distinguishes artistic experience from the detached acceptance of information."

24. Paul Valéry, "Philosophy of the Dance," in Copeland and Cohen, *What Is Dance?*, pp. 59–60.

25. Immanuel Kant, *Critique of Pure Reason*, trans. N. K. Smith (London: Macmillan, 1956), I, First Part, pp. 65–91.

26. Rudolf Arnheim, *Art and Visual Perception* (Berkeley: University of California Press, 1966), p. 365; see chap. 8, "Movement," and *passim*.

27. See Maxine Sheets's *Phenomenology of Dance* (Madison: University of Wisconsin Press, 1966), which joins Sartre's analysis of time and Merleau-Ponty's treatment of space with Langer's notion of virtual force in elaborating a phenomenological aesthetic of dance.

28. See Fraleigh, *Dance and the Lived Body*, chap. 10, on the continuity of time, space, and movement in dance. The entire book is an extended essay on the embodiment of the human world in dance.

29. See Sparshott, *Off the Ground*, pp. 397–98.

30. See Ellis, "Art of Dancing," p. 239.

31. Ibid. Some aspects of this continuity are explored in my essay, "Aesthetic Function," in Dale Riepe, ed., *Phenomenology and Natural Existence* (Albany: State University of New York Press, 1973), pp. 183–93.

32. Sparshott, *Off the Ground*, pp. 342–48.

33. John Martin, *The Modern Dance* (New York: A.S. Barnes, 1933), pp. 13–16.

34. Ibid., p. 6; Cohen, *Next Week, Swan Lake*, p. 109.

35. Martin, *Modern Dance*, pp. 11–13; "The Dance" in Copeland and Cohen, *What Is Dance?*, p. 22.

36. Jamake Highwater, *Dance: Rituals of Experience* (New York: Alfred van der Marck Editions, 1978), p. 24.

37. Sally Banes observes that in the nonillusionistic virtuosity of postmodern dancers "the gulf between artist and spectator has been irrevocably bridged." " 'Drive,' She Said: The Dance of Melissa Fenley," in Michael Kirby, ed., "Dance/Movement," *The Drama Review* 24 (1980): 14.

38. Highwater, *Dance: Rituals of Experience*, p. 112.

39. See Arnheim, *Art and Visual Perception,* pp. 393–94.

40. Fraleigh writes, "When I join the dancer in her dance, it is through my poetic experience of bodily being. I join her in an unspoken celebration of the poetry of our embodiment as it is danced and silently affirmed between us." *Dance and the Lived Body,* p. 74. Arnheim defines this identity of experience of dancer and spectator as an instance of the psychological concept of "isomorphism." It is "the fortunate correspondence between the dynamic patterns of what the dancer perceives through his kinesthetic nerves and what the spectator is told by his eyes." "Psychology of the Dance," *Dance Magazine* (August 1946).

41. Fraleigh, *Dance and the Lived Body,* pp. 45, 53, 60, 62, 66, 169–70; Mary Wigman, "The Philosophy of the Modern Dance," in Copeland and Cohen, *What Is Dance?,* p. 306.

42. Havelock Ellis, "The Art of Dancing," in Copeland and Cohen, *What Is Dance?,* p. 492. See articles on "Aesthetics, African" and "Asian Dance Aesthetics" in *International Encyclopedia of Dance* (Berkeley: University of California Press, 1991); and Fraleigh, *Dance and the Lived Body,* chap. 4.

43. Havelock Ellis, *The Dance of Life* (New York: Grosset and Dunlap, 1923), p. 280. Fraleigh writes of the creation of the self in dance, and of the unity of the individual and the universal as the proper extension and completion of the dancer's self. See *Dance and the Lived Body,* chap. 2.

44. Langer takes Cassirer's mythical consciousness to be structurally identical with artistic consciousness, although not equivalent to it. Of course she rejects any material equivalence of the mythical fusion of symbol and world with artistic consciousness, for she is guided by her dualism of the actual and the virtual by which each art, including dance, has its primary illusion. See *Feeling and Form,* pp. 186ff. Fraleigh, however, affirms their continuity. See *Dance and the Lived Body,* chap. 8.

CHAPTER EIGHT

1. See Ralph Stephenson, "Space, Time and Montage," *British Journal of Aesthetics* 2, no. 3 (July 1962): 251–52.

2. In a virtuoso analysis of filmic time in *Dr. Strangelove,* Alexander Sesonske shows how the director, Stanley Kubrick, creates multiple simultaneous times in the same shot as well as between shots. While the bomber wing is en route to dispatch its final nuclear load, General Ripper, who has ordered its mission, is intent on killing time until the act is done. For him, time moves excruciatingly slowly, as he doodles and dawdles to help it pass. At the same time, Captain Mandrake, who has discovered Ripper's self-willed, mad scheme, is kept prisoner by the general. For him, time is

speeding on as he attempts to discover the code letters and abort the mission. Simultaneously, Major Kong is joyfully leading the mission, having shifted from the lethargic state of marking time during his tour aloft to the purposeful time of the deadly plan of human extermination. Sesonske shows how at this point the time of the plot (action time) is the same as the time of the viewer watching the film (screen time), implicating the viewer in the action time of the film. Alexander Sesonske, "Killing Time: The Last of the Last Minute Rescues," unpublished paper. In another essay, Sesonske discusses how temporal relations within a film affect the involvement of the viewer in the flow of time, much like the use of tenses does in literature. See "Time and Tense in Cinema," *Journal of Aesthetics and Art Criticism* 38, no. 4 (Summer 1980): 419–26.

3. Erwin Panofsky, "Style and Medium in the Motion Pictures," *Critique* 1, no. 3, and often reprinted.

4. See Arnold Hauser, *The Social History of Art,* vol. 4 (New York: Vintage Books, n.d.), pp. 239, 243ff. See also Gilles Deleuze, *Cinema 1—The Movement-Image* (Minneapolis: University of Minnesota Press, 1986), pp. 2–3. Like Hauser, Langer associates cinema time with the eternal and ubiquitous present, in her case the present of dreams. See Suzanne Langer, *Feeling and Form* (New York: Scribner's, 1953), p. 415.

5. St. Augustine, *The Confessions* (A.D. 398), bk. 11.

6. See George W. Linden, *Reflections on the Screen* (Belmont, Calif.: Wadsworth, 1970), p. 192.

7. These correlative concepts are Panofsky's. See his "Style and Medium in the Motion Pictures."

8. Alexander Sesonske has developed a revealing analysis of "cinema space" (the term is borrowed from him). He distinguishes two aspects: "screen-space," which is the two-dimensional rectangular surface, and "action-space," the three-dimensional space of filmic experience. He takes both as visual only, however, an unnecessary restriction on synaesthetic perception. Nor does he distinguish sharply between the perceptual experience of cinematic space, which is bounded not by the frame of the screen (a border exceeded, moreover, by giant and curved screens) but by the usual limits of foveal and perceptual vision and the analytic and genetic characteristics of such space, that is, being visual and framed. In filmic experience we do not *look at* a film; we *enter perceptually* into cinematic space. Alexander Sesonske, "Cinema Space," in David Carr and Edward S. Casey, eds., *Explorations in Phenomenology* (The Hague: Nijhoff, 1973), pp. 399–409.

9. "While seated in the theater we can at the same time be taken (visually) into the space of the film, see the action as from inside this space, move through it at great or little speed, be rejected or excluded from it. Some of our most vivid experiences of film occur in scenes where we seem

to be deep inside the action-space and wholly immersed within the events of the film" (Sesonske, "Cinema Space," p. 403).

10. Slavko Vorkapich, "Toward True Cinema," in R. D. MacCann, ed., *Film: A Montage of Theories* (New York: Dutton, 1966), pp. .

11. Pierre Rouve, "Reel to Real: The Cinema as Technological Co-Reality," in René Berger and Lloyd Eby, eds., *Art and Technology* (New York: Paragon House, 1986), pp. 96–111.

12. Deleuze, *Cinema 1—The Movement–Image*, pp. 6, 22, 59, 61, 70.

13. Rudolf Arnheim, "Art Today and the Film," *Art Journal* 25 (1965–66): 243. These arguments are well known and are usually the result of regarding film as essentially a recording technology, as Arnheim does in this article, so that it remains realistic even when its imagery is ghostly. Kracauer is usually cited as the classical representative of this position, and it pervades his film theory. See Siegfried Kracauer, *Theory of Film* (New York: Oxford, 1960).

14. John Dewey, "The Postulate of Immediate Empiricism," in *The Influence of Darwin on Philosophy* (New York: Holt, 1910), pp. 227, 228.

15. "Je crois profondément que le film dans ses plus hautes expressions se doit de parvenir à une synthèse ou peut-être à une fusion du rêve et de la réalité, et tout semble démontrer d'ailleurs que cette distinction ou cette répartition est relative à un certain stade du développement de la créature et que métaphysiquement elle doit être dépassée." Marcel, "Possibilités et Limites de l'Art Cinematographique," *Revue Internationale de Filmologie* 5, nos. 18–19 (July–December 1954): 176. Quoted in Linden, *Reflections on the Screen*, p. 90.

16. Kracauer, *Theory of Film*, pp. 159–60.

17. "By this technological molding of the film's syntactic constituents the Reel makes its first bid to assert its ascendancy over the Real." Rouve defines the filmeme as the syntactic unit—a "chronotopic" relation between two frames—that constitutes the basic unit of a linguistics of film, and he painstakingly demonstrates the construction of a cinematographic linguistics. Rouve, "Reel to Real," pp. 105, 121.

18. Vorkapich, "Toward True Cinema," p. 176.

19. Michael Roemer, "The Surfaces of Reality," *Film Quarterly* 18, no. 1 (Fall 1964): 15–22.

20. Rouve, "Reel to Real," pp. 96, 110.

CHAPTER NINE

1. Immanuel Kant, *Critique of Judgment* (1790), secs. 27, 28.

2. See Marvin Farber, *The Foundation of Phenomenology*, 3rd ed. (Albany: State University of New York Press, 1968), pp. 541, 554, 559f.

3. The idea of experience was discussed at length in Chapter One.

4. Roman Ingarden, "Aesthetic Experience and Aesthetic Object," *Philosophy and Phenomenological Research* 21 (1960); expanded in *The Cognition of the Literary Work of Art* (Evanston, Ill.: Northwestern University Press, 1973), pp. 175–87ff.

5. Sondra Fraleigh's paraphrase in *Dance and the Lived Body* (Pittsburgh: University of Pittsburgh Press, 1987), p. 64. See Ingarden, "Aesthetic Experience and Aesthetic Object," in N. Lawrence and D. O'Connor, eds., *Readings in Existential Phenomenology* (Englewood Cliffs, N.J.: Prentice-Hall, 1967), pp. 308–23.

6. The discussions in this book have, I hope, shown the impossibility of an aesthetics of fragmentation, basing aesthetic theory on a part or aspect of the complex aesthetic field. This is considered at length in my earlier book, *The Aesthetic Field* (Springfield, Ill.: Charles C Thomas, 1970), chap. 1.

7. Leo Steinberg, "The Eye Is a Part of the Mind," in *Other Criteria* (New York: Oxford University Press, 1972), pp. 297, 291.

8. "I sometimes wonder if [art] nevertheless does not get its force from arousing some very deep, very vague, and immensely generalized reminiscences. It looks as though art had got access to the substratum of all the emotional colors of life . . . from the very conditions of our existence by its relation of an emotional significance in time and space." Roger Fry, "The Artist and Psychoanalysis," in *The Hogarth Essays* (London: Hogarth Press, 1924).

9. Susanne K. Langer, *Problems of Art* (New York: Scribner's, 1957), p. 59.

10. Eduard Hanslick, *On the Musically Beautiful*, trans. Geoffrey Payzant (Indianapolis: Hackett, 1986), pp. 28–29. See the discussion of this idea in Chapter Six.

11. Roger Fry, *Vision and Design* (1920) (Cleveland: World, 1956), pp. 33–34.

12. Ibid., p. 37.

13. Quoted in John Dewey, *Art as Experience* (New York: Capricorn Books, 1959), p. 113. See Douglas Morgan's discussion of Picasso's *Night Fishing at Antibes* in "Picasso's People: A Lesson in Making Sense," *Journal of Aesthetics and Art Criticism* 22, no. 2 (Winter 1963): 167–71.

14. "When one looks for the limiting definition [of experience], the absoluteness of any separation disappears. It is not that the qualitative difference is not to be relied on, but everything seems to connect to everything else." Dabney Townsend, "On Experience," *Journal of Speculative Philosophy* 1, no. 4 (1987): 311.

15. Lewis Carroll, *Through the Looking Glass and What Alice Found There*, in Martin Gardner, ed., *The Annotated Alice* (Clarkson N. Potter: New York, 1960), pp. 247, 259, 280, 282, 207, 210, 324.

16. Henry James was another: "The success of a work of art . . . may be measured by the degree to which it produces a certain illusion; that illusion makes it appear to us for the time that we have lived another life—that we have had a miraculous enlargement of experience" (1883). Henry James, *Theory of Fiction,* ed. James E. Miller, Jr. (Lincoln: University of Nebraska Press, 1972), p. 93. In a letter to Lou-Andreas Salome in 1903, Rilke recognized that "somehow I too must find a way of making *things,* not plastic, written things, but realities that arise from the craft itself." The postmodern novel, like other arts, has sometimes constructed a counterpoint of multiple ambiguous realities. One extraordinary example discussed earlier is Italo Calvino's *Once on a Winter's Night a Traveler.* Jorge Luis Borges sometimes indulges in the same interplay of realities. Tzvetan Todorov has studied how a text leads readers to construct an imaginary universe by a particular type of reading. "Novels do not imitate reality; they create it." See Todorov, "Reading as Construction," in Susan Suleiman and I. Crosman, eds., *The Reader in the Text* (Princeton: Princeton University Press, 1980), pp. 67–82.

17. Gaston Bachelard, *The Poetics of Space* (Boston: Beacon, 1969), pp. 233–34.

18. J. R. R. Tolkien, "On Fairy Stories," in *The Monsters and the Critics, and Other Essays* (London: Allen and Unwin, 1983).

19. Gaston Bachelard, *On Poetic Imagination and Reality* (Indianapolis: Bobbs-Merrill, 1971), p. 22.

20. Wallace Stevens, "The Noble Rider and the Sound of Words," in James Scully, ed., *Modern Poetics* (New York: McGraw-Hill, 1965), pp. 137, 138, 139, 143.

21. William Pardue, in conversation,

22. *Apollinaire on Art: Essays and Reviews 1902–1918,* trans. Susan Suleiman (New York, 1972), p. 20. Chapter Three explored the continuity and inclusiveness of space in landscape painting.

23. Alexander Soper, "The Rise of Yamato-e," *Art Bulletin* 24 (December 1942): 375–76. Recounted in Sherman E. Lee, *Reflections of Reality in Japanese Art* (Cleveland: Cleveland Museum of Art, 1983), p. 4. Lee's catalog essay, "Kinds of Reality," is an excellent commentary on Japanese realism and the larger aesthetic questions it raises.

24. E. H. Gombrich, *Art and Illusion,* 2nd ed. (New York: Pantheon, 1961), p. 111. Chap. 3, "Pygmalion's Power," pursues the question of the power of the image. "The test of the image is not its lifelikeness but its efficacy within a context of action. . . . It must work as well or better than the real thing" (pp. 110–11). In the world of the child there is no clear distinction between reality and appearance (p. 99). Even when one has outgrown

childhood, the division is not always clear: "For the world of man is not only a world of things; it is a world of symbols where the distinction between reality and make-believe is itself unreal" (p. 99). Gombrich, in fact, ends the book on this note: "The true miracle of the language of art is not that it enobles the artist to create the illusion of reality. It is that *under the hands of a great master the image becomes translucent*" (p. 389; my italics).

25. Otto Demus, *Byzantine Mosaic Decoration* (Boston, 1951), p. 8. Cited in Gombrich, *Art and Illusion*, p. 113. Arthur C. Danto explores the interconnections of art and life in characteristically provocative and insightful fashion in "Art and Disturbance," in *The Philosophical Disenfranchisement of Art* (New York: Columbia University Press, 1986), pp. 117–33, esp. pp. 126ff.

26. Art history has its share of accounts of naive observers who fail to grasp the difference between an artistic portrayal and the "real thing." The intent in citing them is to ridicule the simple-minded response that fails to see art as different from actual objects and events and that does not impose the special attitude that places art in its own distinct region. Yet this dismissal is equally simplistic in not recognizing the connections that link these spheres.

27. Danto, *Philosophical Disenfranchisement of Art*, pp. 73–75, 78.

28. No attempt has been made to reproduce these paintings here, for it is virtually impossible to duplicate the subtle presence of the originals in a small-format book illustration. These cases, however, point up a truth about all great art.

29. Quoted in Pierre Rouve, "Reel to Real: The Cinema as Technological Co-Reality," in René Berger and Lloyd Eby, eds., *Art and Technology* (New York: Paragon House, 1986), p. 116.

30. Maurice Merleau-Ponty, "Eye and Mind," in J. M. Edie, ed., *The Primacy of Perception* (Evanston, Ill.: Northwestern University Press, 1964), p. 188.

31. Wassily Kandinsky, "Reminiscences" (*"Rückblicke"*), in R. L. Herbert, ed., *Modern Artists on Art* (Englewood Cliffs, N.J.: Prentice-Hall, 1964). (Translation by Mrs. Robert L. Herbert is slightly revised.)

32. See Chapter Eight.

33. Jean Piaget, *The Construction of Reality in the Child* (New York: Basic Books, 1954), p. 217.

34. Arata Isozaki, *Ma: Space-Time in Japan* (New York: Cooper-Hewitt Museum, 1979), pp. 12–13, 14, 15.

35. Piet Mondrian, "Plastic Art and Pure Plastic Art" (1937), in Herbert, *Modern Artists on Art*, p. 130.

36. "Whatever is discriminated in any way (whether it is encountered or produced or otherwise related to) is a natural complex, and no complex is

more 'real,' more 'natural,' more 'genuine,' or more 'ultimate' than any other." Justus Buchler, *Metaphysics of Natural Complexes* (New York: Columbia University Press, 1966), p. 31.

37. See my essay, "Art without Object," in Stern, Rodman, and Cobitz, eds., *Creation and Interpretation* (New York: Haven, 1985), pp. 63–72.

CHAPTER TEN

1. Arthur C. Danto, "Philosophizing Literature," in *The Philosophical Disenfranchisement of Art* (New York: Columbia University Press, 1986), p. 169.

2. The allusion here, of course, is to Danto's argument for the "end of art." See Danto, "The End of Art," in ibid., pp. 81–115.

3. There are movements and directions in aesthetics deliberately not mentioned here that extend the role and meanings of art. To the extent that Marxist theory subsumes the arts under political ends and regards all art as interested and partisan, it fails to recognize the ontological primacy (although not the priority) of aesthetic experience as foundational in culture and society. Freudian theory, the intellectual mythology of the twentieth century, similarly takes the creative and appreciative processes of art beyond the narrow confines of convention but loses them in the quite different domains of psychological development and therapy. Yet neither Marxism nor Freudianism acknowledges the primacy of art and the aesthetic. While this is not intended to dismiss in a word an enormous body of scholarship and criticism that has values of its own, it provides some good reasons for not including them here.

4. My earlier book, *The Aesthetic Field* (Springfield, Ill.: Charles C Thomas, 1970), developed an aesthetic theory based on this model. It carries out in aesthetics the kind of interconnections that are fundamental to work in the phenomenological and hermeneutic traditions. See, for example, Gadamer's discussion of contemporaneity: "Neither the separate life of the creating artist—his biography—nor that of the performer who acts a work, nor that of the spectator who is watching the play, has any separate legitimacy in the face of the being of the work of art." Hans-Georg Gadamer, *Truth and Method* (New York: Crossroad, 1975), p. 113.

5. See Dufrenne's discussion of "the objective world and the world of the aesthetic object," in Mikel Dufrenne, *The Phenomenology of Aesthetic Experience* (Evanston, Ill.: Northwestern University Press, 1973), chap. 5, pp. 190ff.

6. As Stanley Cavell observes, "An event in which we participate is not knowable apart from our knowledge of our participation in it." *The World*

Viewed (New York: Viking, 1971), p. 128. Dewey and Bentley pointed out the interpenetration of the knower and the object of knowledge nearly half a century ago. See John Dewey and Arthur F. Bentley, *Knowing and the Known* (Boston: Beacon, 1949). Much of the most original and important philosophical work of the past half-century has developed in this direction in such areas as the sociology of knowledge, Marxist studies, existentialism, phenomenology, hermeneutics, deconstructionism, and feminist studies.

INDEX

absence, 115, 164
abstract expressionism, 20–22, 34, 49,
  55–56, 61, 79, 111, 133–34, 144,
  162–64, 179, 195, 198–99, 203, 206
Acconci, Vito, *Step Piece*, 23
action painting, 19, 23, 39, 40
activity, xiv, 3–5, 9, 10–12, 16–18, 22,
  23, 26–28, 31, 32, 35, 39, 40, 42,
  45–49, 55, 70, 73, 75–81, 77, 85–
  90, 92, 95, 97, 99, 102, 109, 111,
  112, 114–16, 118–20, 131, 136,
  141, 147, 148, 151–55, 157–59,
  162, 165, 167–71, 182, 184, 189,
  199, 203, 206–7, 212–13
actor, 28, 59, 88, 187
aesthetic appreciation, 53, 56, 153, 212
aesthetic attitude, xii, 5, 12–13, 18, 22,
  25–26, 28, 33, 55–56, 64, 69–70,
  81–82, 120, 200
aesthetic axioms, 11, 13, 20, 43, 210,
  217n
aesthetic dimension, 2, 62, 92, 211
aesthetic experience, xi–xii, xiv, 3–4,
  6, 17–18, 22, 26, 32, 39, 42, 46–49,

60, 75, 92–93, 109, 112, 191, 208,
  212–13
aesthetic field, xi, xii, 4–5, 40, 47, 49,
  92, 117, 157, 170, 192, 208, 211–12
Aesthetic Field, The, xi, 220, 244n
aesthetic function of art, xi, 196
aesthetic need, 2
aesthetic object, 17, 18, 113–14, 145,
  193
aesthetic participation, xii, 4, 54, 149,
  210
aesthetic qualities, 10, 25, 93
aesthetic realm, 6, 16, 208
aesthetic sensibility, 39
aesthetic value, xii
aesthetics, xii–xv, 1–6, 9, 10, 12–15,
  18–20, 24, 26, 31, 32, 43–44, 48–
  50, 66, 73, 77, 82, 84, 91–92, 98,
  100, 103, 113, 132, 134, 151–52,
  163, 167–68, 191, 194–95, 208–11,
  213; basic concepts of, 210; end of,
  209, 211; traditional, xiv, 4, 14, 15,
  18, 19, 24, 63
aesthetics of reception, 113